MARK HEYWOOD

GET UP!
STAND UP!

Personal journeys towards social justice

2C/10/18

Dear Randy,

Yes we Can! If we
Stand up and
try.

Good luck,

Tafelberg

Mark

Tafelberg, an imprint of NB Publishers,
a division of Media24 Boeke (Pty) Ltd,
40 Heerengracht, Cape Town, South Africa 8000
www.tafelberg.com

Set in 9 on 14pt Caecilia
Cover design by Doret Fereirra
Front cover photograph by Joyrene Kramer
Back cover photograph by Thom Pierce
Book design by Nazli Jacobs
Edited by Betty Welz
Proofread by Russell Martin
Index by George Claassen

Printed by **novus print**, a Novus Holdings company

First edition, first impression 2017

ISBN: 978-0-624-08113-5
Epub: 978-0-624-08114-2
Mobi: 978-0-624-08115-9

In memory of
Ellen Lawless Ternan and Louise Bryant,
two of the women I love.

Words to live by

Let us not waste our time in idle discourse! Let us do something, while we have the chance! It is not every day that we are needed. Not indeed that we personally are needed. Others would meet the case equally well, if not better. To all mankind they were addressed, those cries for help still ringing in our ears! But at this place, at this moment of time, all mankind is us, whether we like it or not. Let us make the most of it, before it is too late! Let us represent worthily for once the foul brood to which a cruel fate consigned us! What do you say?

Samuel Beckett, *Waiting for Godot*, 1953

Grand things are ahead. Worth living, and worth dying for.

Ascribed to Jack Reed in the movie *Reds*, 1981

Let us roll all our strength and all
Our sweetness up into one ball,
And tear our pleasures with rough strife
Thorough the iron gates of life:
Thus, though we cannot make our sun
Stand still, yet we will make him run.

Andrew Marvell, 'To His Coy Mistress', c1650

I found that the written word could achieve far greater disturbance than planting a bomb in a supermarket. The written word's a powerful thing and I don't think that was too well considered, at least not in pop music, until I started to write that way.

John Lydon aka Johnny Rotten, *Anger Is an Energy: My life uncensored*, 2014

Arise, ye workers from your slumber,
Arise, ye prisoners of want.
For reason in revolt now thunders,
and at last ends the age of cant!
Away with all your superstitions,
Servile masses, arise, arise!
We'll change henceforth the old tradition,
And spurn the dust to win the prize!

Traditional British version of 'The Internationale', Eugene Pottier, 1871

Contents

Opening remarks:
the end at the beginning

But our beginnings never know our ends!
T S Eliot, 'Portrait of a Lady'[1]

This book is about how politics, love, literature and song intertwine and shape consciousness and commitment. It is about how revolutions are made not simply by passion, but also by art and books and friendship.

In the past great freedom struggles were carried forward by hope. Activists shouldered the real possibilities of death, torture, lengthy imprisonment because they had an abiding hope. They believed in the morality of justice. So the question this book explores is whether good people today still have hope in their arsenal.

I have always been concerned with social justice, yet in recent years I have seen hope begin to fade. And so the core question facing many people who continue to care about our collective future is not 'Should we hope?' but 'On what can we base our hope?' How can we retrieve the promise of democracy and the stolen dream of equality?

Today we have the misfortune of being able to look forward into politics and the future trajectory of our societies with far more clarity than anyone could have done 50 years ago. Of course there are many great unknowns. But to the question 'Will life get any better for the poor and for the people without monetary power?' the inescapable answer seems to be 'no' – if, that is, we continue to feel powerless in the face of the politics of the present.

Why do we feel so debilitated when so many people have so much knowledge of the crisis of human civilisation that has come into being? Has there been a loss of hope?

I started this book on 27 March 2014, thinking while sitting atop a fortress whose remnants date back centuries. The fortress is on the property of the Rockefeller Foundation Bellagio Center in Bellagio in northern Italy. Visible from its ancient stone ramparts, in the far distance were smooth white snow-slopes on a range of mountains whose individual names I do not know, but whose collective grandeur has long been described as the Alps. Below me lay Lake Como shining in the sun, a deep, variegated blue-green, its surface occasionally broken by the wake trailing one of the ferries which cross from one side to the other numerous times a day. A sprinkling of villages along the water's edge showed signs of life – a train cutting along the mountain-side, chimneys puffing smoke. About and above me, a cold March air, clouds that thickened and then thinned again, the small-talk twitter of a band of birds, including a single woodpecker.

The idea of writing a book was of course intimidating – especially a book about justice and hope.

I wanted to start with the great beauty of living and the potential beauty of the human being. Academics and historians debate what it was that marked the dawn of civilisation, but however you date it, after thousands of years the world has become a very civilised place and human beings enormously sophisticated. Generation after generation of humans, age after age, have accumulated knowledge of themselves, their world, their universe, science, shortcuts and long-cuts, technologies, their own physiology, the human genome.

For those who can benefit from this knowledge – and this will be my theme – the world offers a vast accumulation of riches.

Yet, as we know, far too many people cannot benefit from all that we have accumulated and all that we know.

This disparity – the inequality that grows and grows – and the sense of helplessness that too many people feel as they face it are the subjects of this book. It is no wonder then that it has taken three years to complete. I was naïve when I sat down to write it on that first day in Bellagio.

By my last day I knew that the task was far larger and more significant than I had understood. On that day the clouds came down, miraculously materialising out of the blue skies that had persisted for days. For weeks I had watched the snow retreat from the mountain-tops as spring advanced. But on that day the upper hills were dusted with new snow, while everything below was cloaked in a sombre, silent and pondering grey, making it a day for introspection.

I looked back on days of mental wrestling and realised that although A Book was still playing hard to get, it was beginning to struggle through the millions of words from which we make meaning, our multiple analyses and ways of looking at the world.

I returned to South Africa and submitted the manuscript as it then stood to a publisher. Several weeks later the return-to-sender came, accompanied by a letter from Tony Morphet, the publisher's reader, that described it as dry and drab, overly polemical and mildly didactic. A year later I started writing again, taking as my cue Morphet's suggestion that the one part that had excited him was where I wrote about my personal experience of working in London with the Marxist Workers' Tendency of the ANC. Up to that point I had resisted writing about myself and my own experience, but I decided to give it a try. This time the words flowed freely. Looking back over them, I realised that I had told a personal story about politics.

But now I also realise more clearly than ever before that politics can be understood only through personal experiences, mine and many others'. Politics is not an aloof science that can be described as if it unfolds according to objectively established laws. It is the accumulation of personal experiences, the degree to which people engage with their world in order to change it.

I love books. I love words. But when I started to write this book I felt angry with book-writers. So many word-weavers abuse their gift by writing abstrusely and obscurely. Consequently, the people who may benefit from their thoughts – the people who need their thoughts – are not able to comprehend their words and what they tell us about this world.

For some people book-writing seems to be a habit treated with a degree of contempt. They will write books even if they know very few people will read them.

The book I promised myself to try to write was about how to organise for pro-poor social change in the twenty-first century – in simple terms, how to remake the world, make it more equal, steer it away from a path leading towards self-destruction. I wanted to draw on my own journeys to suggest ways we can do that.

That's a big book. That's why it was so difficult to start it.

When I started writing, the Rockefeller Foundation Bellagio Center in northern Italy, a place that was meant to help me write, was making things difficult. Villa Serbelloni is a place where blessed people come to pour out and order their knowledge by writing books. The original villa was built in the fifteenth century. For some 80 years now it has provided a retreat for writers. Its library contains the evidence of their success: there are hundreds of books, each marked with a little red dot, to confirm it was dreamed up HERE, cleaned up HERE. X marks the spot. No wonder I felt intimidated.

All those other books and their clever authors leaned over me and made me feel as if I was in a nightmare facing imminent and rapidly approaching danger. I needed to run fast to escape but my legs just wouldn't co-operate.

Eventually, after a few imagined starts, they began to move.

By the end of this journey I hope I will have earned my red dot.

This book is about all the loves of my life: literature and punk music and, yes, justice. It is a book about being human and so it is a journey into the art of politics by looking at some of the big challenges of our time. Inequality has made epidemics in the last twenty years and alongside many other people, I have done my best to stand against it. That has meant tackling AIDS and public health and education. It has meant standing up for South Africa's Constitution and working hard to protect the human rights of all people who live within our borders.

Ultimately this is a retrospective about the forces that shaped a boy. It is about what made him think and why thinking made him take a stand. At its most superficial level it is about politics. At its deepest level it is about a fear I have that time may be running out in the quest for social justice in South Africa and the world.

This book, then, is an appeal to you, dear fellow human, to take a stand.

1
Expatriate child –
an African upbringing

As soon as you're born they make you feel small
By giving you no time instead of it all
Till the pain is so big you feel nothing at all
John Lennon, 'Working Class Hero', 1970

On 7 June 1977 the Sex Pistols' wonderful anti-anthem 'God Save the Queen' coincided with the British monarch's silver jubilee celebrations and topped the British pop charts. It was my birthday. In the same week the BBC banned it. Somewhere on the other side of the world a four-year-old girl in Durban, South Africa, nestled up to her parents. Her father was probably dreaming of a book he might one day write – a book he had wanted to write in order to fictionalise his own journey.

The year before, deep in the forests of Zaire, after wreaking fear in the tiny town of Yambuku, a new haemorrhagic virus was named after the Ebola River. In June the same year, 1976, an uprising had flared up in South Africa, led by teenagers such as Teboho 'Tsietsi' Mashinini, school students. This fire would burn and burn until apartheid, the system that caused the anger, could no longer hold itself together. The first President of the democracy that replaced it would be a man who had spent 27 years in prison, most of them in one of the most beautiful and desolate spots in the world: Robben Island.

A few years later I would visit Cape Town on holiday. I was only a child and yet the contradictions and impossible connections were hard to ignore. Somewhere in the midst of that trip I fell in love and now I am nearly 40 years into my love affair with South Africa.

My first encounter with this lover occurred in July 1977. I was thirteen. My parents, Alan and Susan Heywood, had just moved to Gaborone, the capital of Botswana. They had arrived to pick up my sister, Mandy, and me from what was then called Jan Smuts Airport, just outside Johannesburg. We were on holiday from our private boarding schools in England. They bundled us into a car and drove us across what was then the Transvaal. Three hours later we crossed through a fence in the scrub, a border

that marked the middle of nowhere. We then drove another 30 kilometres to our new home on President Drive in the small, dusty, arid city
of Gaborone.

Our house had a glittery blue pool!

I have but a faint recollection of the Johannesburg we drove through
back then. In those days Egoli was a big, clean, modern city, with tall
buildings and wide highways. The whites kept it clean; the blacks did
the cleaning. Johannesburg was a kind of plastic Legoland, comfortably
cupped in a bowl of hills. All I knew was its outer sheen. Its streets had
no names or memories yet for me. The landscape was beautiful but
blank: blue skies and the July brown of a Highveld winter.

It. Was. All. New.

At that time Joburg held no associations for me with politics, literature, culture, life and death. It was just an empty canvas. In the years
that followed I became more and more familiar with the terrain and the
four-hour drive to another country. There was a fish-and-chip shop in
Magaliesburg, then we passed the small resort town of Rustenburg, which
has since grown into a brash platinum centre. Lastly we sped past the
very Afrikaans one-horse town of Zeerust. After this it was a mere 50-kilo-
metre stretch and over the Botswana border at the Tlokweng gate.

That first summer I took joy in having both a swimming pool and a
tennis court in my own garden. There is something very colonial in both
but they appealed to my young mind. I found friends and discovered the
little city of 'Gabs', as it was called by the expatriate community of which
we were a part. It was child heaven. I could ride my Chopper bicycle
from one end of town to another. There was nothing to fear.

It wasn't long, however, before I began to puzzle over the evidence that
the South Africa we had driven through and the Botswana we had driven
to were two very different countries.

Botswana was an independent country with a black President, Seretse
Khama. In 1948 Khama, a hereditary leader from a powerful royal family
in what was then the Bechuanaland Protectorate, had married a white
Englishwoman, Ruth Williams, with whom he had fallen in love while
studying for the Bar in London. The couple faced down racism and
opprobrium aimed at their relationship. Their marriage was opposed by
a united front including Seretse's uncle Tshekedi, who was his regent, the
British Labour government and the South African apartheid government,
and in 1951 the young Khamas were forced into exile.

Five years later, Seretse having renounced his hereditary role, they were allowed to return as private citizens. Seretse entered politics and in 1966 was elected the newly independent Botswana's first President, shortly after being knighted by Queen Elizabeth. Sweet justice. By the time I crossed the border into Botswana he had been President for eleven years. Unlike some fellow law students of his time – by then Nelson Mandela was imprisoned on Robben Island – Seretse was able to put his convictions about equality and democracy into practice; his leadership launched a unique ethic of nonracialism and tolerance in the small state in the Kalahari desert.[2] I naïvely idealised Botswana as a nonracial paradise: in July 1980 Seretse Khama's death inspired me to write my first poem.

By contrast, South Africa was a country where an Act of Parliament declared sex across the colour line 'immoral' and made it a criminal offence. In the towns of the Transvaal that we had driven through black people were forbidden to live in the suburbs they manicured. In Gaborone – across a nonsensical line in the scrub drawn by faraway people in Europe – people could live and love as they chose.

One was a free country. One was a country in chains. One was a democracy, the other a dictatorship.

I had grown up as the child of two white middle-class English people. My father was an aspiring bank manager for Barclays DCO (which stood for 'Dominion, Colonial and Overseas' – a title of the times if ever there was one). He was a working-class child from Manchester whose parents had both died before he was fourteen. Having started work at seventeen, he pulled himself up by his bootstraps, and with a bit of luck ended up in a white rather than a blue collar, transported to a very different life. In his own words he 'had no family of any consequence' and the prospect of working in the colonies was enticing.

My mother was the dreamy daughter of a local bank manager in the Yorkshire seaside town of Bridlington. After qualifying she had become a physical education teacher in London. She had fallen in love with the son of a missionary, a man called Stephen Pricket, an English literature student at Oxford.

When he was given a job teaching at a Methodist school in Eastern Nigeria she decided to follow him. As she wrote, she was 'determined to get to Nigeria, but [had] no clue how to go about it'. Her recollection is that by chance, while walking in London, she came across the Women's Migration & Overseas Appointments Society, which was looking for a PE teacher at Queen's College in Lagos.

And so it was that in 1962 she embarked on a path less travelled for people of her class, ending up in Yaba, a suburb of Lagos, in what was then considered quite a dark Africa.

The story that she started writing of her life ends abruptly at the point when, after being robbed, she met a local bank manager, Alan Heywood, 'who set up a loan for me and turned up at a dance being held at Queen's College that weekend'. How exactly she ditched her lover Stephen and ended up with a man very much his opposite, I don't know, but she married my father in August 1963. I was born on Victoria Island, Lagos, the following year.

The teeming city of Lagos was my home for three years. Later we were sent by the bank to Kano and Katsina, towns in far Northern Nigeria. When we were asked to move to Yola, a town my father described as 'having no decent expat schools and the nearest decent hospital being 250 miles away in Jos', he said no, even though, in his even shorter memoir, he relates how he feared that turning down a promotion would jeopardise his career.

So in 1969 they left Africa and were next sent to work in Valetta, on the Mediterranean island of Malta. For a six-year-old child Malta was a pearly paradise, loaded with one excitement after another: the ancient ramparts of the old port and fortress, cliffs you could jump off, grottos, shops stocked with an unlimited supply of Enid Blyton books, wandering freely on an island of a hundred beaches, diving in transparent blue seas, spotting and collecting multicoloured sea urchins, the naïve, idealised, truly scrumptious world of *Chitty Chitty Bang Bang*, falling in love with Julie Andrews in *The Sound of Music* (where even resistance to the Nazi annexation of Austria was all about song, dance and childhood . . .).

Malta was an interlude. By 1972 Alan and Sue Heywood had grown their nuclear family with the addition of two daughters, Mandy and Rachel. They returned to West Africa, this time to the former British colony of the Gold Coast, renamed Ghana on independence in 1957. Over the next five years I grew up in three very different Ghanaian cities. Kumasi is in central Ghana in the middle of a vast tropical rainforest, where mahogany trees are the size of Jack's famed beanstalk. Kumasi is the ancient capital of Ashantiland, the Kingdom of the Ashanti, a proud and historic tribe of Ghana still ruled over by a king, the Asantehene. Next stop was Takoradi, a coastal city situated along Ghana's slave coast. 'Monkey, banana, cocoa, yam,' sang a small roadside trader. Eventually we arrived in Ghana's capital, Accra.

My memories of those years are a mix of pleasurable sensations and smells. The vast mahogany trees of central Ghana; swimming in break-ing waves off the Takoradi coast; staying at the bank's beach house in Ada and fishing in the mouth of the great Volta River, fearful of barracuda that would strip your flesh if you fell out of the canoe.

Before arriving in South Africa I had felt but not thought about the continent around me. In the late 1960s and the first half of the 1970s Nigeria, Malta and Ghana were just a wonderful playground for an ex-patriate child, the antithesis of the perpetual greys of northern England. The Yorkshire town of Bridlington and the Ghanaian port of Takoradi could not be greater opposites. Bridlington had had its glory days in the ninth century as one of the landing points for the Vikings, but over the twentieth century it had settled into a comfortable indolence as the annual holiday destination of the weary working classes of the industrial cities of Yorkshire. Takoradi was the target of another invasion, the blight of slavery. But to me it felt light, vibrant and unspoilt.

So, the great forests of central Ghana, the Volta River mouth at Ada, the beaches and sports clubs of Takoradi were my hang-outs. A ten-year-old must be forgiven for being blissfully unaware of the politics of these freshly postcolonial states, but the seeds of a political consciousness had been sown in that child's mind.

Kumasi exposed me to an ancient African culture and civilisation. The great statute of Kwame Nkrumah in Accra found a place in my memory, to be pondered later. The slave castles which we visited on the outskirts of Takoradi placed me at the scene of one of the worst crimes in human history.

None of it really made sense nor did I look for meaning. But the one thing I took for granted was that humans were humans regardless of their colour. Although considered British, whatever that means, I was a child of Africa, schooled with black children, tutored and cared for by black servants. I was way too young to even notice, never mind question, class inequalities. My teachers, my playmates, were a kaleidoscope of colours and nationalities. Black skins and white skins and brown skins and skins in-between were part of the natural order of things.

Migrant scholar and the discovery of literature

South Africa was a shock; its arrival on the doorstep of my life coincided with an awakening of youthful consciousness that had been stimulated by the quality of the education I was receiving.

By the time I first landed at Jan Smuts Airport in 1977 I had been a boarder for six years at St Peter's, one of the oldest schools in one of the oldest cities in England, York. In 1971 at the tender age of seven I had been packed off to boarding school. My parents had flown with me from Kumasi to Accra before putting me on a British Caledonian flight to London Gatwick. There I would be met by my grandfather, and taken on a train to York and then by bus to Bridlington. A few years later I would be joined on this journey by my two sisters, whose parting from my parents was always traumatic and accompanied by hours of howling and sniffing as the old Boeing 707s traversed the North African skies. For many years this was my routine. I belonged to a generation of British children sent from our homes in Africa or other colonial outposts to private boarding schools in England. The unstated assumption was that schools where we lived were not good enough. Their children's attendance at boarding school was an employee benefit for people like my father.

Members of Manor House (I am in the second row, third from the right)
in 1983, my last year.

St Peter's School had been running for well over a thousand years when I arrived there. Founded in 627, it was steeped in its own history as well as the history of the English nation. Its most famous alumnus was one Guy Fawkes, who had plotted to restore the Catholic monarchy and planned to blow up the English Parliament, the Protestant King James I and all. Fawkes was discovered and arrested on 5 November 1605 and thus ended the Gunpowder Plot. It gave rise to Guy Fawkes Day, a day when the English – known for their love of peace – celebrate the capture of the attempted regicide. Each year they light bonfires on which they perch a home-made 'guy'. St Peter's, however, eschewed the tradition of burning an 'old boy'. Guy Fawkes Day was celebrated with a fire and fireworks, but never with a guy to burn atop the fire!

St Peter's provided me with a different type of playground from what I had at home in Africa. It had ample grounds, a swimming pool and rugby fields that ran more than a kilometre from the school buildings down to the River Ouse. In winter the Ouse would often burst its banks and the floodplain would then freeze, enveloping our swimming pool in an ice-lake.

The main school buildings had weathered centuries. Our boarding houses, the homes where we slept and whiled away weekends, were named after intellectuals from ancient history, mine after Alcuin, an eighth-century humanist and poet. The grounds of Alcuin House were once a Roman burial ground; ghosts came out after nightfall to trudge along extant Roman roads. One, the Grey Lady, was sometimes seen in the vicinity of the school chapel. One of the teachers, John V Mitchell, was York's resident ghost historian and had published a slim book, *Ghosts of an Ancient City*, describing the various ghosts, restless inhabitants still spotted from time to time in that once-upon-a-time Roman city.

In keeping with its association with things beyond the mortal plane, St Peter's School was intimately connected to one of the oldest churches in England, the glorious York Minster. Once a term Peterites would be marched 'down Bootham', a main city thoroughfare, to join in a church service in that hallowed temple. For a time I was the organ boy, turning the pages of music for the organist, tucked away in a nest, hidden behind the vast pipes that bellowed out notes that literally rattled the rooftops.

York exuded history. It is surrounded still by its Roman walls, its ancient alleyways bear wonderful names like Whip-Ma-Whop-Ma-Gate (apparently meaning 'street of neither one thing nor the other') and the River Ouse runs past the school through the heart of the city, under a string of old bridges and out into the beyond. York is said to have more pubs per head of population than any other European city, taverns with such names as the Bay Horse, the Hole in the Wall, the Old Grey Mare.

This was all taken for granted.

The idea that there could be deprivation or inequality of education would be something that came to me much, much later. For me the greatest treasure that was opened by having a quality education and teachers who wanted to be teachers was access to BOOKS, or what we call when we talk of its canon LITERATURE. Literature is indeed a cannon: light its fuse and it may blow you away.

I took O and A levels in English Literature and through the syllabus I met an array of poets, playwrights and authors: some were impenetrable and alienating, some became loves at first sight – George Orwell, William Shakespeare and Philip Larkin.

It's all a mishmash now but somehow over those years I was inducted into the House of Words. I became privy to their feeling, sounds, malleability and multiple never-ending meanings. Ian Lowe and David Hughes, two of the English teachers at St Peter's, inspired me by the way they read parts of our set texts out loud, infecting me with their lust for words. But side by side with traditional fare, in my case four of Shakespeare's tragedies, they let us nibble on the seditious edges of literature. In those days the edges were found in the Liverpool Poets, Adrian Henri, Brian Patten and Roger McGough, as well as in a conservative, ageing librarian, at that time still alive in the drab port city of Hull, Philip Larkin. I was electrified by the transgressive boldness of poems such as Larkin's 'This Be The Verse':

> They fuck you up, your mum and dad.
>   They may not mean to, but they do.
> They fill you with the faults they had
>   And add some extra, just for you.[3]

Somewhere that made sense.

While I was at school my relationship with my father in particular had started to rot. He sent me to school to learn discipline but, perhaps ironically, it was the independence of thought I was exposed to that made us clash. We fought over things political and things personal. He was a puritan disciplinarian. I was finding my soul, helped along by people like Larkin. He upbraided me for everything from putting my feet up on settees to drinking too much coffee. I fought back and there were bitter and sometimes physical conflicts.

For a long time I tried to work out the cause of his anger. One year I wrote a drawn-out, painfully composed and fearfully posted letter to both my parents trying to repair the deepening rift. But neither knew how to handle emotions. In those days feelings were good only for suppressing. The letter went unanswered. Eventually the theory I settled on was that my father had no parental model. His father had died before he was twelve. He was an angry and unsettled man and he wanted me to feel some of his hardship. It's a pity that we never really recovered. As a result of our damaged relationship, I decided to make myself into everything I thought he wasn't. Not a banker. Not a conservative. Not a person with some serious unacknowledged issues about the world's other races.

Larkin seemed subversive. Larkin transgressed. When Larkin linked the word 'fuck' to my parents, I got it. He offered me consolation:

> But they were fucked up in their turn
>> By fools in old-style hats and coats,
> Who half the time were soppy-stern
>> And half at one another's throats.

When it's used in the right way, I have always had great respect for the word 'fuck'. It's traceable back to the 16th century and might have been carried into the English language by Viking invaders, but would be allowed into the modern English dictionary only in 1965. It is one of the most variously used words we have. It first hit me when I came across it in J D Salinger's *Catcher in the Rye*. This book shook my tender fourteen-year-old self. Holden Caulfield was one of my shadow selves (later to be joined by Pete Townshend's Jimmy and Roger Waters's Pink).[4] I knew his alienation and shared his idealisation of his little sister Phoebe (who in my mind was my little sister Rachel). So when I came across the following passage I might as well have been Holden.

Holden's at Phoebe's school when he fears he's going to puke, so he sits down on the stairs:

> But while I was sitting down, I saw something that drove me crazy. Somebody'd written 'Fuck you' on the wall. It drove me damn near crazy. I thought how Phoebe and all the other little kids would see it, and how they'd wonder what the hell it meant, and then finally some dirty kid would tell them – all cockeyed, naturally – what it meant, and how they'd all *think* about it and maybe even *worry* about it for a couple of days. I kept wanting to kill whoever'd written it.[5]

In the years after that fuck, I kept coming across other transgressive fucks in songs and sonnets. Famous fucks, you might call them. But their power lies in how they are placed. In vulgar mouths, fuck becomes just . . . vulgar.

> Fuck this and fuck that
> Fuck it all and fuck a fucking brat
> She don't want a baby that looks like that . . .[6]

rasped Johnny Rotten, the front man for the Sex Pistols, in a taboo-breaking song about abortion.

'Arseholes, bastards, fucking cunts and pricks,' droned Ian Dury, in the inimitable first line of his song 'Plaistow Patricia', on an album bathetically titled *New Boots and Panties!!*[7]

'It's only the children of the fucking wealthy who tend to be good looking,' screamed Jet Black, in a song called 'Ugly' by the punk band The Stranglers from their genre-bending album *Rattus Norvegicus*.[8]

Words. More powerful than bombs. In 1980 or 1981 I met a real live poet for the first time, Andrew Motion, who was to become the British poet laureate in 1999. Motion was Philip Larkin's protégé, a living link to him, and would later be his biographer. Motion had recently published his first collection of poems, *The Pleasure Steamers*.[9] Holding the thin book in my hands was otherworldly. Its newness, the stiffness of its pages, the smell of book, the wriggly words within! And their connection to a real-life, living, breathing person. A man who was a POET.

The problem I had was that I could not read and enjoy literature in the passive. I could not ignore what the words were telling me about life.

As tensions grew with my parents, I agonised: how was it that they sent me to school but wanted me to ignore some of its most profound teachings? For me, wallowing in the beauty of books, discovering their meaning, could not be detached from my life and views. Literature contains instructions for living. With so much of the literature I read being about injustice, or reflecting on injustice, it became impossible for me to remain neutral on the great political questions of the time. The cry of King Lear, probably first heard when I was fourteen or so, is as loud to me today as it was then:

Poor naked wretches, whereso'er you are,
That bide the pelting of this pitiless storm,
How shall your houseless heads and unfed sides,
Your loop'd and window'd raggedness, defend you
From seasons such as these? O, I have ta'en
Too little care of this![10]

But while this assimilation was going on, my access to a first-rate edu-cation was something that I took for granted. It was just there. I didn't ask what it cost, how it was paid for or who paid for it. I was blissfully unaware that I was in a position of privilege, with an exceedingly rich cup of history close at hand for me to drink as much, or as little, as I wanted.

Private school kids with few cares, during my last summer at St Peter's.

I was thirsty and my journey into South Africa coincided with the begin-ning of my journey through books. As that journey progressed, literature made me look at and question South Africa more deeply. And South Africa made me think more deeply about literature.

Several events broke the skin of my youthful conscience. The deepest injury was the killing of black consciousness leader Steve Biko by the security police in 1977. At the time I was probably unaware of the im-port of his murder. I came to know him around 1980 through my own quest to better understand South Africa when I read Donald Woods's biography *Biko*.[11] Woods had had to flee South Africa because his links with Biko and outspoken opposition to the government led to his virtual house-arrest and fears for his family's safety.

South Africa entered my consciousness on two levels: I was also reading another kind of South African story, the novels of Wilbur Smith. They cast a romantic glow across the southern African landscape, with their stories of white people's derring-do against lions and an assortment of evil men. I saw this South Africa through family holidays, which gave me the best of what white South Africa had to offer. Family holidays took us to Cape Town on the Blue Train, a five-star hotel on rails that snakes across the breadth of South Africa, from its departure in Pretoria to its destination in Cape Town and back again. Family holidays took me to the top of the Carlton Centre in central Johannesburg (for many years the jewel of the city's architecture), where you could gaze across the city of gold. Family holidays took us into the Kruger Park to wonder at its wildlife.

But while the rest of my family were oblivious of the well-hidden horrors of the country and my father made excuses for it, my youthful angst grew and grew and enveloped me in sulky silences. From the top of the Carlton I gazed out over the mine dumps to the township of Soweto, hidden in a haze. From the top of Table Mountain I gazed across at Robben Island, made familiar by the names of the great leaders imprisoned there. I found a counterpoint to the Blue Train in Hugh Masekela's 'Stimela,[12] a haunting lament about the trains that carried apartheid's migrant labourers from the rural areas of southern and central Africa to the gold mines of Johannesburg.

In the days that followed I would write my own youthful poems.

> What right have you
> Nationalist bastards
> To suppress
> To oppress
> The people I love?

In the early 1980s I tried to compile my poems into a portfolio. I described the poems that came to me at that time as 'four years of feeling'. I had begun to grapple with my race and what I thought was our complicity, my parents' in particular, in black people's oppression. I think I had a sense of powerlessness. I could and did rage against my parents. I could rage in poetry. But I could not escape.

Joining the South African liberation struggle

The first action that I took to build on my deepening emotional engagement with the liberation struggle was to work as a trainee journalist for a month at the *Rand Daily Mail*. It was the winter of 1980 and I had just turned sixteen. The *Rand Daily Mail* was South Africa's foremost mainstream opposition newspaper. It was liberal at a time when many activists saw this as a positive trait and it was renowned for its exposés of the suffering caused by apartheid. It was that reputation that drew me there.

This was to be my first time living alone in the 'evil empire'. I stayed at the YMCA at the top of Rissik Street. Each day I walked across the city to the *Rand Daily Mail* offices on Main Street. In the 30 years since then nothing has really changed in the city's infrastructure except that the Gautrain station has given the YMCA a new neighbour. My walk to work took me over the Rissik Street bridge, down Commissioner Street and past the Carlton Hotel and Tower. Although I rarely varied my route, I began to know the streets of Legoland and started to fill them with meaning and memory.

I imagine that in 1980 a sixteen-year-old white English boy with an attitude stood out in the newsroom. I wanted it to be known that I was against apartheid. I befriended another journalist, David Capel, who smoked like a chimney. So I did too. Capel told me off, advising me to be more careful about what I said and to whom.

Obviously, all the stories I was involved in were pedestrian. There was no drama, no frontline reporting of deepening political tensions. I celebrated my first front-page byline with the report '23 Killed as Bus Plunges into Ravine'. But I was fortunate because two veteran black journalists, Doc Bikitsha and Sophie Tema, took me under their generous wings. I did not know at the time what legends I had landed beside. 'Doc', by then a gruff, warm man, was a lover of words and literature, a direct link to both the political and literary traditions in which I would later immerse myself. Sophie Tema was a pioneering black female journalist and had been on the scene of the shooting of Hector Pieterson in 1976. They both took me for my first visit to the famed Soweto, acting like protective parents. In Soweto I took photographs of the cramped matchbox houses and compared them mentally with the leafy white suburbs.

The *RDM* archives show stories written around this time by one Helen

Zille. She must have sat beside me in the newsroom but I don't remember her. Years later, however, she would play a prominent part in South African politics as the leader of the Democratic Alliance and the premier of the Western Cape province.

After my month at the *Rand Daily Mail* I was changed. I had become an activist. Anger at injustice was now flowing in my blood. I had made friends who were black, people whose oppression I empathised with deeply and to whom I felt I owed a debt. I had been to Soweto, that place beyond the mine dumps, try as they might to obscure its existence. I had seen parts of the Legoland city that its architects hid from white people.

Everlasting love

In the prologue to his autobiography, philosopher and social critic Bertrand Russell writes that the three passions that governed his life were 'the longing for love, the search for knowledge, and unbearable pity for the suffering of mankind'. Of love, he claimed that it brings ecstasy and relieves 'that terrible loneliness in which one shivering consciousness looks over the rim of the world into the cold unfathomable lifeless abyss'.

John Lennon put it another way: 'Love is all you need.' I too believe that love between two people, not easily achieved, is an essential spring of feeling and empathy, an energy, and my encounters with love have had almost as close an association with the quest for social justice as literature or music.

During that month of July 1980 my days in the newsroom were full of discovery, trepidation and excitement. My nights were lonely, stranded in an echoey vinyl corridor, in a city in which I had no friends. The Christian fundamentalists who ran the YMCA tried to badger me and scared me. One morning somewhere in the middle of this month of fullness and emptiness I received a letter in a stamped blue envelope. It was addressed to me in a spidery immature script, by a person I knew, Bridget Hamilton. Bridget was the girl I was 'going out' with – a quaint term, that; in fact it meant permission to kiss and hold hands. That permission had come about after we had fallen into each other's arms one intense night while the wind and rain beat against the shutters of Wath Hall, a baronial farmhouse in Malton, Yorkshire, where Bridget lived with her family. The house was not as austere or isolated as Wuthering Heights, but that evening felt as intense as the coming together of Cathy and Heathcliff.

Back in 1980 expressions of love had a very close association with letters. Since the Royal Mail was first made available to the British public by King Charles I in 1635, the postal service had spread its reach along the tentacles of colonialism. In those days letters were special. They arrived in the morning, rather than every second in an email, so they were looked forward to. I opened the envelope. Inside was a single blue sheet of paper and in the same script a mere five words:

> Dear Mark
> I love you.

There could be no words more powerful. They had been stamped and sealed, carried from Wath Hall, passed through postmasters' hands, across continents, through airports, into other hands. Finally, with the same accuracy as the modern-day internet, they arrived at their destination and found their target.

When I returned to England a month later Bridget was going out with another young man. It seemed impossible to comprehend. I learned then that the power and strength of love is measured by its loss. That was an early lesson, not fully appreciated at the time, but oft repeated.

Epiphany: Never take the intensity of youthful first love for granted: it may mark you for life. I have sought true love all my life and there are times when I have found it and times when I have lost it.

My first politically motivated act of defiance took place in an unusual location. Once again I was home in Botswana for the Christmas holidays – a four-week escape from the darkness of an English winter.

In Botswana, as in many other postcolonial African states, the centre of expatriate life was often the golf club. Wherever they are, golf clubs are centres of snobbery. It was there that white families gathered over weekends to play golf, eat and drink. It was there that youngsters like me, home for the holidays, gravitated to make friendships.

On New Year's Eve 1982, the Gaborone Golf Club was the place to party. I was there to party too, but sometimes things just happen, thoughts and feelings well up and dictate your actions. Perhaps alcohol had a little to do with it as well. Just before midnight, the emotions and anger embedded somewhere in my psyche after my stint at the *Rand Daily Mail* welled up. Somehow I managed to get hold of the microphone, draw the young black caddies together and make a short impromptu speech. I reminded the revellers why they should remember the atrocities going on across the border, I used the word 'apartheid' and asked them to think about the murdered Steve Biko and the imprisoned Nelson Mandela.

Then, together with the caddies, I launched into one of my earliest renditions of the African anthem, 'Nkosi Sikelel' iAfrika'. I had learnt the

South African version of this beautiful hymn, written in 1897 by Enoch Sontonga, by listening to recordings, memorising the words and patiently singing them back to myself because there was no one else I could sing them to. This was how I embraced the liberation struggle practically.

Young man in transition. The British Anti-Apartheid Movement's button, a badge I wore for many years, as a signal of the person I wanted to be.

This harmless little act of solidarity might as well have involved setting off a bomb. I was immediately ostracised. A few days later the golf-club elders, sticklers for decorum, summoned my father, who in turn summoned me and angrily told me that I would have to apologise or be barred from the club.

Thereafter I gained a reputation across Gaborone as a rebel with a cause. The Soviet Embassy was directly opposite our house on President's Drive. One holiday somebody graffitied 'Solidarnosc' across its white walls in large red letters. Solidarność (Solidarity) was the independent Polish trade union movement led by Lech Wałęsa which in the early 1980s was rattling the chains of the Stalinist government. The graffitist was widely believed to have been me.

I supported Solidarity. I supported every struggle for freedom that I knew about. But for the record, it was not me.

I completed my A levels and finished school in late 1982. I had nine months to fill before taking up my place at Oxford – what these days is termed a 'gap year'. Understanding my passionate interest in South Africa, my mother had somehow arranged for me to be a volunteer at the Wilgespruit Fellowship Centre near Johannesburg.

Wilgespruit was an ecumenical and multiracial initiative founded in the late 1940s. It aimed to create a psychological free space for people to meet. Wilgespruit was also home to the Agency for Industrial Mission (AIM), an NGO whose major focus was to promote a broader understanding of the social costs of the migrant labour system. It used Lesotho as the focus of its study, running vacation seminars for theological students and using them as researchers. Some students were placed in villages among the wives and families of migrant workers, some at the recruiting station near Maseru, some were themselves recruited as migrant mineworkers to live in hostels and work in the belly of the mines and others worked alongside church chaplains who ministered to mineworkers. A booklet called *Another Blanket* was compiled from the students' diaries: the title came from a song sung by the migrants as they crossed the Caledon River into South Africa and 'assumed another blanket'. A young priest called Jo Seoka co-ordinated AIM. Much later he became Bishop of Pretoria and President of the South African Council of Churches (SACC), and retained his empathy with mineworkers. He was involved in assisting miners and their families before, during and after the 2012 Marikana Massacre. I would meet him again much later in life.

Another Wilgespruit project, the Self-Help Associates for Development Economics (SHADE), initiated programmes that aimed to ameliorate the worst effects of apartheid, empowering people from rural areas through self-help projects, assisting black women to find markets for traditional crafts in gleaming white shopping malls or through solidarity markets overseas run by Oxfam and other groups. Wilgespruit was also one of the few residential conference centres in the early 1980s that refused to comply with petty apartheid and bar black people. It was thus a magnet for churches, trade unions and quasi-political groupings, a hub for the growing opposition to apartheid.

Wilgespruit was situated in a place of great natural beauty on one of the quartzite ridges that run across Johannesburg and its surrounds, looking out over rolling hills and plains of the Cradle of Humankind. In the early 1980s it was close to the western limits of white Johannesburg.

To reach Wilgespruit you had to drive through whites-only areas that sometimes felt hostile; to its neighbours and the security police who constantly monitored it, Wilgespruit was an aberration. But once you hit the dirt road it was like entering Narnia: you were in another country.

To be in South Africa in early 1983 was to be at the heart of an awakening social movement. Much of it was organised through or given some form of cover by the progressive SACC, and I was fortunate to find myself on the periphery of one of its fronts. At Wilgespruit I encountered a string of committed and passionate people taking a stand against a hardening regime. They would change my life. Dale and Laetitia ('Tish') White were united in their opposition to apartheid. They possessed a huge energy that seemed to belong to many opponents of the system.

But they were opposite in character: Dale was warm but reserved and hard to penetrate, an Anglican priest in a Soweto parish; Tish was raucous and rebellious and took no prisoners. She chain-smoked and swore like a trooper. But different as they appeared to be, both were dedicated to each other, their community and freedom.

The Whites' house was perched on top of the ridge, with a beautiful view out across to the Magaliesberg. They shared it with their two teenage daughters, Anastasia (known as Stacey) and Natasha, both of whom had boyfriends whom apartheid classified as 'coloured'. Since the young women themselves were classified as white, their relationships were risky in those dark days. This eccentric, unusual, committed family inspired me with wonder and admiration. They fostered my anger and were surrogates for the love and conviction that I felt were denied in my own family.

Dale White's parish was in Jabavu, a vibrant part of Soweto. The trips I took to his church while I was at the Fellowship Centre renewed and deepened my encounter with the most interesting and powerful part of the black urban community in South Africa. I experienced at first hand the swelling political momentum that was gathering under the guise of song and prayer at places such as Regina Mundi Roman, the Catholic church, and Dale White's St Paul's, the Anglican church.

I was not religious myself but for six months I lapped up the spirit. I wrote, I read, I absorbed, I witnessed, I wondered, I wrote angry poems dedicated to each new death I heard of, Saul Mkhize, Mzukisi Nobadula, Neil Aggett; I wrote a poem the morning after the SA Air Force dropped bombs on suburban Maputo; I wrote poems for Cedric Mayson and Breyten Breytenbach.

I felt what it was to fear the security police, describing in a letter to Helen Hudson, one of my first loves, how one afternoon 'I thought the security police were following me, and even after they overtook the car I was driving I had a prolonged case of the shakes, and thus, unable to control my shaking legs, I drove the car into the back of a stationary car at a garage.'

Over this time I won the trust of Dale and Tish and was admitted into the family and the more hidden parts of its politics. The mark of trust came when you were included in the little groups that would wander away from the office to hold huddled discussions beyond the reach of bugging devices, or who wrote notes on bits of paper that were burned immediately after being read. Under such circumstances, in April 1983 I found myself on the periphery of a plan to smuggle Cedric Mayson out of South Africa. I felt I had come of age.

Mayson was a Methodist Church leader who had been charged with treason and membership of the ANC. He had already spent 15 months in prison when his trial was unexpectedly adjourned. He was given bail after a statement he made to police under torture was ruled inadmissible by the judge. Even under apartheid the rule of law sometimes yielded unexpected results.[13] Nonetheless it was feared that when the trial resumed it might be used to implicate the Rev. Beyers Naudé; besides which, Mayson might be found guilty and receive a lengthy prison sentence.

Tish told me that the plan was for Dale to slip away from Wilgespruit one night, pick up a disguised Mayson and drive him to a point close to the Orange Free State town of Ficksburg. From there he would hike through the mountains and over the border into Lesotho.

My role in this plot was as little more than a confidant, one of the small group who were aware that Dale would be gone for a few days. The night he left I sat up very late with Tish. We were afraid that the police might intercept them on the way. For just over 24 hours we huddled under that blanket of fear and uncertainty. There were no cell phones and there would be no way of knowing whether the operation had been successful until we saw Dale driving his Toyota Corolla back down the hill to the offices at Wilgespruit. A failure to return within a day would in all probability indicate that the plan had fallen apart.

Dale returned. Then, dramatically, on the day Mayson was due back in the Pretoria Supreme Court he announced his presence in England. The operation had been a success. We had cocked a snook at the security police and the apartheid state.

But Mayson's flight focused security police attention more closely on Wilgespruit and, at least this is how I have understood it all my life, on the young white English volunteer who was increasingly trusted and involved in its work. Perhaps it was just my imagination, part of the heroic narrative that I was subconsciously beginning to construct for myself, but I thought that I began to get more direct attention from the security police. I was followed several times when I drove off the premises at Wilgespruit. The intimidation culminated one day in June when, as I was sitting having lunch alone in the Carlton Centre, I was joined at the table by two black security policemen. They sat down without saying a word and placed a pouch on the table in which I could see the shape of a gun. I didn't imagine that. I gulped my food down and left.

That was enough. I was scared. I must have decided at that point that I was too young, too white and too lily-livered to stand up to police interrogation, torture or prison. I decided to leave South Africa earlier than planned, to run away from my fear of possible detention. I said my goodbyes to the Whites and within days I had hitchhiked my way back to Botswana and crossed over at the Tlokweng border post. I returned to the safety and blessed life of an expatriate child: swimming pools, the Gaborone Golf Club – and love. But I had lost my naïvety. Johannesburg was beginning to fill up with memories.

The discovery of politics –
introduction to Johnny Rotten, Leon Trotsky and Martin Legassick

*That line, 'I wanna destroy the passer-by' . . . I was talking about all those
kinds of people, the complacent ones that don't contribute, that just
sit by and moan and don't actually do anything to better themselves or
the situation for others. The non-participating moral majority. . . .
'Your future dream is a shopping scheme'? That's turned out pretty accurate,
didn't it? Seems to be the way of the world now. I seen it coming.*
John Lydon, Anger Is an Energy[14]

After hastily beating a retreat from South Africa in July 1983, I was angry and impassioned. But I was also young. The late summer of 1983 in England was to be the last time in my life when for a lengthy stretch of time I would behave as if I was completely carefree. I had several months to waste before going up to Oxford, so I took a job as a bartender at the Friendly Forester, a pub in Bridlington. One night, after a flirtatious dance around our class differences that had gone on for several weeks, I lost my virginity to a young married woman who worked as a bartender with me.

When not pulling pints I was falling in and out of love, joying in the beauty of some of the young women who were my friends, taking day trips to the beautiful Yorkshire moors, strolling on the Bridlington promenade, living to the backdrop of the Boomtown Rats' 'I Don't Like Mondays' and Cliff Richard's 'We Don't Talk Anymore'.

It was a sort of hedonistic exhalation after the intensity of South Africa.

But joy and despair can mirror each other. I had returned to an England in the midst of an angry, wrenching transition. It was a country frequently characterised by various stripes of angry young men, the Vandals and vandals, punk rockers and striking mineworkers. The lead singer of the punk band the Sex Pistols, Johnny Rotten, was the troubadour of the time, the real poet laureate. His partner in crime, who had aptly renamed himself Sid Vicious, was the symbol of disaffected youth. Vicious would die at the age of 22, self-destructing in a blaze of heroin addiction. Rotten still lives. The political and social movement that they inspired

screamed about misery, ennui and contempt for the existing order and
any future order.

> There is no future
> In England's dreaming
> Noooooo fu-ture
> Nooooooo fu-ture
> Nooooooo future for YOU![15]

. . . rasped Rotten as he rang out the chorus of their banned anti-national
anthem, 'God Save the Queen'.

In May 1979, in the wake of what the media termed 'the winter of discontent', Margaret Thatcher had been elected British Prime Minister. By
1983 she had settled in at 10 Downing Street, fought off her enemies
within the Tory party and begun dismantling the welfare state. Thatcher's
was a mission to break up and weaken the power of the trade unions,
a protective bulwark between the welfare state of the post-war boom
period and the everyone-for-themselves free fall of the now-familiar age
of neoliberalism.

People were angry. No longer could they take for granted the certainties of the post-war period: quality education, a job, the famed National
Health Service (NHS) and the welfare state. Class differences were
strained and sharpening – and in the midst of all this I was on my way
'up' to one of the established and ancient bastions of class privilege,
Oxford University.

In 1982 I had won a place to study English Language and Literature at
Balliol College. Oxford or Cambridge had never been part of my plans,
but my A level results had surprised even me, putting me in that small
elite of students who were considered clever enough to sit the Oxbridge
exams. I returned to St Peter's for what was called a seventh term, solely
to study for and sit the Oxbridge exams. I was considered a bit of a no-
hoper. During that term I surreptitiously worked as a barman at a local
hotel. I sat the exams, travelled to Oxford for an interview and walked
away with low expectations of success. Then in December 1982, back
home in Gaborone, a letter arrived to inform me that I was in.

I was not a great scholar but at the time I believed I might be a yet-to-
be-discovered poet. During the seventh term, I sent a collection of angry

juvenilia to Balliol. I hoped they would see – before I had even been awarded residence – a famous alumnus, and that that might make up for my shortcomings as an academic. Whether my poems had any impact on their decision to accept me, I will never know.

The universities of Oxford and Cambridge operate through a system of autonomous colleges, each with different traditions, benefactors and histories. Both universities (collectively described as Oxbridge) have for centuries been the training grounds of the Establishment and its ruling class, what a 2014 official report called a 'closed shop at the top' whose graduates made up 75% of senior judges, 59% of cabinet posts, 57% of permanent secretaries, 50% of diplomats, 47% of newspaper columnists, 44% of public body chairs and 33% of BBC executives.

Balliol College is as Establishment as the rest, but it also has a reputation for radicalism and difference. It was founded in 1263 and is one of Oxford's oldest colleges. I chose to apply to it because of its reputation and also because some of my favourite poets (think Gerard Manley Hopkins) and politicians (Seretse Khama) had studied there. It was said to take students on merit and character and not just on the strength of their noble lineage. Nonetheless, at Oxford the Establishment can't be avoided. Boris Johnson went up the same year as I did and we were in the same year at Balliol. Just over the bridge, David Cameron was a student at Brasenose College.

Balliol is in the very centre of Oxford on Broad Street, a street where in 1555 and 1556 the Protestant martyrs Hugh Latimer, Nicholas Ridley and Thomas Cranmer were burnt at the stake. Here was an interesting parallel. I had been educated at a school one of whose 'old boys', Guy Fawkes, was executed in 1606 for plotting the restoration of the Catholic Church and the Pope. Now I was about to study at a college outside whose front gate three leading Protestant theologians and reformists had been burnt for advocating the disestablishment of the Catholic Church and a break between England and the Papacy.

Many years later, shortly before he died, my father gave me a seven-page account of his life 'as a trainee with Barclays Bank in the 1950s and what happened next'. In a paragraph praising the Bank's 'more than benevolent interest in the welfare and progress of its employees', he stated that 'from a personal viewpoint, I believe that the BBI Chairman in 1983 played a helpful role in gaining my son's entry into one of the best Oxford colleges'. I had always thought I won a place at Oxford on my own merits and discovering that assertion so much later in my life came as a shock. I hope it was not true. But if it was, I'm sorry . . . family connections, 'the old school tie', have for centuries been the way many children of the British upper classes gain entrance to Oxford and Cambridge.

Nonetheless, for whatever reason, in September 1983 I stepped off Oxford's Broad Street, entered the Porter's Lodge and crossed the two grassy quads to my new home on Staircase XIII.

Now for a second confession. While still at school in York I had joined Maggie Thatcher's Conservative Party. Why? I don't know. Perhaps it was because it allowed me access to the Conservative Club, which had a bar that took a flexible approach to underage drinking. Perhaps it was because I had acquired the habit of taking political clippings each day from the *Daily Telegraph*, a Tory-backing conservative broadsheet whose opinions I may somehow have imbibed and which I read in full every day for several years.

My experience in South Africa made a radical of me, but my politics were contradictory and ill-informed. I considered myself a part of 'the struggle', but my outrage was largely based on the offence to my morals, my sense of injustice and a rejection of inequality and the indignity apartheid imposed on black people. As I bobbed about in my sea of anger I began to seek explanations of the world and its inequalities. I wanted an answer to The Who's question: Who are you? Briefly I thought nihilism suited me. I came across Samuel Beckett and his three bleak novels, *Molloy, Malone Dies* and *The Unnamable*, exploring and trying to depict his sense of ennui and nothingness, captured my imagination. His play *Not I* took modernism and my sense of alienation to its limits – a play with no character, only a voice.[16]

I really wanted to be an '–ist' of some sort. Being an '–ist' meant that you stood for something. I soon shuffled off nihilism and decided I was an existentialist, which meant you asked for nothing. All was bleak and hopeless. But in sharp contrast to *Not I*, Jean-Paul Sartre's trilogy *Roads to Freedom* spoke to both my anguish and my growing sense that there was a need to act, to take a stand. Sartre was political. His memoir *Words* was subtitled 'I loathe my childhood and all that remains of it . . .' I felt I agreed. Childhood was about impotence and dependence, adulthood about agency.

In *Troubled Sleep*, originally translated as *Iron in the Soul,* the third book in the trilogy, I found the iconoclastic purpose that I so admired in his resistance hero Mathieu. The words in which Sartre describes the last fifteen minutes of Mathieu's life spring with life and death:

> He made his way to the parapet and stood there firing. This was re-venge on a big scale. Each one of his shots avenged some ancient scruple. One for Lola whom I dared not rob; one for Marcelle whom I ought to have left in the lurch; one for Odette whom I didn't want to kiss. This for the books I never got to write, this for the journeys I never made, this for everybody in general whom I wanted to hate and tried to understand. He fired and the tables of the Law crashed about him – Thou Shalt Love Thy Neighbour As Thyself – bang! in that bugger's face. Thou Shalt Not Kill – bang! at that scarecrow opposite. He was firing on his fellow men, on Virtue, on the whole world. Liberty is Terror. The Mairie was ablaze, his head was ablaze. Bullets were whining around him free as the air. The world is going up in smoke, and me with it. He fired: he looked at his watch: fourteen minutes and thirty seconds. Nothing more to ask of Fate now except one half-minute. Just time enough to fire at that smart officer, at all the Beauty of the Earth, at the street, at the flowers, at the gardens, at everything he had loved. Beauty dived downwards like some obscene bird. But Mathieu went on firing. He fired. He was cleansed. He was all powerful. He was free.
>
> Fifteen minutes.[17]

Many years later a woman I loved deeply bought me a second-hand copy of *Iron in the Soul*. She had marked page 225 with some code that made sense to us then but the meaning of which I can no longer fathom. Once more I recovered so much emotion compacted into so few words.

But Sartre's place in my pantheon was not uncontested. George Orwell, J D Salinger, Alex Hailey, Nelson Mandela and many more vied with each other. These were writers who either fed my emotions or suggested phil-osophies or ideologies that helped me begin to understand or explain what I now considered the unfair state of the world.

In September 1983, as a fresher at Balliol, I prepared to settle in for three years at Oxford. I had a comfortable room on the fifth floor of a century-old building with a view of St Giles' Church. At the foot of the staircase was the Balliol Bar. I didn't even have to go outside to access it! In addition, I quickly made friends with attractive and intelligent women. I could have settled in. But I was feeling raw and restless: my brief encounter with the South African liberation struggle made me easy picking for the radical left, in my case the Tendency.

Militant years

In the 1980s the Militant Tendency was an unwanted scion that grafted itself onto the Labour Party in Britain. It espoused a traditional purist Marxism, updated according to lessons learnt (or not) from the rise and demise of the 1917 Russian Revolution. It drew much of its inspiration from the life and writings of Leon Trotsky, who, until his murder in Mexico in 1940, was the individual most singly committed to exposing the crimes of Stalin and the hijack of the fledgling communist state. After his death the baton was picked up by the founder of Militant, one Ted Grant.

Trotsky was a dashing and romantic revolutionary who surfed on the crests of the great social and economic waves that tipped the nineteenth century into its successor. His energy, intelligence and commitment can still be felt in his voluminous and varied writings. His brief affair with the painter Frida Kahlo while in exile in Mexico, then his assassination by means of an ice pick brought to an end an extraordinary life. Ironically I had first encountered mention of Trotsky in 'No More Heroes', a 1977 song by the punk band The Stranglers.

> Whatever happened to
> Leon Trotsky?
> He got an ice pick
> That made his ears burn[18]

In contrast, Ted Grant had been a shabbily dressed and dour person, a man who had exiled himself from his native South Africa in 1933 to seek a more relevant theatre in which to prosecute the struggle for socialism. By the time I met him in the 1980s Grant was plucking the fruits of many years of preaching in the wilderness: the post-war economic boom had made Marxism seem irrelevant. Militant was on the rise. Among its supporters it counted two Labour MPs and its followers dominated several city councils, most significantly in Liverpool. In 1985 it moved into a modern and refitted headquarters in Hackney paid for entirely out of its 'supporters' subscriptions (its entryist position in the Labour Party meant Militant had to publicly claim that it did not have members). Grant confidently prophesied the imminent collapse of capitalism in Britain and internationally, something that would take place 'within five, ten or fifteen years' – a mantra we learnt to mimic.

1980s Britain was a time of insecurities and turbulence, with social and class ruptures deliberately created by Margaret Thatcher – a civil war in Northern Ireland – and a military adventure to recapture the Falklands from the 'Argies', as the Argentinians were called by the gutter press. It was a time of opportunity for a left that, given the certainties of the post-war consensus, had for decades found itself near-redundant.

It happened that the student on the floor below me on Staircase XIII hailed from a working-class background and had already joined the Militant before coming to Oxford. Greg Wilkinson was donkey-jacketed, chain-smoking, gruff. My unfocused outrage collided with his rational and reasoned explanations of politics, history and philosophy. Suddenly it all made sense. I found my '-ism' and became an '-ist'. Before long I found myself transitioning from being a 'contact' of the Militant to a fully fledged 'recruit'.

Thus began a ten-year association and a deep intimacy with the left. Thus began many hours of branch meetings, reading groups, paper sales of *The Militant* outside the British Leyland factory in Cowley (a working-class suburb on the outskirts of Oxford) and trips to London to participate in conferences and meetings. Thus I encountered Trotsky's *History of the Russian Revolution*, Lenin's *What Is to Be Done?* and of course Marx's forbidding *Capital* – a work of science and imagination that several years later I would read out loud, from start to finish, line by line, under the tutelage of Rob Petersen, a self-exiled South African lawyer, in his flat in a dank council tower block in Hackney, East London.

With hindsight I could say – with justification – that there were many better ways to spend three years at Oxford. Instead of punting on the River Cherwell I would be up early in the morning riding my bike through empty streets to stand at the gates of British Leyland, trying to sell copies of each week's *Militant*. 'Labour's Marxist newspaper!' I would call out with my middle-class accent to a weary, uninterested workforce, starting a new day's shift, lunch-box and *The Sun* in hand. When it was almost too late I discovered the wonders of seclusion in isolated sections of the vast, ancient Bodleian Library and then the beauty of Christ Church Meadow.

Perhaps one day I will reclaim my lost time at Oxford University. I don't regret its loss: Oxford will always be there, but that moment in political time will not. My involvement with the Militant Tendency gave me a ringside seat from where I could view a different type of politics from that which I had experienced in South Africa.

Britain's struggles were made of grit and coal, they were oily and industrial, more complex and less easy to idealise or romanticise than the South African struggle. It was a politics that my middle-class personality found hard to identify and associate with.

I was suddenly in a strange and unanticipated place. Class difference confused me. At St Peter's School in York, where I had lived sheltered in a boarding house with ample grounds, I had experienced class in the form of working-class youths who lived on the other side of the school walls. We called them 'bovver boys' and 'skins'; they prowled the perimeters of the school grounds, beating up or threatening sheltered toffs like me if they ran into us on the streets. Every Saturday morning we were allowed to leave the school grounds to go to buy sweets and comics at a nearby grocer's shop in Clifton. The 1970s was the golden age of comics and in 1976 my and many others' favourite was the violent *Action*. Even the comic strips reflected the changing of an age. Soft titles like *The Beano*, *The Dandy* and *The Beezer* made way for brutal stories like 'Hook Jaw', 'Kids Rule OK' and 'Dredger'.

If I am to be truthful I have to say that the working class frightened me. On the days when there was a soccer match involving York City Football Club the violence of disaffected working-class youth came closer to home. Terrorising private-school boys was one of the games that followed the match, and would be more violent on the days when York City lost (which it did frequently). We were instructed by our teachers to stay indoors. Later, I experienced the differences between classes through my fear of skinheads, another brand of socially estranged youth expressing their alienation through vandalism, racism and violence.

The sharpest expression of the disaffection of working-class youth was in the music of the late 1970s.[19] When in 1976 the Sex Pistols burst upon British politics, they both frightened and fascinated me. They seemed to gleefully break every hypocritical taboo in the Establishment book. Their clothes were ripped, their ears safety-pinned, their language a new liturgy of obscenity, their targets the Establishment, particularly the Queen. But for me, once I became familiar with the thunderclap that was their one and only album, *Never Mind the Bollocks, Here's the Sex Pistols*, their music was like a new form of terrorism, with Johnny Rotten and Sid Vicious literally spitting their contempt at the post-war consensus while (almost unintentionally) creating music with a political power that is still unprecedented.

Socialist literature, to which the Militant Tendency introduced me, was much safer than punk rock, which I began to love from a safe distance. My rapid trawl through socialist history and literature began in 1983. Ironically, Trotsky's romantic vision for humanity felt safer for me – it was more intellectual and idealistic than the grimy working-class struggle for what I thought were mundane things like jobs.

In those good old days it was assumed that grown-ups got jobs and that mass unemployment happened only during economic slumps; joblessness was the exception, rather than the norm. In those days the battle was not for employment but for a better quality of employment. In the words of Linton Kwezi Johnson (aka LKJ) in his poem 'More Time':

> wi want di shawtah workin day
> gi wi di shawtah workin week
> langah holiday
> wi need decent pay
>
> more time fi leasha
> more time fi pleasha
> more time fi edificaeshun
> more time fi reckreashun
> more time fi contemplate
> more time fi ruminate
> more time
> wi need
> more
> time[20]

I romanticised the rich lives of such revolutionaries as Leon Trotsky, Rosa Luxemburg and Karl Liebknecht. Trotsky's essays published as *Literature and Revolution* offered a different perspective from the Establishment literary canon I had come to know at Oxford. His *Problems of Everyday Life*,[21] intended as a practical guide to new values under the Bolshevik administration, looked at life shorn of the cant of the middle-class social denialism I was brought up with. It made sense because here I was, a student at Oxford University, lapping up a millennium of English writing that had started with the epic Anglo-Saxon poem *Beowulf* and ended (in my studies) with George Orwell, but tormented that I had access to this world only because of privilege and not by right.

'I have seen the future, and it works,' remarked the American journal-ist Lincoln Steffens after a trip to the early USSR.[22] In socialist literature I thought I had too.

Unfortunately Steffens was dreadfully wrong, or perhaps he was right? Perhaps the Soviet Union's descent into totalitarian Stalinism was the future. One thing is certain, though: in my lifetime the practicability of the socialist dream has been dashed.

On some days I think back over the last 30 years (not just my years, but the world's years) and wonder about the dreams of equality we seem to have given up. In my early years as an activist equality meant equality of access to the world's treasures, equal opportunity for each human being to fulfil his or her human potential, not just economic potential. I dreamt of a different world, one where, as Lenin was said to have said, 'a cook could be a prime minister', one where class differences and inequality would dissolve and where the treasures of humankind, in literature, music, architecture or art, would be opened to everyone. These days we have descended into struggles for basic dignity and decency, for toilets or school textbooks.

During her first years as head of government, Thatcher's objective was to break the power of the trade unions. Her first target was the National Union of Mineworkers (NUM), the strongest component of the labour movement. The British Coal Corporation was a nationalised industry and unprofitable pits were being closed so as to make it more attractive for privatisation. Thatcher provoked the NUM into an industrial action and between March 1984 and March 1985 over 100 000 British mineworkers went out on strike to defend their jobs.

I joined the resistance.

At the outset a mineworker was an alien thing to me. In my naïvety I couldn't understand the reason for their strike. Why, I asked myself quietly, protest against pit closures when the pit was the source of many an accident, darkness, dust and hard labour? My understanding of mining was cerebral, brought to me first via the horrors of exploitation described in novels like Emile Zola's *Germinal* – or, more appropriate in 1984, the novels of the Welsh communist Lewis Jones, particularly his tales of the struggles of Welsh mineworkers in *Cwmardy* and *We Live*.

Nonetheless, once the strike got underway I joined a miners' sup-port group, rattling collection tins every Saturday morning on Oxford's

A photo of a mounted policeman riding at full gallop, his baton aiming for the head of a member of Women Against Pit Closures, has stayed with me all my life. Orgreave, 1984
© John Harris[23]

Cornmarket Street, calling out 'Support the miners!' to passing shoppers. Yet what I came to learn from the strike was more about the nobility of resistance and solidarity than about politics. I was being drenched in Marxism at branch meetings of the Militant, meetings I attended far more frequently than lectures. But despite this I would properly understand the politics and economics of these first years of 'neoliberalism' only many years later. By contrast, the trips I made to colliers' villages in South Wales, seeing the hunger, witnessing the violence the police meted out to the strikers, got me emotionally involved with the miners' cause. I attended benefit concerts by the likes of Billy Bragg, whose version of 'Which Side Are You On?' helped me understand the gut-wrenching disgust attached to the word 'scab'.

> It's hard to explain to a crying child
> Why her Daddy can't go back
> So the family suffer
> But it hurts me more
> To hear a scab say 'Sod you, Jack'[24]

After a long, long year the NUM was defeated. The miners fought heroically to keep the coal mines open but Thatcher considered herself on a historic mission; she could and would hold out longer than them. As the strike dragged on workers were split, families turned on each other, anger occasionally morphed into murder, unity into division. Eventually the strike was broken and in March 1985 the remaining strikers returned to work, defeated but unbowed.

In manifold ways the politics of Thatcherism and my membership of the resistance permeated my Oxford years. My early struggle CV, proving my credentials as an immature socialist, would have read something like this:

1985	Arrested for the first time during a demonstration attempting to prevent Thatcher giving a lecture at Oxford's All Souls College. Tried in Oxford Magistrates' Court.
1984–1989	Member of the Militant-controlled Labour Party Young Socialists (LPYS). Participated in its annual conferences at the seaside resort of Brighton.
1984–1986	Numerous trips from Oxford to Militant's grand modern headquarters and printing press in the hollowed-out former industrial area of Hackney Wick, a building bought with money raised from members' subs and sacrifices.
1986	Marched on the streets of Liverpool in support of the Militant-dominated Liverpool City Council, which had sinned against the Tories by building new houses for working-class people in a period of recession.
1988	Fought the Poll Tax.
1988	Participated in grand political rallies organised by a rising Militant at the Alexandra Palace and the Royal Albert Hall, veritable symbols of the Establishment, which the growing Militant appropriated to advance the cause of socialism.

Not too long after the miners' strike I found myself embroiled in another defining struggle over union power. This time Thatcher was out to break the print unions of Fleet Street. To do this she joined forces with the noxious Rupert Murdoch. Murdoch's News International titles, including *The Sun* and *The Times*, moved physically away from the Fleet Street area, the centuries-old home of the print media, to brand-new headquarters in Wapping, East London. It became known as 'Fortress Wapping' because of its razor-wire barriers, floodlights, watchtowers and the heavy police presence.

One evening in 1986 a last-ditch picket of Wapping aimed to prevent the new HQ from becoming operational. I was there. The memory remains fresh: the great wall of razor wire around Wapping; the floodlights on the ramps leading lorries into the building to collect their newspaper cargo; an army of tense police squared up against an opposing phalanx of striking print workers and thousands of their supporters. Both sides lined up outside the gates. Lorries moved up the ramps to collect their cargo and move on through the building into the night, to the chant of 'scab, scab, scab . . .' Then the police charged, bricks were thrown, strikers arrested. That night I fled the riot and ran home through the back streets of East London, taking care to avoid what we then called the pigs. I sensed people's powerlessness to hold back the tide of a new but then unrecognised political movement, 'neoliberalism'. The demonstrations made good theatre but they were futile: the strike collapsed early the following year.

In the early 1980s something profoundly different was developing in politics and economics. Institutions and systems that had been built to protect the working class were being overrun, and old certainties and philosophies were being dug up and destroyed. The Militant Tendency struck a chord but unfortunately the left was so hamstrung by its dogmas, ideologies or lethargies that it was able neither to define nor to resist the new age. A refrain loved by Marxists then and now is that society had reached 'a fundamental turning point'. For example, a July 1984 article in *Militant* stated that 'under the impact of this strike the entire landscape of British society is being redrawn. When it is over, nothing – socially, industrially or politically – will have been left untouched.'

That was true, but not in the way the Militant Tendency saw it. The common belief on the left was that in the miners' strike we were witnessing the death agonies of capitalism, rather than its bloody rebirth and the acquisition of a new lease of life. Thatcher was administering the C-section. Her friend President Ronald Reagan was doing the same thing by taking on the air-traffic controllers in the United States. But the resistance, although determined, was ultimately unsuccessful.

Activist in exile

The Anti-Apartheid Movement (AAM) was also on the rise during this period and Thatcher's policy of 'constructive engagement' and opposition to sanctions was correctly the focus of its ire. The AAM organised huge protest marches and was the cause of my taking additional bus and train trips between Oxford and London. AAM demonstrations often targeted the grand colonial South Africa House, its place on the edge of

Trafalgar Square proof that South Africa was once a jewel in the crown of the British empire. On one demonstration I had my head split open as a bottle, loosely aimed at South Africa House by someone who was hidden among a group of Class War anarchists, landed instead on me. I was knocked out, dragged through the police lines, spat on and sworn at by one weary pig and put into one of the fleet of waiting ambulances.

The play in which I was a bit player was an English one, yet South Africa was always in my foreground; that was my struggle. And the backdrop to the British resistance to Thatcher was an ever-rising revolution in South Africa. It was for South Africa and a reconnection with the politics of the liberation struggle that I yearned. Fortunately, by the second year of my membership of the Militant Tendency I was trusted enough to be introduced to its secretive South African 'section', the Marxist Workers' Tendency (MWT) of the ANC. Being invited to London to attend their meetings felt like being drawn into the real struggle again. Working with exiles close to the ANC fed my starved imagination.

The heart of the MWT was the 'gang of four', as they were described in ANC exile circles. The four were not a naturally cohesive group of people but had been thrown into each other's arms by exile and ideology: David Hemson (who wrote under the names 'Jake Wilson' or 'Ken Mark') had participated in the 1973 Durban strikes as a student and was an ardent trade unionist; Rob Petersen ('Paul Storey'), a lawyer who had briefly been National Chairman of the Young Progressives before gravitating to organising workers and thence to Marxism; Martin Legassick ('Richard Monroe'), the well-respected radical historian; and Paula Ensor, a political activist who after several years of exile in London had chosen to live in Gaborone, Botswana.

The four had journeyed into exile via different paths at different points in the 1970s. In this respect they were like a trickle of other radicalised white youth who sought to avoid military conscription and/or to join the ANC. What brought them together in England was their common endeavours to shift the ANC to the left and to encourage the growth of an independent workers' movement in South Africa. But an independent brand of socialism was not wanted. So it was that despite their closeness to some senior figures in the ANC, including Oliver Tambo and Ruth First, the four had been suspended from the ANC in 1979 and then expelled in 1985.

After their suspension they worked to set up the Southern African Labour Education Project (SALEP), an organisation that focused on exposing the exploitation of cheap labour by British multinationals and produced good-quality political educational material for use by trade unions in South Africa. But their primary mission was to organise a Marxist current inside the ANC which, it was hoped, would in time become a majority.

Working with them at the SALEP office were several other exiles: Victor Mhlongo ('Sam'), Weizmann Hamilton ('Winston'), Darcy du Toit ('George'), Anneke Poppe and Margie Struthers. Several others – seconded to work with the MWT – made up the team, notably Leon Kaplan, Paul Moorhouse, Norma Craven and April Ashley.

The late Nimrod Sejake, one of the founders of the South African Congress of Trade Unions (SACTU), the predecessor to COSATU, and a 1956–1961 treason trialist, was also part of the group. Nimrod lived in Dublin and so was at our offices only infrequently. He was an eccentric and spirited elderly man, with a silver goatee. He had chosen Dublin as his place of exile because his sister worked as a domestic worker for an Irish family in South Africa: as a result he identified with the Irish people's struggle against the English. Nimrod spoke at the Tendency's big events because nobody could question his struggle credentials or legitimacy: a photo of him talking to workers adorned the cover of *Organize . . . or Starve!* – a book about the history of SACTU.[25]

It was at one of these meetings that I first encountered Zackie Achmat. For several years Zackie remained a mystery. 'For security reasons' (a common refrain in those days) he was known as Michael. He had shoulder-length hair, a scrubby youthful beard and a sense of fun. He would arrive in London without warning, be huddled in discussions for several days and then disappear again. He was the leader of the MWT in 'the interior' (as we called it then). But his person was clouded in secrecy; he was a man about whose personality we could not ask questions 'for security reasons'. I did not even know he was gay until I came back to South Africa in 1989 and shared a flat with him in a Johannesburg suburb.

In the years ahead Zackie Achmat became a comrade and friend who would shape the direction of my life. For many years I was in awe of him, slightly intimidated, afraid to reveal the more human side of my character for fear of being thought 'petit bourgeois'. I was afraid to smoke in front of him and rarely drank. However, after 1994 our relationship developed into an enormously creative collaboration as we worked together to build the Treatment Action Campaign. He befriended Ciaran, my first living son, and I became a frequent guest at his home in Muizenberg in Cape Town, witness to some of the pain and anxiety that came with his HIV infection. In the midst of his depression I was often the only person who could cajole him out of bed in the morning. But once he was up, our different strengths and perspectives worked together perfectly. But hold on, I'm jumping times and journeys . . .

Somehow I muddled through Oxford. My real preoccupation was with the struggle for socialism: my studies were very much on the periphery. I felt as if I were an exile. Wherever possible I sought out the company of South Africans. These included Jann Turner, the elder daughter of Rick Turner, the Durban-based philosopher-activist who had been shot dead by unknown assailants in January 1978.[26] I romanticised Jann; we became good friends; she felt to me like Burger's daughter in Nadine Gordimer's eponymous novel. 'I love Lionel and Lionel's daughter,' I wrote in a poem of the time. Secretly I was in love with her. I yearned for the afternoons we would sometimes spend at her little flat on the banks of the River Cherwell. But my heart was broken when she started a relationship with my housemate, Greg Wilkinson, the gruff working-class student and friend who had recruited me for Militant.

But despite my preoccupation with revolution I was attentive enough to my studies to deepen my knowledge and love of literature. For three years we were made to gallop through English literature: an author a week, a century a term. I sat Finals in June 1986. Not surprisingly I emerged with a lowly II-2. A few days of the traditional Champagne Charlie debauchery followed. Then I was ready to move.

On one of my trips to London I had been summoned to a Discussion (with a big D) with Rob Petersen and Leon Kaplan and asked to work full-time for SALEP (read: the MWT). Leaving Oxford University to go and live on the bleak working-class estates in the East End of London was an act of defiance against my conservative parents' expectations. My father had started work at the age of seventeen and had pulled himself out of a difficult working-class background in Manchester. He was convinced that with a bit of effort everybody else could do so too. He was a standard-bearer for the 'pull yourself up by your bootstraps' generation; Thatcher fodder, persuaded that unemployed working-class youth were nothing more than 'yobs' or – in the self-parodying words appropriated by the Sex Pistols to describe themselves – 'lazy sods'.

He was an ardent armchair Thatcherite, the type of person with whom her appeal to individualism resonated. From the time I started to form political opinions different from his own, our relationship had never been

A rare photo of me from my Oxford days. In the Quad at Balliol with my close friend Anna Cressey after finishing Finals in June 1986.

good: now it deteriorated further. On my occasional trips back to the family home in Farnham, Sussex, the heart of Middle England, the banker belt, we fought about capital punishment, which he supported and I opposed, the Falklands War, which he supported and I opposed, the miners' strike and so on. There was little space for common ground and we hated each other.

My going back to rough working-class housing estates was in part taking a stand against him. A 'fuck you'. Oxford University graduates were meant to assume careers that led them up the invisible ladder into the Establishment. Boris Johnson, my peer at Balliol, started on a trajectory that led him to become Mayor of London, a controversial leader of the Conservative Party and a bumbling advocate of Brexit. Oxford graduates like me were not meant to sign on to the dole, feigning unemployment so as to have a few pounds to eat, drink, pay rent and advance the socialist revolution in South Africa and globally.

But that's what I chose to do.

So it was that in July 1986 I moved from the dreaming spires to late Cold War recessionary London. Initially a council flat was arranged for me on a wretched place called Pembury Estate in Hackney, East London. I shared it with Ruth Williams, a young working-class Welsh woman with dyed red hair and a loud voice to match. She was a full-time employee of the Militant Tendency. Pembury Estate was everything I never wanted to live in: great squat blocks of flats separated by tarmac, and only the occasional patch of green grass. Dog shit, brawling couples sounding like cats in the night and the vulgar uncultivated lumpenproletariat. My flat was what John Cooper Clarke, the punk poet, termed 'a fully furnished dustbin' in his poem 'Beasley Street'.[27]

After a year I left Pembury Estate for an even worse abode. This time my home was in the same building as the SALEP (MWT) office but on the ground floor. A more unpleasant place you could not imagine, damp, dark and unwelcoming. When I moved in shit flowed from a broken pipe outside the front door. I walked out into the shit. It was a 'home' that propelled you four floors upstairs to work. It was a far cry from the manicured quads of Oxford colleges and the dreaming spires.

My first 'office' at SALEP was little better. The MWT occupied four abandoned flats on the fourth floor of a burnt-out block of flats in Hackney. Secrecy and suspicion pervaded the operation. The balcony of the flats was sealed off by a large, impenetrable iron gate. Access to the fourth flat was limited to a very few people. One of the meeting rooms was padded with foam in a doubtless vain attempt to block listening devices planted by a probably imaginary security police. 'Sensitive' organisational discussions took place in the nearby London Fields park. This was a practice I had first encountered at Wilgespruit Fellowship Centre; it's a very struggle thing. The assumption in those days was that buildings held listening devices – but today it's so last Tuesday. In the age of the cell phone you can be listened to almost anywhere.

Yet my romantic self welcomed the cloak-and-dagger stuff. I felt it meant I was involved in a serious struggle. Initially I wrote under the name of Peter Davies. Later I was allowed to choose another name and for the next three years I became Sean Kelly, my real name unknown even to my lovers or close friends.

I adopted a faint South African accent, not because I wanted to deceive but because I wanted to be more legitimate in the eyes, or rather the ears, of the real South Africans I worked with. I wanted to be a bona fide South African revolutionary. I worked eighteen hours a day and every weekend. I wanted to prove myself to my leaders, to blot out my petit-bourgeois background, to hide my Englishness and thereby win enough trust to do undercover work in South Africa.

I cut links with my Oxford friends, had little contact with my family, avoided falling in love or developing more than half a handful of close friendships. I wanted to be ready at any moment to pack up and go. So on an emotional level these were years of limbo, living corporeally in one place yet spiritually and imaginatively inhabiting another.

And yet those years were formative and important. In some ways this was University phase two. Oxford lined my soul with literature. Hackney taught me to make another type of sense from it.

Everlasting mountains

On a long journey you need a place where you can rest. On the journey towards social justice you need places to hide from the madding crowd. You need to retain enough energy to want to explore alternative routes, take paths less travelled, find environs where you may surrender to each of your five original senses.

My escape from Hackney was to the mountains of the Lake District. The Lakeland paths have been painstakingly hand-drawn and described by one Alfred Wainwright. Wainwright was an eccentric. He eschewed the life of a cotton mill-worker to explore the contours, nooks and crannies of his beloved hills. A fell-walker. I was guided by Wainwright's little book of drawings and commentary, A Coast to Coast Walk. It maps the path Wainwright took from St Bees Head on the west coast of England to Robin Hood's Bay on the east. Wainwright's philosophy for the book is that 'one should always have a definite objective, in a walk as in life – it is so much more satisfying to reach a target by personal effort than to wander aimlessly. An objective is an ambition and life without ambition is . . . well, aimless wandering.' [28]

Wainwright was a socialist. He had a soulmate in Karl Marx, who said of patient study, research and reading that 'there is no royal road to science, and only those who do not dread the fatiguing climb of its steep paths have a chance of gaining its luminous summits'. [29]

From Wainwright I learned an affinity not only with mountains but with those who seek solace in their embrace. Mountain revellers have something special. We get through our humdrum days because we know about something unique, something not purchasable at supermarkets or downloadable from the internet. Our kindred souls reach across the ages. Samuel Taylor Coleridge wrote that, coming down from a mountain in the English Lake District, he 'lay in a state of almost prophetic Trance and Delight' at 'the sight of the Crags above me on each side, and the impetuous Clouds just over them, posting so luridly and so rapidly northward'.

That was in 1802. I know that feeling.

In August 1987 I ventured further afield. I fled Hackney to hitchhike across Scandinavia. One evening, somewhere between Trondheim in Norway and Östersund in Sweden, I came across a mountain. That day hitching lifts had been easy. I was ahead of time. The sun cut through a deep blue sky. On the spur of the moment some feeling pulled me off the road and onto the mountain. There was no path. I set my compass towards the sky and started walking.

Mountains have a spirit. If you make yourself vulnerable to their ministrations, they will possess you. I climbed around or over cliffs, towards then beyond the treeline. The further forward, the more impossible to turn back. In winter these slopes are covered in snow. Now they were rocks and green grass. My wise self said 'go down'. My possessed self refused.

After several hours I stood upon the summit. Marx and Wainwright were right. The effort was rewarded. Luminosity. A perfect vista in every direction, unbroken, as far as the eye could see. Mountain-tops at eye level, lakes far below.

It was too rare a moment to give up. I decided to stay the night. Impulse always fights inertia, conservatism, a tinge of fear. Impulse won. I camped on the summit, feeling very alone. Me, my pea-pod tent and the mountain.

The next morning when I poked open the tent the world had changed. Clouds sat thickly upon the mountain. 'As far as the eye can see' was reduced to 'as far as the hand can reach'. A continuous drizzle leaked out of the grey blanket. Panic. Down I went through the fog, risking the cliffs I had carefully skirted the evening before. Down, down, down. Eventually I stumbled back onto the road. I had been foolhardy but I had survived.

I never will know the name of that mountain. But the passion and mixed emotions of that one-night stand will linger forever, resident in some recess of my brain until life force is extinguished.

I would die happily on a mountain. In Memoirs of a Fellwanderer, with old age firmly upon him, Wainwright wrote, 'all I ask for in the end is a last long resting place by the side of Innominate Tarn on Haystacks, where the water gently laps the gravelly shore and the heather blooms and Pillar and Gable keep unfailing watch. A quiet place. A lonely place. I shall go to it, for the last time, and be carried – someone who knew me in life will take me there and empty me out of a little box and leave me there alone. And if you, dear reader, should get a bit of grit in your boot as you are crossing Haystacks in the years to come, please treat it with respect. It might be me.'[30]

The 'gang of four' were a remarkable and unusual group of activists with whom I shared three years of close company. There was a lot to learn from them.

The leader was Rob Petersen, taciturn, outwardly unemotional, immensely intelligent, the brains behind the operation. His character contrasted sharply with that of Martin Legassick, chain-smoking, dishevelled, literally frothing at the mouth when he gave any speech that lasted longer than ten minutes. Legassick died in 2016: his remarkable achievements as a historian and his lifelong commitment to socialism deserve proper study.[31] His is one of the South African revolution's untold tales.

Then there was David Hemson, a Durban trade unionist and one of the architects of the 1973 Durban strikes, a friend of Richard (Rick) Turner. He had been in exile in Zimbabwe, but in 1985 he and thirteen others had been arrested for propagating Marxism and opinions critical of ZANU-PF. He spent seven weeks in prison before being deported. Hemson was the most human and warm of the group and also lived on the bleak Pembury Estate with his wife Trish and their two young boys.

The secretive Paula Ensor was the mystery card. She had been banned under the Suppression of Communism Act and left South Africa in May 1976, travelling to the Botswana border illegally, crossing it at night, alone and on foot. After some years in London, and after her suspension from the ANC, she went to work in Botswana where she was at risk from both the South African state and the Stalinists. Paula never came to the office. When she occasionally visited London, meetings with her were held in a nearby flat.

The flagship of the MWT was its publication *Inqaba ya Basebenzi: Journal of the Marxist Workers' Tendency of the African National Congress*. Its title means 'Fortress of the Workers' in Zulu. The first edition had been published in January 1981, proclaiming that it stood 'For a mass ANC with a socialist programme!'

Although it was written and printed in London, enormous efforts were made to ensure that it reached a layer of conscious political activists within South

The first edition of *Inqaba ya Basebenzi*, January 1981.

Africa. With brilliant minds like Petersen's and Legassick's, it was a content-rich and high-quality source of analysis of southern African politics and history. Had he been writing as a professor at a university, Legassick's 'Lessons of the 1950s'[32] might today be regarded as a classic text of South African history with the same reputation as his other seminal academic writings of the late 1960s.

Among all stripes of Marxists, from the days of Marx himself, the 'theoretical journal' has been the centrepiece of organising. It is meant to arm followers with a theoretical understanding of politics, demonstrate analysis in practice and provide the 'advance guard' of the revolutionary masses with their marching orders. *Inqaba* was published as an alternative voice to the Stalinist *African Communist*, described as 'the theoretical journal of the South African Communist Party'. Its articles were long and complex because they were meant to be studied and not just read in passing.

Strange as it may seem for someone who had just completed three years studying English language and literature at Oxford, researching and writing for *Inqaba* was where I learnt to write. Under the tutelage of Petersen and Legassick I became a published writer for *Inqaba* in February 1986 when it had reached issue 18/19 – at that time I was still at Oxford.[33] I attended editorial board meetings that lasted for several days, picking over words while suffocating in an airless, lightless, foam-padded room.

Every word of a draft article would be placed and interrogated as to its connection to the next word and its relevance. Petersen was a lawyer and law is the discipline that, at least when practised well, makes the best use of words, carefully examining each for its meaning, not settling for words that might be misinterpreted, pushing from the page words that are surplus to requirements. Very different from poetry.

In these meetings we endured the merciless slaughtering of our favourite sentences and theories. In early 1988 I had to rewrite an article analysing the Freedom Charter 'from a Marxist perspective' three or four times before it was considered good enough for publication.[34]

Not surprisingly, these meetings became known as the abattoir.

Writing for *Inqaba* became the lens through which, for the next three years, I closely observed South Africa's unfolding revolution. Weekly phone calls would take place with leaders back in South Africa, usually with Zackie but sometimes with other leaders such as Shafika Isaacs, Noor Nieftagodien and Lederle Bosch. These intricate political discussions analysed South Africa's rapidly developing politics. They were tape-recorded, transcribed, pasted into notebooks (eventually running to many volumes) and then intricately discussed by members of the Political Committee.

The late 1980s heralded the beginning of the communications and internet revolution, the launch of the internet and the World Wide Web. Petersen made a mission of closely following the development of this new technology. As a result of his knowledge the MWT was able to take advantage of what was then the latest in communications technology. As desktop computers started to make way for laptops, we were owners of one of the first 'portable' Amstrad computers – an instrument the size of a small suitcase. This machine was considered a minor miracle. Twice a week I would put it in a rucksack and carry it on my bike across London to a safe house. There we would link it to a phone and in a complicated process transmit encrypted files down the line to a public telephone box in Cape Town where Zackie would be situated with a similar device.

Thinking back to those days helps me realise the practical consequences of the communications revolution. Among many other things it has revolutionised the struggle for human rights; the new machines have saved on labour. On one occasion, to avoid detection and interception by the security police, I made an eight-hour train and ferry journey across the English Channel to the German city of Frankfurt so as to post copies of the latest edition of *Inqaba ya Basebenzi* to various addresses in South Africa. Today you would save the journal as a PDF file, attach it to an email and press 'send'!

3

One of the great revolutions
of the twentieth century

Kaydar
e ad to go
Zhivkov
e ad to go
Husak
e ad to go
Honnicka
e ad to go
Chowcheskhu
e ad to go
just like apartied
will av to go
Linton Kwesi Johnson, 'Mi Revalueshanary Fren'[35]

In the last three years of the 1980s I learnt a great deal about politics and Marxism. But holed up in my flat in Hackney I lived the life of a monk. With a few exceptions I eschewed close friendships and kept sexual relationships to fleeting, fumbling encounters which I could disengage from should need be. The tower blocks of Hackney were my skyscape. Occasionally I would escape on my bicycle and ride through the London streets to the banks of the Thames, where I would revel in a sense of freedom and release.

Essentially it was a time of waiting.

Then in August or September 1989 I received the news that I had hoped for since I started working in London. One day Rob took me for a walk, away from the imagined microphones of the security police. In his clipped and precise manner he told me what I already knew: the political situation in South Africa was white-hot and changing rapidly.

The apartheid state had begun making concessions under pressure from trade unions and township rebellions on one side and capitalists on the other. The latter realised that the game was up: apartheid, a political system they had taken advantage of for 40 years in order to amass enormous riches, was now not just a liability but a threat. Small pre-democratic spaces were opening up.

In mid-1989 the MWT had launched *Congress Militant*, a more frequent and accessible Marxist newspaper. Rob asked that I go to South Africa for three months to provide political education to two groups of young activists, one from Dobsonville in Soweto and the other from the coloured Johannesburg suburbs of Westbury and Bosmont.

I was asked to lose my British passport, with its telltale South African immigration stamps, and apply for a new one. In my small circle of comrades and friends, nobody was to know I was leaving: I was just to disappear. One day I would be gone. Into the empty space where the day before I had lived and worked, my friends would insert their understanding of where my physical being had been removed to.

I was not planning to tell my parents, from whom I was anyway estranged. But a few weeks before my departure my grandmother Ada Masser suffered a stroke. She was the person with whom I had one of my strongest family relationships, the matriarch with whom, since the age of eight, I had spent weekend exeats and half-term holidays. I travelled back to Bridlington, in effect to say goodbye.

I was right. Ada Masser eventually died in 2001 and I would see her only once more. But on this occasion my mother too was visiting Bridlington and I told her of my imminent departure. Our conversations were so strained in those days that I cannot remember her reaction.

Thus it was that in October 1989 I boarded an Olympic Airways flight to South Africa via Athens, with a small suitcase of clothes. I was pretending to be a tourist. I was half expecting to be detained at Jan Smuts Airport or, if I was lucky, to be returned immediately to Europe. As I anticipated (or imagined), at the immigration desk a steely-faced Afrikaner official ordered my passport temporarily removed for closer inspection. As it disappeared my heart fluttered nervously. But within minutes it was returned.

I grabbed my single suitcase and walked through the arrivals hall into what would become a new life. In what I thought was a breach of security I was surprised to be met by a cheerful Michael (Zackie Achmat). I hurried past, telling him under my breath that I thought I was being followed. I wasn't. Within an hour I was moving into my new home, a flat shared with Zackie in Judith's Paarl, a small Johannesburg suburb.

The late 1980s were a time of ferment, a time that was shaking the old South Africa and shaping the new one. It was a time of blood-letting and of the blooding of the people who would become leaders of a democratic South Africa.

From London we had watched and written about the rise of the Congress of South African Trade Unions (COSATU) after its launch in 1985. We had observed and analysed its young General Secretary, Jay Naidoo, who many years later would become a friend and comrade. We studied such trade union leaders as Moses Mayekiso, Cyril Ramaphosa and Chris Dlamini, each of whom engaged in brief political discussions with the Tendency.[36]

We had spoken on the phone weekly to my friend Lederle ('Laddy') Bosch, whom the MWT had sent from Cape Town to build branches in Natal. With his assistance we analysed and provided commentary on the civil war between Inkatha and the United Democratic Front (UDF) in Natal. We warned about the culpability of the ANC leadership in advancing the career of the treacherous Chief Mangosuthu Buthelezi and the state-funded Inkatha. In 1986 I co-authored with Zackie (I under the name Peter Davies, he as Daniel Lackay) an *Inqaba* article titled 'Inkatha – This Spear of Counter-Revolution Must Be Broken'. When smuggled copies reached South Africa the article caused a breakdown in peace talks between Inkatha and the UDF that aimed to halt the deepening civil war in Natal. Somehow Buthelezi, the leader of Inkatha, got hold of a copy of that issue of *Inqaba*. He demanded that the UDF repudiate the article. They did. Peace talks resumed. But they didn't bring peace.

Our analysis was spot-on. Inkatha was a front of the apartheid state, not a genuine Zulu nationalist movement. Its raison d'être was to legitimise the Bantustan system and later to wage war on the Zulu people's rebellion against apartheid. Soon after I arrived in South Africa the civil war was transported to the hostels and townships of Johannesburg. At this point the murderous role played by the Inkatha Freedom Party (IFP) became plain for all to see.

Learning a second literature

My three months passed quickly.

As South Africa teetered on the edge of fundamental political change, I taught small groups of young activists from Soweto and Bosmont/Westbury about Lenin and Trotsky. We held political discussions to forewarn them about the class character of the ANC leadership, which would lead to their betraying the socialist aspirations of the mass of workers. We met

A collage of newspaper articles reporting the UDF's repudiation of the article Zackie and I wrote, and the advertisement itself.

for political discussion at the back of a small church in Braamfontein, which many years later would be converted into first a restaurant and then the Orbit jazz club. I paid discreet visits to Dobsonville in Soweto to meet with youth activists. I forged lifelong friendships with 'Tsegie', 'Keith', 'Nadia' and 'Cindy', all aliases for well-known activists in the coloured suburbs of Bosmont and Westbury. One weekend we slipped away to a two-day planning meeting at a farm near Sterkfontein, a place later to be declared the Cradle of Humankind.

The interest of young activists in the MWT was growing. People sensed big change and were thirsty to try to understand the swirling politics around them. In this context, imagining a bright future ahead for the growth of a mass Marxist following, in early 1990 Achmat and Petersen (I imagine) decided that I should extend my stay in South Africa. I was asked to make arrangements to remain indefinitely.

But to do so I needed a cover.

Thus it was that one day I wandered into the African Literature department at the University of the Witwatersrand wearing Balliol College on my sleeve. I don't believe in God, but there have been moments in my life when I have wondered about fortune, the existence of some hidden spirit or formula that fortuitously puts you in the right place at the right time. This was to be one such moment. In that nondescript corridor in a nondescript corner of the university were to be found two of the greatest living writers of South African literature, E'skia (Zeke) Mphahlele, author of *Down Second Avenue*, and Njabulo Ndebele, author of *Fools and Other Stories* and more recently *The Cry of Winnie Mandela*. I hit the jackpot at the end of that corridor.

But being star-struck was not my mission. I made a point of befriending the head of department, Peter Thuynsma. I asked whether I might be eligible to register for an MA in African Literature. My proclaimed interest: the influence of the teaching and reading of Shakespeare on black South African writers in the nineteenth century.

I must have been sufficiently convincing. Before long I was being asked to lecture to undergraduate students. Through my new studies and research I came to know of Tiyo Soga, Samuel Edward Krune (S E K) Mqhayi, Sol Plaatje, Thomas Mofolo, Herbert Isaac Ernest (H I E) Dhlomo, Can Themba, Phyllis Ntantala, William Plomer and many others. I was even allowed to teach their writings to first-year students at Wits University.

For my MA dissertation I focused on the writing and life of Archibald Campbell Jordan, husband of Phyllis Ntantala and father of the ANC intellectual and stalwart Pallo Jordan. A C Jordan was the author of the much under-appreciated Xhosa novel *Ingqumbo Yeminyanya / The Wrath of the Ancestors*.[37] I had read his English translation, but wondered why he had prefixed to the original text a quote from Shakespeare's play *Richard II*:

> For God's sake, let us sit upon the ground
> And tell sad stories of the death of kings.

'Why Shakespeare?' I wondered. Thus began my journey into an unknown (to me) literature, one that felt much more alive, more resonant and relevant, more closely tied up with issues of contemporary justice and injustice than the body of literature I had studied at Balliol.

I had intended my MA as a cover for political work, allowing me to apply for a student visa and remain in South Africa. It served this purpose and from time to time I would skip into the department, give a class, attend a lecture, maintain a presence. But in 1993, as the time approached for delivering a pile of words to my supervisors, I had to get more involved with my dissertation. So I took a couple of weeks' 'leave' from political activism and travelled to Alice.

I walked through the modern remains of Lovedale. In the overgrown gardens and in the shadow of the older buildings I could still feel an energy exuding from the space. Lovedale is now a Technical and Vocational Education and Training (TVET) college – so its connection to education is not entirely squandered. Yet, I wondered then, why is this patch of land, the source for so much of the intellectual energy of the subsequent history of South Africa, not a national monument or museum? Why did that sacred spot feel abandoned to me?

I had no money – thankfully in those days political activism had not yet been turned into a profession. So I set up my tent in a campsite on the edge of Grahamstown. The only other occupants were a couple of mandrax addicts. During the day I sat in libraries at Rhodes University, digging up century-old letters between missionaries, student and mission newspapers and reports. The extant archive of Lovedale College restored to life the period, its people and its conflicts in my imagination.

The picture that emerged was not how mission schools or the roles of missionaries were typically depicted. Instead, the Lovedale I found was a hotbed of dissent, discussion and independence, sometimes directly encouraged by mission teachers. For example, the first principal of Lovedale, the Rev. William Govan, clashed with his superiors and the Cape Colony government over whether and how literature should be taught and for what purpose. He was accused of creating too much independence of thought among the black students, introducing them to ideas and knowledge they would have no need of as labourers or a 'Native pastorate'.

Lovedale's first principal,
the Rev. William Govan.
Lovedale Missionary Institution,
South Africa, Photographic Views,
Lovedale Press, 1884.

80 years later Robert H W Shepherd, the last Principal of Lovedale before it was closed under the Bantu Education Act, would quote an inter-

nal church report of the time as stating that the black students, 'though destitute of classical and scientific education, may be endowed with such gifts and graces as to constitute an effective Native pastorate for the rural districts'. The school, Govan's detractors argued, should provide only a primary and an industrial education. As a result, in 1870 he was removed from his position and replaced with a missionary of 'sterner stuff', James Stewart.[38]

William Govan returned to Scotland, where he died in 1875. But his influence endured. In his early years in South Africa he had nurtured the like of Tiyo Soga, one of the first African students at Lovedale. Also among those he influenced was Skelewu, a local chief who had married the educated daughter of a Methodist preacher. They named one of their sons Govan. Govan Mbeki was educated at Healdtown, another mission school in the vicinity. He was a proclaimed disciple of English literature, was the father of a future President of South Africa and was a revolutionary and intellectual in his own right.[39] Sometimes, as I have frequently discovered, history does its own dot-joining.

I titled the final dissertation 'Books Made the White Man's Success, They Said, and It Shall Make Ours: Lovedale, Literature and Cultural Contestation, 1840–1940'. It relates the findings of an investigation that started with my question why Jordan, an avowed Africanist who wrote his novel in Xhosa rather than English, nonetheless prefaced that novel with a couplet from Shakespeare's *Richard II*.[40]

Trying to answer that question led me back to the 1850s, to the dawn of the African written literary tradition in South Africa. It took me to a small village named Alice, in what was then known as Kaffraria, part of the modern-day Eastern Cape and the frontier in many of the colonial wars against the Xhosa chieftainship. It led me through the front doors and into the inner chambers of Lovedale College, a mission school set up by the Glasgow Missionary Society in 1840. There I found Shakespeare and the whole canon of English literature present in its well-stocked library.

At Lovedale, once again, I found literature and social justice bound to each other. It had not been an easy relationship. Many settlers felt that the teaching of Shakespeare, far from being an instrument of denigration and imperial subordination, was being received by students as a source for a developing liberation philosophy. For example, on 2 December 1872

The library at Lovedale in College in 1884. *Lovedale Missionary Institution, South Africa,* Photographic Views, Lovedale Press, 1884.

A view of Lovedale College in the mid-1880s. *Lovedale Missionary Institution, South Africa,* Photographic Views, Lovedale Press, 1884.

The Kaffir Express, a newspaper produced at Lovedale, carried an article warning:

> Food to a starved man is apt to produce lightness of the head, and a kind of intoxication. It is the same with knowledge to a starved mind. Pope probably knew very little about Kaffirs, and cared a great deal less, when he wrote, in application to *Criticism,* his oft mis-quoted and mis-placed lines:
>
> > 'A little learning is a dangerous thing!
> > Drink deep, or taste not the Pierian spring;
> > There shallow draughts intoxicate the brain,
> > And drinking largely sobers us again.'

> These lines should find a conspicuous place in legible characters in
> every school, and in all class rooms of native institutions. For they suit
> exactly the state and condition of those indigenous African youth,
> whose conceit and presumption vex the missionary, and astonish or
> amuse the Superintendent-General of Education.[41]

The missionaries were instructed to pour cold water on the growing
ambitions of their students.

The teaching of English literature did indeed give impetus to the
development of an independent and indigenous literary tradition. This
tradition, once established, openly proclaimed its debt to English literature. The finding of inspiration in literature continued right through to the
assassinated leader of the South African Communist Party, Chris Hani,
who also received his education at Lovedale and Fort Hare. Hani frequently declared his love of Shakespeare, *Hamlet* in particular, as literature that inspired and emboldened him.[42]

My research excavated parts of our history. It brought people involved in
early struggles around the content and quality of 'native education' back
to life, making connections, providing names, revealing the emergence of
traditions that are uniquely ours. I would happily have surrendered all
my time to it. But South Africa was in the middle of a revolution.

Everlasting literature

*Since the advent of democracy there has been a lot of fiddling with educational
policy and practice, much of it misguided. But one thing that is hard to understand is why the educationists charged with devising a non-racial curriculum, one
suitable for all South Africans, did not see the value of teaching our children and
adults about Africa's rich literary and cultural history. The fact that access to
these treasures is largely limited to universities and experts stunts our national
soul and sense of identity.*

*I have been a soul-gatherer from an early age. On the beaches of human
literature I have scavenged for words that make meaning where there was no
meaning before, or words that stand out like a cowrie shell, rubbed and polished
by tides of time, once inhabited by an author, now vacated.*

*We should not take words for granted. Some people take great trouble with
words. John Keats was one of those. He laboured as if working with stone. For
others they just come easily.*

*Words are our immortal remains. They are shards of our soul that we use to
etch with on blank pieces of paper.*

There is no end to words. No limit to their permutations.

In the poem 'Lament', Jim Morrison assured himself 'words got me the wound and will get me well / if you believe it'.[43] But the meanings formed out of collections of words do not always make you well. Their fascination with the play of 'words accompanied Jim Morrison, Sello Duiker, Virginia Woolf, Phaswane Mpe, Sylvia Plath and many more to an early grave. The young and dying John Keats carried with him to Italy letters from Fanny Brawne that he didn't open. He instructed that his gravestone state, 'Here lies one whose name was writ in water'. Those driven to suicide gave up their bodies, mistakenly, because in doing so they silenced their imaginations. But their words couldn't be drowned even by themselves. Their words are here with us forever. They will be read until the last day of time. They are trapped in books, and books of words find ways to sneak in everywhere. We owe it to them to read them.*

Coming out in Hillbrow and Alexandra

While I was popping in and out of Wits University, preparing tutorials and working on my MA, I was living a very different life a short way away at my flat in Caroline Street in Hillbrow. Hillbrow, the flatlands suburb of the Johannesburg inner city. It was the melting pot of apartheid's disintegration, going from white to grey to black. It was a bustle of awakening and experiment, a compressed square kilometre of nonracial cinemas, bars, sex. It was the geographic testing ground for a deracialised South Africa with an Exclusive Books, its famous Mini Cine cinema and Tandoor, a laid-back restaurant specialising in tandoori chicken and an ever so sweet and tasty suji. As elderly white people retreated from its once decorous streets, a new generation started to move in. It has continued to change ever since. It was the site of my coming out, both as a person who could afford to love again and as an above-ground activist.

Working for the MWT involved recruiting and consolidating what we wishfully imagined 'objective conditions' would produce: a mass current in the ANC. The differences between the MWT and the ANC were ideological. The MWT traced the origins of the ANC to black elites, chiefs and churches, which we warned would betray the hopes of the people because of their 'unwillingness to break with capitalism'. We opposed what we termed 'individual terrorism' – the planting of bombs by MK – advocating instead mass mobilisation. What I think really upset the exiled ANC leadership was our criticism of Stalinism, something that stung because the ANC was heavily dependent on the USSR for funding, arms and military training. My days often involved teaching Marxism to anyone willing to listen, to small sections of an awakening people, a people sensing the imminence of liberation and anxious to secure its fruits.

In the early 1990s the exiled leadership of the MWT had cautiously made a return to South Africa. Our block of flats in Hackney was abandoned for another city's inner city. We set up a secret office on Plein Street in Hillbrow, again in a flat, where we began the local production of *Congress Militant*.

In this guise, and now going by the name of 'Jim', I began to spend more and more nervous time as a conspicuous white man in the segregated black communities of Alexandra, Dobsonville, Meadowlands and Katlehong. In this way I became witness to the actual aspirations of a flesh-and-blood people throwing off a centuries-old yoke.

This was also the time when, after years of being Sean Kelly, I began to come out again as a person called Mark Heywood. Being Jim moved me closer to my real personality; James was my middle name and Jim the name of my mother's father. Coming out also allowed a rediscovery of the self that I had suppressed since leaving Oxford University.

During this time I met and fell in love with a comrade we called 'Anne'. We met in early 1990 after she moved from Pietermaritzburg to Johannesburg to escape from her domineering mother and to be more actively involved in the struggle. I was asked to go and assess her political commitment and to start to integrate her into our Johannesburg structures. I discovered a bubbly, attractive, enthusiastic young woman. We sat across from each other in a flat in central Johannesburg, talking Trotsky, but feeling something else. Before very long she and I surrendered to that gravitational pull that comes with attraction and, later, love.

Her real name Sharon Ekambaram. In the classification system of apartheid South Africa she was an Indian. In the parlance of our struggle she was a black woman from the working-class community of Northdale in Pietermaritzburg. Her father, who died in 2005, had worked all his life in a shoe factory. Her mother stayed at home, looked after the house and oversaw the raising of their five children.

As our flirtation progressed, one more 'mixed couple' was born – something still rather rare in those days. Fortunately, the notorious Immorality Act, a law prohibiting sexual relationships between whites and nonwhites, had been repealed in 1985. But mixed couples still had a stigma to contend with. We drew glances and comments in the street and on a rare camping holiday were denied access to the campsite. One night I

smuggled her into my flat in Hillbrow, anxious to avoid the cen-
sorious eyes of the racist landlord.
That one night spilled over into
many more and before long we
found ourselves living together.
Still, for several months 'Anne'
did not know my real name.

She was both lover and comrade. She soon became a central
pillar in the work of the MWT. I
was inspired by the brave way she
would get into taxis and travel
alone to Alexandra Township to
establish branches of the MWT,
a woman in a world of men, an
Indian in an African township.
When she started to call me Mark,
I knew that the transition from
the underground was complete.

Now that I was half-out I could

'Anne' (Sharon) in 1992,
a photo taken during a trip she made to
Sweden to participate in the Militant's
international congress that year.

start to engage in politics personally. The MWT was an 'entrist' organisation. This meant that rather than building its own open movement, its
cadres joined whichever organisation where the mass of the poor and
working class congregated and then waged an ideological battle inside
this organisation for Marxist policies. In Britain this was the Labour Party;
in South Africa it was the ANC. The political explanation for this strategy
was that poor people were being misled into believing the ANC was a
revolutionary party and as a result had picked up its banner in the
1980s. In reality, we explained, the ANC leadership represented a class
that was inherently hostile to the poor and would ultimately betray
their aspirations.

On this basis I joined the ANC for real. In those days the ANC had a
vibrant branch in Hillbrow. Some of the future leaders of the ANC in
Gauteng were cutting their teeth there. Meetings were held in Highpoint,
a landmark skyscraper, and were serious affairs – so serious that one
evening when I walked into a meeting with Sharon's bra hanging loosely
over my shoulder (she had taken it off at home and thrown it at me), it
took half an hour before Sandy Singh gingerly pointed it out.

I threw myself into the work and in 1992 I was elected an office-bearer, a position I held until after the democratic elections in 1994. With other ANC members I participated in the first attempts to drive democratic urban renewal, setting up organisations such as the Johannesburg Inner City Community Forum (JICCF) to make demands of and present the people's vision to the still racially segregated organs of local government.

From being a spectator and analyst from a squalid corner of East London I now found myself in the place I had always dreamed of: a quiet participant in an actual revolution. From being a theorist of Revolutions Past I found myself more and more an activist in a Revolution Present. I came to feel the much more nuanced tos and fros of a revolution, its ebbs and tides, its eddies, its moments of ferocity and lull, murder and remaking.

One of my stomping grounds was Alexandra Township – Alex. In Hillbrow I was Mark. In Alex I was still Jim.

Part of my work in building branches of the MWT of the ANC involved proselytising about Marxism to the urban proletariat. This meant visiting industrial areas close to neighbouring townships where we could sell *Congress Militant*. While selling our newspaper we struck up conversations with workers at factory gates or busy pedestrian intersections.

Politics doesn't rest. The story of South African politics is mostly a story of surfaces. The underbelly has hardly been touched by historians. So at the same time as the world was enjoying the first month of Nelson Mandela's freedom, on 23 February 1990 a group of drivers for the apartheid bus company PUTCO, based at the Wynberg depot close to Alex, had embarked on a strike over a rationalisation of bus routes by the PUTCO managers. In April 'the bosses' had responded, as bosses do, by closing the depot and later by sacking 400 workers.

'Anne' had met the PUTCO strikers through selling *Congress Militant*. It is probably a rule that striking workers, particularly those left high and dry by their trade unions in the heat of battle, have a raised political consciousness and are more susceptible to people who profess radical alternatives. In reality, it just means that they are susceptible to anyone who will listen to them, show them support and respect. Through the PUTCO drivers I came to know Alex, where most of them lived: its dark, dirty streets and its resilient residents. One of the leaders of the strike was a quiet, genial, humorous man called Dan Chepape. Dan lived on

Fourth Avenue in a ramshackle half-house, half-shack with his wife Stella and young children. It was here, as well as in the cellar of the house of Sara Mtembu, a political matriarch who lived in one of Alex's original houses on Fifth Avenue, that we would meet for MWT branch meetings.

Alex is one of Johannesburg's oldest townships and bears a heavy burden of history. It started life in 1912, securing its status as a 'native township' just before the racist law of mass dispossession of indigenous people from their lands, the Natives Land Act, was passed in 1913. Alexandra was then a farm on the outskirts of Johannesburg where black people were, unusually, able to acquire freehold tenure on land and build homes.

Over the years Alex survived many attempts to remove it. It emerged as a hotbed of various colours of political resistance to apartheid. For the purposes of my story there is merit in describing the Alex I came to know in the early 1990s.

Alex was and is a rabbit warren. There are a myriad pathways between houses and shacks, playing as important a role as the official roads. In those days these pathways offered routes for activists to move undetected by police who patrolled the streets in armoured personnel carriers painted in SAP yellow and colloquially known as Mellow Yellows. And anyway, the roads were only just being tarred.

Leering over the community are Alex's three sinister hostels. They were built in the early 1970s and '80s and are the remnants of a plan that apartheid town planners had hatched to turn Alex into a hostel city and demolish all the houses. The women's hostel, now named Helen Joseph, was just down Fourth Avenue from Chepape's home. Compared with the men's hostels it was relatively open and accessible, overcrowded yes, but not impenetrable and dangerous. Unlike the men's hostels it had integrated itself into the community. Some of its residents, notably Violet Mvubu and Thembeka Mthabela, were leaders of the Alexandra Civic Organisation (ACO).[44]

I had been going in and out of Alex for several months when on 17 March 1991 the Inkatha Freedom Party (IFP) invaded the township. That Sunday morning Sharon and I were driving into Alex when we witnessed a battalion of buses parked on Louis Botha Avenue. An Inkatha rally was due to take place that day. The buses were offloading a red-headbanded impi, thousands of Zulu men from other parts of Johannesburg and KwaZulu in Natal. Many openly wielded metal rods and pangas, others hid high-powered R5 assault rifles under blankets. After they had gathered they began a destructive march into Alex. Their objective was to take over the Madala and Nobuhle men's hostels, to provide reinforcements to the Inkatha members already resident there.

That day a young activist, Philemon Mauku, was one of the Nobuhle hostel residents who were forced to flee their home. He left his belongings and ran for his life in the face of an advancing impi, who were being given cover by the police.

Fortunately, the women's hostel was not touched.

In the months that followed, a vicious civil war developed in Alex. On 14 April 1991 a massacre of fourteen people attending a funeral vigil, many of them children, led to a visit to Alex by Nelson Mandela. He called on residents to arm themselves and form self-defence units (SDUs). The township became a war zone. Hundreds of people were murdered or injured by Inkatha. One of the worst-affected areas close to the hostels was renamed Beirut. Inkatha were supported with weapons and intelligence by the South African Defence Force (SADF). They used the height advantage of the multi-storey hostels to make a no-go area out of all land and houses within shooting range of the hostels. Madala and Nobuhle hostels were transformed into fortresses reminiscent of the castles of mediaeval Europe. Occasionally marauding impis left the hostels to intimidate, attack and kill residents. The hostels became dens into which women were pulled and raped and where men, yanked off the streets, disappeared to be tortured.

The violence in Alex was the latest military offensive in a war that had started in July 1990 in other townships across what was then known as the Pretoria-Witwatersrand-Vereeniging (PWV) region. Inkatha impis, supported by the police and the SADF, invaded and took over the hostels, driving out all but the Zulu-speaking residents. As the MWT had warned repeatedly in the pages of *Inqaba ya Basebenzi*, Buthelezi's Inkatha had prostituted itself to what was known as the 'third force' – apartheid's secret and murderous security forces. Their mission was to foment ethnic violence that would create the impression of 'black-on-black' violence and weaken the ANC in its urban strongholds. Once they were under Inkatha's control, the hostels, an apartheid relic mainly occupied by migrant workers, particularly workers of Zulu ethnicity, were used as the launch pad for an assault on ANC-supporting communities.

Hostels fell across the East Rand and Soweto. But because of its political traditions and unity Alex was almost the last township to be conquered. Before that fateful day in April 1991 residents had fought off several earlier attacks. Philemon Mauku's first-hand description (archived at Wits University) offers a frontline account from the perspective of one of those who lived in a hostel:

> In Nobuhle Hostel where I was staying there were Zulu-speaking people, and others were used to come and stay with us, were also Zulu-speaking people. There was no problems, but only overcrowding in that room. In order to overcome the problems we had to join hands with the township residents. I met Mzwanele Mayekiso who is the general organiser of the Alexandra Civic Organisation (ACO).
>
> I have tried to visit Madala Hostel and had meetings to avoid violence. Fortunately, some have understand, but some of the IFP leaders who were staying there were the best perpetrators of violence against the comrades. More people belonging to the IFP came in full force to convince others to join and fight against the comrades. The councillors played a key role in the perpetration of the violence and Prince Mokoena told Moses Mayekiso – who is the President of ACO – that he will get him. The violence was there to get him.

Despite Mandela encouraging the formation of SDUs, and despite the mythical heroism attributed to the ANC's armed wing Umkhonto we Sizwe, neither arms nor MK soldiers were made available to communities to defend the ANC-supporting townships. This necessitated the formation of independent SDUs, small groups of ANC members who took upon themselves the protection of the community. SDUs acted mainly to gather intelligence but also acquired arms, primarily for defensive purposes.

But where were the SDUs to find the weapons they needed?

The State v Philemon Mauku: the defence of necessity

Anyone who is committed to actively pursuing human rights and justice has to be prepared for the unplanned and unpredictable. There are times when you must be willing to take a leap into the unknown or else retire quietly. From my safe middle-class background I had never contemplated becoming directly involved in an armed struggle. We had once been asked to store weapons at our flat in Hillbrow. We declined, partly out of fear, partly out of uncertainty as to where they would end up. I was not a pacifist but neither was I an advocate of armed struggle. But the reality we all witnessed was of innocent people being killed and maimed on the streets of Alex and elsewhere. According to one report by the Human Rights Commission (in those days an NGO), 3 180 people were murdered between July 1990 and June 1991. It was a state of undeclared war. Communities could not defend themselves with texts from Trotsky. They were not being protected by the police. They needed weapons.

Twenty-four-year-old Philemon Mauku was a young activist we had recruited through the PUTCO campaign. He worked for Edgars. His elder brother Titus was one of the striking bus drivers. Philemon had lived in Nobhule hostel, was a member of its committee and was an ACO activist involved in trying to improve living conditions in the hostel as well as to integrate its residents into the surrounding community. Squat, thoughtful and committed to social justice, one day Philemon branched away from our Marxist reading group and asked Sharon whether the MWT would assist him to get arms for the SDU that had been formed by the hostel committee. Sharon spoke to me. I spoke to Rob Petersen. There was no getting away from our duty to try to assist.

Soon after, huddled in a shack in Setswetla, a dense and overcrowded area of Alex, we met with the other five members of the SDU. After several careful discussions it was agreed we'd try to help.

Obtaining weapons was new to all of us. Within months, the resulting trail of errors led to Philemon's arrest. For his first exploratory trip Sharon lent him the car belonging to her brother Paul – without telling him why it was being borrowed. Philemon disappeared for several days longer than we expected. We became fearful that he had been arrested. The tension rose with each passing hour. One afternoon we sat in the Nu Metro cinema on Plein Street in Hillbrow, watching *Thelma and Louise*. It was a fun and fast-moving film, but I was hardly able to pay attention. We were deeply anxious about Philemon's possible capture and torture. We worried too that his possession of Paul's car would bring the security police knocking on our door. I was counting my final hours of freedom. Never had a movie felt like such a luxury.

Then we got word that Philemon was back – but he hadn't succeeded in getting arms. The car was badly battered. A second trip was necessary.

Several weeks later, in September 1991, he set off again, this time headed for Mozambique. One residue of the proxy battles of the Cold War, fought out in the anticolonial struggles of the liberation movements, was the piles of AK-47 assault rifles the USSR provided to Frelimo, Mozambique's independence movement. When the civil war ended these guns were hidden and many were now in the hands of former combatants or criminals. This was where the SDUs purchased their weaponry.

Once more Philemon did not come back on time.

Once more days passed.

Once more there was nothing we could do. We did not know where he had gone. Cell phones did not yet exist. For obvious reasons we could not report his disappearance to the police. We did not know if he was dead or being tortured. We considered looking for his body in mortuaries. Then, two weeks after his disappearance, having given him up for dead, we were contacted out of the blue by the relative of a prisoner at Nigel prison. He told us that Philemon had been arrested at a police roadblock in Brakpan. He was in prison. But he was alive.

Sharon was dispatched to visit him. He told her that the taxi he was travelling in had been stopped at a police roadblock. The police searched his bag and discovered that he was carrying two AK-47s and ammunition. He had told the police that the weapons were for use by a self-defence unit. In the words of the arresting officer:

> Ek het die beskuldigde toe om 'n verduideliking gevra, waarop hy 'n rapport aan my gemaak het. Hy het aan my gesê dat hy op pad is na die Alexandra woonbuurt in Johannesburg. Hy het aan my gesê dat hy die wapens gaan gebruik om 'n 'defence unit' te stig.[45]

After his arrest, according to Philemon, 'the police hid me in many police stations, Brakpan, John Vorster Square, Morning Side, Nelspruit and Komatipoort police stations. After the first three days I have managed to get one of the lawyers from the ANC who came to see who I was and to know how did I get arrested. I explained I had been arrested on political grounds but he blamed me for doing it without the consultation of the executive of the branch.'[46] However, although the ANC had learnt where Philemon was, they informed neither his family nor his comrades in Alex. He remained 'missing' for a further three weeks.

After we found him we paid his R5 000 bail as quickly as possible, arranged a safe flat in Yeoville with a friend we called 'Slow Rob' and began to discuss the plans for his defence. Philemon suspected that he had been set up by 'Lawrence', another comrade we worked with.

The Philemon Mauku Defence Campaign was my first experience of using the law to advance justice and combining it simultaneously with a political campaign. On the advice of Rob Petersen, who had returned to South Africa in May 1990 and was now known as 'Andrew', it was decided to mount a novel legal strategy. Although Philemon had admitted to the illegal possession of the two AK-47s and 55 rounds of ammunition when he was arrested, we decided that he would plead not guilty. His legal defence would be that he had broken the law out of *necessity*, a legal justification for otherwise unlawful conduct. He argued that Alexandra was under murderous attack from Inkatha and that those tasked with protecting the peace – the police and the SADF – were actually fomenting the war by aiding Inkatha.

We contacted Mohamed Bham, an attorney who was also a secret supporter of the MWT, who agreed to act for Philemon. We applied for legal aid, which of course was denied.

Side by side with the legal preparations we began to mobilise support for Philemon within Alexandra as well as to campaign for the right to 'armed self-defence'. In addition to the dropping of charges against Philemon we demanded 'the immediate release and indemnification of all those presently being held for organising self-defence' and that the state 'issue firearm licences to all members of genuine community self-defence units'. This way the Philemon Mauku Defence Campaign – soon to be known as the PMDC in typical South African abbreviated fashion – came into being.

Following the best tradition of human rights law in South Africa, we turned Philemon's arrest into a political trial rather than a criminal one. MWT members in Alex went door to door, shack to shack, street to street, collecting signatures and over R5 000 in small donations to support his legal defence. Oliver Schmitz, a respected local filmmaker and the director of the acclaimed 1988 film *Mapantsula*, was a friend of Hugh McLean, another long-time friend and a founder member of the MWT in South Africa. We asked him to make a documentary about Philemon, which we then used to raise international support.[47]

Preparation for the trial involved using methods that I would later return to and finesse in litigation around the rights of people living with

HIV. We compiled evidence of the terror, took affidavits from its victims and collected statistics on the numbers of deaths and reports from the Alex clinic where most of the injured were taken.

We persuaded three people to give evidence in Philemon's defence. David Robb, who headed the Alexandra Clinic, provided testimony on the scale and type of injuries that were being dealt with by the clinic. The clinic had admitted over 664 people to casualty between March and December 1991, mostly with gunshot and stab wounds. There had been more than 100 such deaths in less than a year. The trajectory of many gunshot wounds entered through the upper back and exited lower through the chest, showing that they had been fired from a height – nailing the two Inkatha-occupied men's hostels as a source of the terror.

In addition a priest, Rev. Benjamin Mzamo, and Mzwanele Mayekiso, an ACO leader, testified about the fears of the community, its attitude to obtaining arms in self-defence and efforts to negotiate with the police.

Philemon's trial started in the Brakpan regional court in April 1992 and ran for several days. We bused scores of PMDC supporters from Alex to Brakpan. The transcript of the trial provides a unique window on the violence that took place during that period.

The trial placed the civil war in Alex under a spotlight. The prosecutor's aggressive cross-examination only made the political nature of the trial more obvious. Painstakingly a picture was drawn for the magistrate of the nature and barbarity of the assault on Alex. But, as was expected in those days when the legal system upheld the apartheid state, and before respect for human rights and equality had entered the law, he was not to be persuaded. We anticipated this. Indeed, Rob Petersen had written to Philemon shortly before the start of the trial, warning him against any 'imagined impartiality of "the law"'. In his words:

> This is, after all, only a magistrate's court of the old South Africa, hoping to survive into the new. It is an organ set up for domination of a minority over a majority; **it is in no way an expression of the people's will**. Formally, it is you Philemon who are on trial before the court. But we have to show also in this trial that it is the state apparatus (of which this court is but an arm) that stands trial before the people **on the question of its association with the Inkatha killers**.[48] (Emphasis in the original)

In those days we were not savvy in working the media. Social media had not yet been born. In addition, activists were still in a political limbo. The outcomes of a negotiated settlement were far from certain. This meant we could not risk being completely open about our involvement with the SDUs. Because of their antagonism towards the MWT, the ANC and the ACO also actively tried to suppress information about the trial and divide Philemon's supporters.

Predictably, the magistrate was not persuaded by the defence of necessity. He agreed that the circumstances were 'difficult' but found they did not justify Philemon's actions. By his reasoning, the fact that at the time he was found in possession of the weapons Philemon faced no immediate danger to his life undid his justification.

On 18 May 1992 he was found guilty and sentenced to five years' imprisonment with two years suspended. Given that possession of illegal weapons could carry up to 25 years this was a relatively lenient sentence. When notified of Philemon's intention to appeal the magistrate stated, 'if I erred in my sentencing . . . it was to pass a sentence that can be seen as too light'.[49]

Nonetheless leave to appeal was granted, although the magistrate immediately rescinded Philemon's bail. Philemon Mauku was escorted down to the holding cells and was then sent to Modderbee, a prison near the town of Springs on the East Rand. His freedom was over.[50]

After several months at Modderbee and Nigel prisons Philemon requested to be transferred to Leeuwkop, because it was closer to his family (and comrades). Leeuwkop Maximum Security is part of a prison complex set in those days in beautiful agricultural surrounds on the outer edges of northern Johannesburg. Since then it has been enveloped by bland suburbia.

Over the next two years we visited him almost every weekend, parking on the outer perimeter of the prison and then taking a prison bus stuffed with prisoners' families through Leeuwkop's tranquil gardens to the gates of the maximum security prison. After searches and questions we would be escorted into the visiting area. Initially we could talk only through a glass screen, but in February 1993 good behaviour earned Philemon the right to contact visits. Contact visits allowed different kinds of conversations to begin. During the weekly visits messages and letters on tightly wrapped-up sheets of paper were passed surreptitiously to Sharon.

Philemon's letters opened a window on life inside the prison.

Unanticipated, another campaign was about to start.

At Leeuwkop Maximum Security, Philemon had quickly established relationships with other political prisoners. These prisoners were predominantly men who had been overlooked in the formal negotiation process between the ANC and the government to identify and release political prisoners. It was no accident that they had been left behind. Behind the bars of Leeuwkop Maximum Security – as well as in many other prisons – were the 'young lions' who had taken at face value calls made by the ANC in the 1980s over Radio Freedom to 'make the townships ungovernable'. These young men saw themselves as soldiers and acted on instructions to root out and, if necessary, kill informers and collaborators. They were part of the post-1976 generation whose heroism and self-sacrifice made apartheid unworkable.

But in the early 1990s they found themselves effectively disowned by the ANC.

Most of the young men at Leeuwkop Maximum Security had been found guilty of murder. The groups imprisoned there included the 'NUMSA Six', the 'Katlehong Five' and the 'Daveyton Two'. Their crimes included 'necklacing', the practice that took hold in the 1980s of placing a petrol-filled tyre around the neck of an informer or other victim and setting it alight. Some had burnt down the homes of the hated stooge town councillors. The NUMSA Six had killed scabs from the Inkatha-inspired United Workers' Union of South Africa (UWUSA) during a bitter strike.

All were serving long sentences. Several had been previously sentenced to death and spent time on death row in Pretoria. They had formed a Political Prisoners Committee and I got to know its intense young members very well. Apart from Philemon, two became friends as well as comrades: Mthuthuzeli Nqandu, a member of the Port Elizabeth Youth Congress (PEYCO), had necklaced a policeman in his township in the Eastern Cape. He had been sentenced to death. Phineas Ndlovu, a member of the Daveyton Youth Congress (DAYCO), was one of a group of six young comrades who had thrown a petrol bomb into the house of a town councillor, causing his death and that of his children.

A few year later I would read the gruesomely vivid details of the violence they inflicted in the records of their trials. But sitting across from me in the visiting room of Leeuwkop they were just thoughtful, intense and intelligent young men. They were anxious and unhappy because the ANC had been unbanned, the liberation they had fought and risked their lives for was getting closer and closer ... but they were still in prison. These men were not what my youthful imagination had envisaged murderers would look like. In the visiting room I gained an understanding of how otherwise peaceful people can be driven to commit extreme violence that those of us who live 'ordinary lives' would never have to contemplate.

Life is not as simple as many would have it.

With Philemon organising prisoners on the inside and Sharon organising their families on the outside, we set up the Leeuwkop Political Prisoners Support Committee (LPPSC) and began a campaign for these prisoners' release.

One thing I have learned from the many campaigns I have been involved with is that they work best through small coalitions of like-minded individuals who, in the heat of a campaign, can find a way to capture public imagination. In the thick of a life-and-death issue, be it AIDS or the release of political prisoners, solidarity and support shift from abstract to practical, discussions become real rather than theoretical, actions are needed more than words. Action draws the attention of both your enemies and friends you may not even be aware of.

The PMDC and later the LPPSC were an irritant to the ANC, because it was known that they were driven by the MWT. We held demonstrations outside the CODESA negotiations between the ANC and the government, wrote letters, pricked the consciences of those with and without a conscience. This way we caught the attention of Paula McBride, who, as we started our campaign, had already acquired years of experience in her own long, often lonely campaign for the release of her husband, Robert McBride.

Paula is a woman of political acumen and resilience. The lack of interest today in the dense tapestry of the South African liberation struggle means that the story of her stand against the death penalty is one of the rich threads that stand to be lost.

Paula became a friend and comrade. Her life has strange parallels with my own. She is the daughter of an Anglo American executive, was born in Kenya, grew up in Zambia and had a stint in an English boarding school.

Her family had moved to South Africa in 1973. This was a somewhat unlikely background for a human rights activist – a bit like me. But, in Paula's own words, 'I think it was the contrast between Zambia and South Africa that led me into politics and into many years of trying to get rid of the system of Apartheid.'[51] She is also the sister of John Leyden, the songwriter/singer of one of South Africa's most loved pop bands, Mango Groove.

Paula was one of a small team working with its national director, Brian Currin, at Lawyers for Human Rights. Her unbounded energy and fearless 'don't give me no bullshit' attitude got things done. Paula had met Robert McBride while she was working on the Lawyers for Human Rights (LHR) political prisoners programme and visiting prisoners awaiting execution on death row in the prison known as Pretoria Maximum.

McBride was the leader of an Umkhonto we Sizwe unit in Durban. His unit planted a car bomb in Durban in 1986 that killed three young white women and injured some 70 other people. This led to him being sentenced to death in April 1987 and taking up residence on death row in Pretoria Central Prison. The 'Magoo's Bar Bomber', as he came to be known, was demonised by the media and hated by most of white society. In exile and in the townships, however, McBride was a hero, the epitome of the liberation soldier.[52]

I can't claim to know the intimacies of how a relationship between Paula and Robert developed but it did, and on 10 May 1989 they were married on death row.[53] The journalist John Carlin reported that 'the honeymoon, in the presence of a warder, lasted 40 minutes'.

The release of political prisoners was a contentious issue throughout the negotiations between the ANC and the government.

In his famous speech in Parliament on 2 February 1990, President F W de Klerk had declared a moratorium on the death penalty. He had also unbanned a number of political organisations and announced that 'people serving prison sentences merely because they were members of one of these organisations or because they committed another offence which was merely an offence because a prohibition on one of the organisations was in force, will be identified and released. Prisoners who have been sentenced for other offences such as murder, terrorism or arson are not affected by this.'

When negotiations between the ANC and NP got under way, the issue of political prisoners was high on the agenda, as is evidenced by the Groote Schuur Minute of May 1990. Certain categories of prisoner were relatively easy for the NP to agree to release, such as people in prison for no other crime than their membership of a banned organisation. Others were more tricky, so the issue dragged on.

For its part, in the early 1990s the ANC leadership, now returned from exile or released from prison and involved in delicate negotiations, was concerned with establishing its credentials as a moderate party. Foundations were being laid for the philosophy of rainbowism. In this context Robert McBride presented them with a problem typical of many other political prisoners. The ANC leadership did not want to admit that the Magoo's Bar bombing had not been the unilateral act of a maverick who had misunderstood 'the call of duty'. In fact the order to carry out the bombing had come through the MK command structures.[54] For many years McBride, ever the loyal soldier, chose not to disabuse the public of this pretence, setting the record straight only in his application for amnesty. This meant that he had to live with a horrid comparison with the maverick white racist Barend Strydom, the self-proclaimed 'Wit Wolf' and murderer of eight people in a 1988 shooting spree in Pretoria that wounded a further sixteen.

Before the February 1990 moratorium on the death penalty a campaign by LHR, Paula and many international anti-apartheid activists made it difficult for the government to instruct the hangman to lead Robert McBride – public enemy number one in the eyes of most white people – up the 52 stairs to the gallows level, to handcuff him, put the hood over his head and the noose round his neck, and then throw the lever that would open the trapdoor underneath his feet.

After February 1990, however, the issue remained controversial. Again it was Paula and LHR, later joined by us, who prevented politically inconvenient political prisoners being forgotten. The 26 September 1992 Record of Understanding between the ANC and the government dealt inter alia with the release of political prisoners. On 28 September 1992 McBride and Strydom were among 150 political prisoners freed. Additional progress seemed to be made later that year when the Further Indemnity Act recognised that an act with a 'political objective' could result in a purely criminal conviction, such as for murder or kidnapping.

But these developments were cold comfort at such prisons as Leeuwkop where young activists continued their wait behind bars.

Looking back I can see how the campaign to draw attention to the plight of the Leeuwkop political prisoners was a dry run for many of the activities that have become part of my stock in trade: working with the media to expose injustice, raising awareness within sympathetic communities, lobbying politicians and (when other means fail) putting into effect threats of litigation or other sanctions.

My archive covering that period is preserved in the William Cullen Library at Wits University. It contains many of the letters smuggled out of Leeuwkop – letters the prisoners wrote to the ANC, to F W de Klerk, to Nelson Mandela, to Winnie Mandela; letters to the prisoners from overseas; reports and minutes of meetings; research into and profiles of the prisoners.[55]

But after two years letters, pickets and pleas had yielded little more than lip service to their plight. An occasional visit by a high-profile ANC leader such as Walter Sisulu was no longer enough to raise their hopes. Their levels of frustration and despair were enormous. They can be felt in a letter Phineas Ndlovu surreptitiously handed to me in late 1992:

> My seventh Christmas in prison is an agony. My family never thought I would spend another Christmas in jail. I fought at the face of a very dangerous enemy, demanding, among other things, the release of ALL political prisoners. The Rivonia comrades were still behind bars and on the Island and the future looked bleak at the time but we NEVER said die and fought with courage and determination to bring about a just society worth living in.
>
> Against this background I am still languishing behind bars frustrated in the neglect of the beloved nation I fought for sacrificing my life in the process.[56]

The Leeuwkop prisoners felt they had run out of options and resolved to go ahead with a hunger strike.

The hunger strike is not an activity very often drawn out of the armoury of social justice activism. We knew it was a risk, a form of brinkmanship with unpredictable results. I didn't really know how we were going to support it. Media would be essential, so in the days leading up to the hunger strike we tried to solicit the interest of British journalist David Beresford. Beresford had reported intimately on the hunger strike of prisoners from the Irish Republican Army (IRA) in the notorious H-blocks in

1981. He had written the standard account of that tragedy in *Ten Men Dead: The story of the 1981 Irish hunger strike*,[57] describing graphically the manner in which the human body withers away when deprived of food. He was one of the closest witnesses to the death through starvation of IRA prisoner Bobby Sands and nine others. On the basis of these prior experiences Beresford was initially dismissive of our attempt to attract his interest. His response was to advise that we contact him again after the strike had gone on for twenty days.

So on 1 May 1993 Philemon and 21 other prisoners started refusing food. On 6 May they were moved from their communal cells to solitary confinement. A week later, with their numbers now reduced to fifteen, they were admitted to the prison hospital. It was at this point that the ANC panicked and hastily arranged for a senior delegation, including Winnie Mandela and Paul Mashatile, to visit the prison. This group was able to persuade the prisoners to suspend their strike. Weary, hungry and ever prone to hope, they started eating again.

And yet once again the Leeuwkop prisoners were made to wait. A meeting of the Further Indemnity Committee the following month failed once again to set them free. Although Philemon Mauku was released after serving his sentence – a week later than Nelson Mandela – others remained. The ours-but-not-ours political prisoner issue remained an intractable one that the ANC never took full responsibility for. It was only after the first democratic election that a behind-the-scenes solution was quietly agreed with Dullah Omar, the new Minister of Justice. Omar appointed Brian Currin, National Director of LHR, to head a committee to make further recommendations for the release of the remaining prisoners.

Throughout my young adulthood my father would ask me when I was going to get a 'real job'. I never had a suitable answer. However, in July 1994 I was asked by Currin if I would work for him as his sole researcher. I would even be paid! This was my first salaried job, although probably not the type of 'real job' my father had wanted for me.

Currin asked me to trawl through the transcripts of political trials and other documents stored at the Indemnity Committee, and to identify people who were still in prison whose offences, however heinous, could be deemed to have a political motive. In July and August 1994 I drove each day to the Committee's offices on the edge of Church Square in Pretoria. Once there I sat in a dark storeroom ploughing through the files of prisoners who had applied for indemnity and had been turned down. I worked in that lightless office beholden to an apartheid apparatchik who made clear his dislike of me. I had to request specific files from him –

files of people I already knew, files of the comrades at Leeuwkop. My job was to write up a summary of each case and make an accompanying recommendation to the Indemnity Review Committee.

Not only was this my first real job, it was the first time I was involved with real law. To make things worse, sometimes the trials whose transcripts I had to read had been heard in an Afrikaans that I could barely understand. But through my acquaintance with quite a number of the prisoners, lack of knowledge of law or language aside, I felt I had a deep enough understanding to discern the motives of people who under ordinary circumstances would not have committed such crimes.

I was fair. I looked at the applications of opponents and supporters of apartheid. Unsurprisingly the latter were a much smaller number. I wrote up my recommendations for Currin's committee, which deliberated on them and then passed them on to Justice Minister Dullah Omar. This way groups of political prisoners began to be released, including Mthuthuzeli Nqandu. Sadly some, including Phineas Ndlovu, remained behind bars, trapped by a clause in the Further Indemnity Act that required offences to have been committed before 9 October 1990. Another twelve-day hunger strike took place in November 1994. We continued to campaign on their behalf for another year, now negotiating directly with leaders from the liberation movement such as Ahmed Kathrada and Dullah Omar who were now in government.

As prison doors opened and indemnity applications closed, another unplanned chapter of my life was over. Taking a stand leads you into many an unintended space. What started with a campaign to support a group of striking PUTCO drivers had ended in an office in Pretoria recently occupied by the apartheid government and with the release of over 100 prisoners.

Lesson for lawyers: beware, public impact litigation sometimes has a long tail.

Making sense of liberation

Rewind a little.

On 10 April 1993 Philemon was still in prison. I was talking to his brother Titus, a taxi driver, on Quartz Street in Hillbrow as the first reports of the murder of South African Communist Party leader Chris Hani arrived on the ghetto grapevine. I could see the news rip and ripple along the streets, passed from person to person like a Mexican wave of disbelief. Shock and then anger soon followed.

The next few days were the first time I felt that my whiteness stood out and drew hatred from some black people. I rode the wave and Sharon and I attended Hani's emotionally charged funeral service at the Orlando Stadium in Soweto. As we sat in the stands a group of men sitting behind us began to threaten me, banging sharpened iron rods, menacing, chanting, moving closer and closer. I felt helpless. I knew how the anger of a crowd can quickly become irrational and can give way to murder. I was perhaps moments away from injury or death when an ANC marshal clad in military fatigues noticed what was happening and waded through the stands to escort me to safety.

But in the five tumultuous years of 1990–1994, that was the only time I felt fear. It seemed obvious that this was a dangerous moment. It took Mandela's huge moral authority to quell the anger of April 1993. I did not really appreciate at the time that this was the closest South Africa had come to a racial civil war.

Yet in every other respect those were unforgettable days for those of us fortunate enough to be on the side of the Revolution Present. In many ways they chimed with William Wordsworth's oft-quoted paean to the French Revolution:

> Bliss was it in that dawn to be alive,
> But to be young was very heaven!— Oh! times,
> In which the meagre, stale, forbidding ways
> Of custom, law, and statute, took at once
> The attraction of a country in romance!
> When Reason seemed the most to assert her rights,
> When most intent on making of herself
> A prime Enchantress—to assist the work
> Which then was going forward in her name!
> Not favoured spots alone, but the whole earth,
> The beauty wore of promise . . .[58]

It started as we sat listening to the radio on 2 February 1990 as F W de Klerk, the last white President of apartheid South Africa, made his unexpected announcement of the unbanning of the ANC as well as, unthinkably, the SACP and Umkhonto we Sizwe. I was there to witness the televised release of Nelson Mandela on 11 February and I was really there two days later, part of the tide of humanity that took over the roads and marched to Soccer City, the biggest football stadium in Johannesburg, to jam the stands to mark his triumphant return. Later that day I was somewhere on the inside of seething crowds that greeted Nelson Mandela on his return to his home in Vilakazi Street, Soweto. Mine was usually a singular white face among tens of thousands of black people – yet experiencing no animosity.

Chris Hani's horrid murder, together with the violence being inflicted by what we described as a 'third force', was evidence that people were at work trying to stymie democracy. This led to the speeding-up of the negotiation process. The main election day was set for 27 April 1994. This drew us more and more into open politics and campaigns to secure an ANC victory. The Hillbrow ANC branch canvassed support and organised community meetings, and during the election itself we acted as observers at three voting stations in and around Hillbrow. As the voting days gave way to night, we continued work, now overseeing the transfer of boxes and boxes of ballot papers from Hillbrow police station to Nasrec, the showgrounds wedged between Soweto and Johannesburg where the votes were being counted.

It may seem odd, but I lived those days so intensely, was so much a part of them, that I have little recollection of the detail of the morning after or of subsequent days. We worked too hard to be storing up memories. We were lost in the minutiae of the moment. I must have gone to bed for a few hours, I must have woken up. I did drop in on the ANC's celebration party at the Carlton, then an ostentatious hotel in the very centre of Johannesburg. I was there to witness one of the great liberatory moments of the twentieth century.

After 350 years of subjugation, starting in 1652 with the arrival of one Jan van Riebeeck in what became Cape Town, the original inhabitants of the lands of South Africa were now free to determine their own destiny.

But what about mine?

The election results were announced on 6 May 1994. The ANC had won 62.5 per cent of the vote. We had now accomplished national liberation. Contrary to my Marxist teachings, I had learnt that a revolution need not always involve overthrow or seizure of state power. What had just happened to us smelled like a revolution. It tasted like a revolution. But according to Trotskyite theory, the achievement of one-person-one-vote was just a phase in an ongoing struggle, something we called the 'permanent revolution'.

According to the theory of permanent revolution, the 'illusions' the masses held in the ANC would shatter as it quickly became clear that capitalism could not meet their material needs, summarised as bread, peace and land. That way the ground would be laid for a mass embrace of the struggle to 'overthrow' capitalism. There was not even to be time to stop and catch your breath. There should be no work to consolidate the new state, because it was inherently contradictory (a term loved by Marxists) and fragile. It was also incapable of providing bread, peace and land to a hungry people. Ironically, the order given by the MWT leadership (which included me) was that all our efforts should be directed at exposing the contradictions of the new government, weakening its hold on the masses, hastening its demise. The Trotskyites (that was me again) sneeringly contrasted the idea of permanent revolution with the Stalinist 'two-stage theory' of achieving national liberation first, developing and deepening the 'national democratic revolution' and then gradually moving on to socialism. Both theories were equally dogmatic and equally wrong.

The theory of permanent revolution modelled itself on a revolution that had happened 77 years earlier. It held that as in pre-industrial Russia, the Menshevik leaders of the February Revolution (read ANC) would be found wanting and be turfed out by the Bolsheviks (read MWT) and an October Revolution, thus instating a socialist state – which would follow as surely as night follows day.

What happened in those heady months in Russia is beautifully described by Jack Reed in *Ten Days That Shook the World*. If you have the appetite the best insider account is Trotsky's own *History of the Russian Revolution*.

But that was then and this was now, and the world had changed quite a lot in the middle.

In the early 1990s history and politics started refusing to behave according to Marxist theory. Perhaps the Marxists could be forgiven for getting it wrong, because 'qualitative changes' had erupted into world politics and economics. That term too needs explanation. According to the theory of 'historical materialism' the dynamic of history involves multiple slow, subterranean, 'quantitative' shifts which accumulate over time to a point where they are 'unsustainable'. Then they explode, erupting volcanically, into periods of uprising and revolution.

A time of qualitative change in the world was certainly what we were living through. In space of the last years of the 1980s and the early 1990s we witnessed the Chinese students' uprising in Tiananmen Square,[59] the fall of the Berlin Wall and East Germany, and revolutions across the states of Eastern Europe. People who had been chained under a variety of grotesque and debauched Stalinist dictatorships had spectacularly exercised their power to throw off these carbuncles. These wonderful uprisings were heralded by Marxists as the long-awaited workers' revolution against Stalinism – but the workers then chose capitalism rather than the democratising of the planned economy, as we Marxists had long been predicting. People wanted TVs and consumer goods, fashions and freedom, liberation: not a set of new dogmas.

The entry of millions of eager new consumers into the world market led to an intense if relatively short-lived economic boom.

As a result, contrary to the 'five, ten, fifteen years' theory of Ted Grant, aped by many of his followers (that was me again), capitalism did not fall apart. The fact that Margaret Thatcher and Ronald Reagan were able to defeat the trade unions in the manner I have described earlier allowed them to usher in a new economic and political period in history.

To my former fellow travellers, however, let me say that this did not mean for one second that capitalism had escaped its contradictions – or that it could meet the expectations of the 'masses' (as we have now seen). It was not, as Francis Fukuyama proclaimed, 'the end of history'. Far from it. It was the beginning of another history.

Disobedient reality put severe pressure on Marxist analysis. In the early 1990s this led to splits in the Militant in England. The unthinkable happened: long-term collaborators turned on each other as the founder of Militant, Ted Grant, split from its General Secretary, Peter Taaffe.

Militant was the strongest section in an international network of mini-Militant Tendencies, called the Committee for a Workers' International (CWI). Sections of the CWI existed in many European states, Pakistan, India and several Latin American states. A group was even established in China after the Tiananmen uprising. Every two years the separate national sections met at an International Congress somewhere in Europe. In 1988 I had been trusted enough to attend one of these in the Belgian city of Ghent. The mini-Militants were made up of brilliant and bright people, and the discussions about 'the coming world socialist revolution' (termed International Perspectives) were exciting and persuasive because they were so located in economics.

But a chain that breaks at its strongest link is as fragile as one that breaks at its weakest. Before long these cracks had reached South Africa. Over several years comrades started to grow apart. We were visited in South Africa by members of both opposing factions in the International. As a real revolution was raging around us, we discussed world perspectives, South African perspectives, strategy and tactics till the cows came home. As post-apartheid South Africa began reconstituting itself, we continued our debates.

Eventually an acrimonious break-up of the MWT mirrored that of the Militant in England. Weizmann Hamilton, Martin Legassick and Norma Craven opted to remain with 'the majority' in the CWI. They continued their pursuit of the programme based on state ownership and central planning as the way to socialism, despite the radically changed conditions globally and nationally which had made this obviously unrealistic. They remained hostile to the negotiated settlement. They were unwilling to re-evaluate programme, strategy and tactics. In their opinions the permanent revolution must go on.[60]

Rob Petersen, Sharon and I, together with several others, ended our years of involvement with the Tendency and chose to continue our quest for socialism and social justice by different routes and with different people.

Soon after apartheid ended, so did the MWT of the ANC. In 1995 I gathered up my back copies of *Inqaba ya Basebenzi* and *Congress Militant*, my notes and campaign records, and symbolically surrendered them to the Historical Papers archive at Wits University. The end of the Militant years and the beginnings of liberation meant that in some ways two strands of my life had reached an end point of sorts.

South African liberation, my preoccupation since the age of thirteen, had been achieved. Starting with the Berlin Wall, walls of all sorts had come down, including the apartheid wall. But capitalism, a system whose collapse I had believed to be imminent since joining the Militant at Oxford University in 1984, appeared triumphant across the world. In South Africa billboards proclaimed 'Free Enterprise Is Working'. Although it wasn't clear whether this was a statement of triumph or of self-deception, it seemed highly improbable that the South African working class would follow the formula of permanent revolution, so loved by myopic Marxists.

Theory – and here this would apply to Marxism – was characterised by Trotsky as providing 'the superiority of foresight over astonishment'.

But in truth the left's attempts to apply the theories and method of Marxism had become a recipe for blindness. Astonishingly in this time of global political ferment, a socialist revolution was nowhere to be found.

And for me a new journey was about to begin.

4

The AIDS Law Project –
into the world of HIV and human rights

Life is one big road with lots of signs, yes!
So when you riding through the ruts, don't you complicate your mind:
Flee from hate, mischief and jealousy!
Don't bury your thoughts; put your dream to reality, yeah!
Bob Marley, 'Wake Up and Live'

In the middle of 1990 the Human Immunodeficiency Virus (HIV) entered my life. One evening Zackie Achmat came home trembling to Strathbogie Mansions, the flat we shared in Caroline Street, Hillbrow, and told me that he had been diagnosed that day with HIV. As if in anticipation of a rapid decline in his health he packed a bag and went to stay with another friend, one who could give him more comfort and support. I would not see him for the next four years, as he hid away from sight (mine at least) in Cape Town.

I didn't know how to process Zackie's disclosure. In 1990 HIV was a different proposition from what it is now. It was a dark and fearful diagnosis, an almost certain death sentence. Zackie had been told that he would live for another six months. Such was the sense of impending doom that Martin Legassick wrote him a letter in which he invoked the Dylan Thomas poem, 'Do not go gentle into that good night . . . Rage, rage against the dying of the light.'

In 1990 there was no antiretroviral (ARV) treatment; the efficacy of these medicines would be validated only six years later. The virus was little understood by medical science – in fact it was misunderstood. After Zackie left Johannesburg I pushed HIV as far away from me as possible. For several years I lived with an irrational fear that I might have been infected, having shared a flat with Zackie for the six months since I had arrived back in South Africa.

Fear not. All activists start from positions of relative ignorance about the issues they are moved to take up. History records how every new social movement started with the imagination of one or two individuals. Since that evening HIV and I have become well acquainted.

Four years passed. After the 1994 election I was exhausted. It had been a roller-coaster four years since arriving in South Africa, full of stress, tension, occasional fear and constant work. I had decided to retire from political activism and instead seek to feed my love of literature. Somehow, in the early mornings at the beginning of 1994, as a revolution raged around me, I had put over 200 pages of words together, so that they neatly told the story of Lovedale College, its teachers and its pupils. My dissertation had been highly commended and I had received a letter awarding me an MA in May 1994. One of my two assessors, Tim Couzens, a person whose own research and writing on authors such as the playwright H I E Dhlomo I respected immensely, had recommended it for a distinction. He also took the unusual step of proposing that I convert it into a PhD and continue research to bring it to finality. Stephen Gray, the other assessor, was much less enthusiastic. Obviously I went with Couzens's proposal, even though this meant freezing my right to an MA. But, I was assured, with another two chapters I might find myself with a doctorate in African literature.

This was what I planned to do: I hoped to be the first person to publish a book about A C Jordan, thereby bringing him to the place in our literary pantheon that he deserves. I applied for a position in the English Literature department at Wits University, thinking this would give me the peace and place I needed to complete the PhD. But I was unsuccessful.

As I contemplated how to live in a free South Africa, HIV was not part of my plans. It had crossed my path twice: first at Balliol College, when in the early, fearful days of the AIDS epidemic in England members of the Junior Common Room had held a collection for the Terrence Higgins Trust, an organisation – named after a man who died of AIDS in 1982 – that supports people living with HIV. The second time was through Zackie.

However, in much the same way that Zackie had inadvertently shaped my life during my years in the MWT, he was to play a catalytic and influential role in my next phase of political activism, bringing me into full-frontal confrontation with the social and political meaning of HIV in South Africa and the world.

In February 1995 my PhD proposal was approved by the Higher Degrees Committee. But in late 1994, just as I had set about reordering my life, Zackie reappeared. In the intervening years I had had little contact with him. He had not gone gently into that good night – in fact the opposite.

He had gone to film school, made an award-winning documentary and quietly started his journey as an AIDS activist. He was also involved in queer politics and lobbying for recognition of equality for lesbian and gay people in the new Constitution. After befriending human rights lawyer Edwin Cameron, he had decided to take on HIV. When I met up with him again he was working with Cameron at the AIDS Law Project (ALP), a project of the Centre for Applied Legal Studies (CALS) at Wits University.

One of the hard skills I had developed while working at the MWT was in graphic design and the layout of pamphlets. For several years I had been the principal person responsible for the layout of *Inqaba ya Basebenzi*. In this capacity I had become a master of the early software programs that were revolutionising the print industry, PageMaker in particular. Finding myself short of money and somewhat short of purpose, I was easily persuaded by Zackie to take on a short-term contract with the ALP to develop five user-friendly pamphlets on HIV and human rights. The pamphlets were on the right of people testing HIV-positive to confidentiality, the right to be tested for HIV only after providing informed consent, and how to draw up a will and a living will.

Thus began my life with HIV, human rights and law. I have still not cashed in my MA. My PhD is still in the deep freeze. A C Jordan still cries out for a biographer.

Sometime in July 1994 I walked from Hillbrow to Wits University for a different purpose. I crossed the lawns of the East Campus and entered the D J du Plessis Building, a squat turtle-shaped edifice on the edges of the School of Law. This was where the ALP was housed. I was planning to give it a few months.

At the ALP I quickly came to see a continuity between the struggle against apartheid and the struggle to prevent and treat HIV infection. Freedom is vital for dignity and autonomy, the opportunity to be and become. It is meant to offer equality. This is what people in the liberation struggle had fought and died for.

But as apartheid was shoved kicking and screaming off the stage, HIV was unobtrusively shuffling on: in fact HIV had been quietly entrenching its position in the blood and bodies of the people of South Africa since the first cases were detected in 1982.

Before the advent of ARV treatment HIV first robbed people of their dignity before it robbed them of their life. AIDS was associated with various rare types of skin cancer and lesions, diarrhoea, wasting, tuberculosis and only then premature death. It was also heavily stigmatised, as a result of the fear that engulfed it but also because of blame. From the beginning, AIDS has variously been a white person's disease, a gay person's disease, a disease of sex workers, 'loose' people, 'immoral' people, foreign people, drug-users – a 'brought-it-on-yourself' disease.

It was a cruel trick of history that the culmination of the great positive movement for national liberation, bringing with it a million tasks of constructing the laws and institutions of a democratic society, coincided with and largely eclipsed the need for a similar movement to stop AIDS from assuming epidemic proportions.

In the early 1990s there were only a few lone voices of warning. In April 1990 Chris Hani, the greatly loved and respected SACP leader, had warned that AIDS could 'ruin the realisation of our dreams' at the Fourth International Conference on Health in Southern Africa. At that point the prevention of an AIDS epidemic was still possible and the conference had strong words on why that should be prioritised.

Although the conference eventually resulted in the formation of the National AIDS Convention of South Africa (NACOSA) in 1992, as with so many conferences little action followed. Yet the consequence of not carrying out that conference's resolutions has been as many as ten million preventable HIV infections, including an estimated 3.5 million deaths due to AIDS that had occurred by 2015.[61] In April 1990 there were fewer than 500 recorded cases of AIDS. Three years later, in 1993, the actuary Peter Doyle had developed a model that predicted an epidemic of up to five million people if HIV prevention was not made a political priority.

In 1992, before forming the ALP, Edwin Cameron had established the AIDS Consortium, a motley collection of organisations, ideas and the individuals needed to develop a human rights approach to AIDS as part of the national response. Cameron had been aware of his own HIV infection since December 1986 but was not at that time open about it.

Once a month members met in the cavernous basement of the D J du Plessis Building. It was here that for me AIDS suddenly became real. It became about people and people's dignity. Among those present I saw deep wellsprings of humanity and empathy, features that come to the fore when people are under siege, whatever the form of threat or oppression.

Assembled in that dim room was the cast who in the years to come would shape the medical and political responses to HIV. There were Peter Busse, the future Director of the National Association of People Living with HIV and AIDS (NAPWA) and Mercy Makhalemele, the first woman to live publicly with HIV. Both were warm, loving, thoughtful individuals, and for me their HIV infection typified the tragedy of AIDS – here were rich, promising lives that risked being cut down by a virus. Then there were James McIntyre and Glenda Gray, two doctors who pioneered research into medical interventions to prevent mother-to-child HIV transmission (PMTCT), and clinicians such as Dr Reuben Sher, Dave Johnson and David Spenser, among the few doctors at that time caring enough to treat people with AIDS; Sister Sue Roberts, a nurse who started the first public-sector HIV treatment clinic, at Johannesburg's Helen Joseph Hospital where she worked; and Eric Xayiya, much later on to become an adviser to the Gauteng Premier.

I formed a close bond with Mercy in particular, a young woman whose four-year-old daughter was to die of AIDS in 1995. Mercy refused to give up. In September 1995 she and I travelled together to Kasane in northern Botswana, to participate in the first conference to be organised in Botswana of people living with HIV. At the meeting point of four countries, on the banks of the great Chobe River, we helped to draft the Botswana HIV/AIDS and Human Rights Charter. Botswana has a tiny population but nonetheless the venue in Kasane was chosen to be as far away from the few towns as possible to protect the identity of the participants, all of whom carried their burden of HIV infection secretly. Encounters like these, with a group of about twenty young men and women, some already ailing, knowing that most might not live for more than a few years, witnessing their fear and persecution, were what made me understand the full human dimensions of AIDS. The deeper I got into the epidemic, the more difficult it became to leave it.

The AIDS Consortium is where we really find the beginnings of the civil-society-led fightback against AIDS. It was co-ordinated by Morna Cornell, an energetic and vibrant woman, whose efficiency gave it its life.

In this context my dreams of acquiring a PhD and publishing a book about A C Jordan faded into the distance. I came to realise that AIDS was one of the great human rights issues of the late twentieth century and that it involved an unprecedented struggle by millions of people for dignity, equality and ultimately life itself.

Being so close to death, witness to others' fear of death, made me much more aware of the value of being alive. It shaped my conviction that those of us who have health and opportunity must exploit every second available to us; we must maximise life and living. Life cannot be taken for granted. It can't be spent in bed.

Later that year I accompanied the small troupe that was then the ALP to a planning meeting at the home and guesthouse of the late Barry McGeary in Nylstroom (now Modimolle). Again, AIDS was being given a human meaning. In 1991 McGeary had been the first person to bring an AIDS case to a South African court, with Cameron as his counsel. His doctor had breached confidentiality by revealing McGeary's status to others and McGeary sued for damages. I remember watching his pathetic AIDS-ravaged figure being wheeled into court: he died that September before the trial was over. The court found against him and it would take another two years for his case to succeed on appeal in September 1993.

But I wasn't to work directly under Cameron for long. In late 1994 he was appointed by President Mandela to chair a commission of inquiry and a few months later he was made a judge of the Johannesburg High Court.

My reconnection with Zackie Achmat was almost as short. For as long as I have known him, Zackie has had a habit of proving unreliable at crucial moments. For example, in late 1989 he disappeared on the eve of a secret political youth camp that the MWT had organised in the Magaliesberg. I was left to lead the meeting alone.

This time he disappeared to become deeply involved in and lead the National Coalition for Gay and Lesbian Equality (NCGLE). He became the driving force behind one of the first movements to combine social mobilisation and litigation and successfully test the new Constitution's promise of equality and its prohibition on discrimination on the grounds of sexual orientation. As a result of his and others' efforts, on 9 October 1998 the criminalisation of 'sodomy' was declared unconstitutional by the Constitutional Court.

Learning about (AIDS) law

As its name suggests, the work of the AIDS Law Project hinged on law. Yet in all my preceding years of political activism I had given very little thought to the place of law in society, its role in establishing and policing norms and in regulating private, public and commercial behaviours. I had been taught that the law was used as an instrument of oppression. Interestingly, law was another place where literature and politics came together: in a more subtle and nuanced way I could find support for anti-law in Shakespeare's jovial cynicism towards lawyers. Bassanio's comment in *The Merchant of Venice* addresses a theme encountered often in Shakespeare's plays:

> In law, what plea so tainted and corrupt,
> But, being season'd with a gracious voice,
> Obscures the show of evil?[62]

'The first thing we do, let's kill all the lawyers,' suggests Dick the Butcher in *Henry VI Part 2*. And what about Timon of Athens, who proclaims, 'Crack the lawyer's voice, / That he may never more false title plead . . .'? I sympathised. Consequently I had *never* thought that law had any potential to be an instrument for liberation. The crude Marxist line is that the legal system, its laws, courts and lawyers are part of the class superstructure of bourgeois society, always protecting the interests of the capitalist class, inherently stacked against the working class. Legal institutions and the courts are structures of capitalism that will have to be reformed after the socialist revolution, and that will gradually 'wither away' as class conflicts disappear. While Marxism constantly refers to and seeks to explain the relationships between politics and economics, very little modern left thought seems to have interrogated the potentially progressive and transformative role of law. Much of Marxism continues to dismiss it.

The first time I had combined use of the law with social mobilisation was in the criminal trial of Philemon Mauku. But I must admit that in that first foray my attention was much more on the politics – law was just a means to a political end. I did not consider that some more profound potential might inhere within it. I didn't really appreciate it at the time, but *The State v Philemon Mauku* had been my baptism in public impact litigation.

With Edwin Cameron and Zackie Achmat gone, I found myself manning a ship I felt unqualified to captain. I didn't know whether to take hold of the helm or get into one of the lifeboats. After a year of prevarication I chose the former. So, with neither a law degree nor a deep understanding of AIDS, in 1997 I was appointed to head the ALP.

I was an unlikely head for a public-interest law firm. At the time I was barely able to differentiate between an advocate and an attorney. I was oblivious of the distinctions between the various forms of affidavit in a legal process. I was untutored in the ways of the guild, the mysterious and outwardly impenetrable language of law. Somebody told me that if I could not remember the sequence in which affidavits are meant to follow each other in an application (as opposed to a trial) I should recall it as FAR: Founding, Answering and then Replying. A bit like 'Every Good Boy Deserves Food', the way we had been taught in music to remember the notes on the lines of the treble clef.

To make things worse, the ALP I inherited had little legal capacity. After Edwin and Zackie departed I was left with a ragbag of individuals, lawyers who came and went with varying degrees of real commitment to AIDS and human rights. Cameron and Achmat had left the ALP as a shell, largely built around their own powerful personalities and capacities. My job was to give that shell a body, some blood and, in a word loved by donors, 'sustainability'. It would not be easy.

As for individuals: we started as a hotchpotch, a motley collection mostly of lawyers led by a person who knew lots about Marxism but next to nothing about law and legal process. But as time passed there was growing internal coherence. The most important addition to the ALP came in late 1996 when a young lawyer, Fatima Hassan, joined the ALP for three months straight after completing her articles. Fatima came from a conservative Muslim community. She told me that she 'couldn't even tell them she was working at the ALP'. But she had been politically active as a black student. As an Indian woman she had the lived experience of race discrimination but, on her own admission, she knew nothing about HIV.

With Fatima, at last the ALP had a 'real lawyer', someone with both the capacity to practise law and the desire to combine it with her political vision and personal commitment to human rights; a dream of using legal advocacy and litigation in a way that would make a difference. Fatima existed in a state of constant outrage against injustice, something that translated into a frenetic energy in law. She had one other essential characteristic: real and deep empathy. Her three months eventually grew to ten years.

Such individuals, I have learnt, are an essential ingredient of the ability to effect social change. Sadly, they are few and far between. I learnt that there are two types of people who work in human rights organisations:

those who are there by accident or for self-advancement, and those who are there because they have a real commitment to human rights and equality. The challenge is to weed out the former and find and hold on to the latter.

But ill-equipped though I may have been, I knew I had been given a rare opportunity and I was intent on seeing if I could build an effective public-interest law firm, following in the best traditions established by such organisations as the Legal Resources Centre and Lawyers for Human Rights.

Somewhere I recall Trotsky asserting that it's imagination that sharply distinguishes human beings from other mammals. Imagination is day-dreaming, building work in the soul. The advantage humans have is the ability to bring to life stuff that starts in the mind, to turn a subjective thought into an objective reality. It starts with an idea.

I imagined the ALP as a vibrant and effective law practice, able to respond to the many slights and injuries of people living with HIV that I was becoming aware of. I imagined an organisation that could pursue and realise the vision set out in the 1992 Charter of Rights on AIDS and HIV that Cameron and colleagues at the AIDS Consortium had pioneered. This is the founding document of the human rights response to HIV in South Africa. It was launched on World AIDS Day 1992 after a political campaign soliciting the signatures of leaders as diverse as Chris Hani, Mangosuthu Buthelezi and Nelson Mandela.

Building an institution from scratch is arduous and painful. However, in a life of organisation-building, one of the things I have learnt is that public interest organisations are not constructed in the abstract; they build themselves in the course of concrete campaigns that seek particular results. Campaigns require organisation; out of focused campaigns networks of people begin to emerge, together with ideas and eventually an organisational architecture. The campaign, because it requires action rather than waffle, is where the process of natural selection of activists, the sorting of wheat from chaff, takes place.

Lesson for social justice activists: Never try to build an organisation as an end in itself. You won't succeed.

In the mid-1990s, when the ALP and the AIDS Consortium were the only political and human rights voices on AIDS, we had plenty to campaign and complain about. Although I did not understand constitutional law at the time, the coming into effect of the final Constitution in February 1997 changed the human rights game in South Africa. Human rights were now embedded in the supreme law of our country. The state was under a duty to respect, protect, promote and fulfil these rights. This gave legitimacy and a great fillip to the work of the ALP.

Learning about loss

In mid-1994 Sharon and I joyed in the discovery that she was pregnant. We would have a child. It goes without saying that pregnancy is a special time for any couple, but it is an especially special time for many women. The experience of another being growing within you is one that a man can only imagine. It can be seen in the sense of wellbeing that radiates from women who are happy in their pregnancy. For nine months the body of a pregnant woman is in a constant process of creation. However habitual to human nature, indeed to any nature, it remains wondrous.

Sharon's pregnancy was a happy and fulfilling one. Like an eternity of star-struck parents we watched her body grow, felt the little kicks, began to imagine an identity for the child within. One thing we did not do was worry; we were in the care of struggle doctors Helen Rees and Fazel Randera. We assumed everything would be fine. Then out of the blue tragedy struck.

After years of unpaid work for freedom we were poor. So, like millions of others, we were dependent on public hospitals for our healthcare. Our plan was that Sharon would give birth at what was then called J G Strijdom Hospital in the suburb of Brixton, Johannesburg – the same hospital that I would visit a few years later to meet doctors at the start of the TAC case on PMTCT.

In March 1995, 36 weeks into the pregnancy, excited and expectant we went for our first scan. This would be the first glimpse of the baby within, the time when we would find out its sex. Instead we had the breath knocked out of us. As the radiographer passed the head of the ultrasound wand over Sharon's swollen belly, she froze. She used the tannoy to call other medics in the vicinity to 'come and see a very clear presentation of hydrocephaly'. The curious doctors arrived, went into a huddle, whispered and peered. The radiographer rested a book on Sharon's tummy. When Sharon asked what the sex of the baby was, the response was that 'right now this is the least of my concerns'.

In the moments after, we were told bluntly that our baby had extreme hydro-cephalus, a swelling of the head caused by water on the brain, and that the prospects for the baby's survival were nil. The devastation was indescribable. We went into a whirr of pain. Meetings with doctors, meetings with expert ob-stetricians, informing our families, managing our own lost hope.

A decision was taken to terminate the life of the baby. There was none other possible. For several days Sharon lay in a public ward in J G Strijdom waiting for her child to die within her. I sat at the end of the bed for hours and hours, haunted by a test tube of blood attached to the drip that went into her body. Why was it there? What did it signal? We were never told.

Our son did not die easily. He took two days. Eventually a Caesarean section was undertaken to extract his body. Soon after I went to find him in the mortuary in the bowels of the hospital. Then on to the crematorium. Hope, despair, death, birth, death, dissolution overlapped. Greater pain you could not imagine.

The boy we called Joe is buried in a quiet spot in the Magaliesberg, a place where Sharon and I had shared moments of happiness during the crazy years of politics. We scattered his ashes in a pool at a point where the stream rests after it has tumbled over rock, forming a pool overhung by an ancient tree, whose gnarled roots have edged their way down a cliff-face over many unseen years. We carved the letter JE into the tree, for Joe Ekambaram.

In late 1995 Sharon became pregnant again. This time we were cautious throughout the pregnancy. We had watched our baby grow, feeling a terrible anxiety at every appointment with the radiologist. We knew our daughter, whom we had named Caitlin, was healthy. Caitlin timed her disengagement from Sharon's womb on an Easter weekend. Because it was a holiday there were re-duced staff at the Marymount Hospital. After the trauma of the year before we had decided to have a natural birth. But almost exactly a year after Joe's death the same tragedy repeated itself. That early morning the midwife was inattentive and tired. Sharon's labour was drawn out and the midwife did not notice that Caitlin was in stress. By the time she picked up the fact that something was wrong, Caitlin had breached the scar of the previous year's Caesarean, the place where Joe had simultaneously entered and exited the world. Panic took over. But because it was an Easter weekend, the hospital had a skeleton staff. It took over an hour for an anaesthetist to arrive. By the time a Caesarean could be carried out, Caitlin was dead.[63]

I was the horrified witness to the instant birth and death of my second child. I looked at her and nothing made sense. She was a beautifully formed little girl who would have had a life. Sharon woke from the anaesthetic to the news that her baby had died. She was sedated. Later, I placed Caitlin in her mother's arms. There is a photograph of this somewhere. A photo I will never be able to look at.

That night I slept under the hospital bed in the ward where this trauma had taken place. For a second time I felt helpless in the midst of the screams and sobs and agony of a mother who had lost her child.

Days later Caitlin's ashes joined her brother's in that little pool. Her initials too were carved into the tree.

In this article, published by the *Sowetan* in 2000, I disclosed my experience of losing a child and how it helped me understand the pain of so many other mothers and fathers.

Mr 'A' and the Airways

Through the rest of the 1990s most of the ALP's work involved putting into place protective legal frameworks for people with HIV in relation to access to employment and medical benefits and in prison. With the assistance of Fatima Hassan we represented the little Nkosi Johnson as his school initially tried to prevent his admission. We had to negotiate with another pre-primary school who refused an HIV-positive child on the grounds that he might bite other children. The dread of stigmatisation meant that relatively few individual victims of discrimination sought out our services directly. When they did, we had to call them after hours and avoid using the ALP letterhead, such was the fear. Cases were often brought to us by the indefatigable Sister Sue Roberts. But when people did seek our help we took up their cases and causes passionately. The seminal case of a young man called 'A' who found the courage to take on South African Airways (SAA) was where I cut my teeth.

What came to be known as *A v South African Airways* was the first ground-breaking constitutional case that I, and my small team, can lay claim to. A was a young black man with a dream. If he was alive to tell his story I imagine it would be of his high hopes for opportunity and the new-found dignity that came with the start of democracy only three years before. He had qualifications, he was attractive and personable. But he also had HIV. This, he discovered, was a new form of apartheid.

In 1998 A walked gingerly into our offices to seek assistance.[64] The story he unfolded was that after sitting exams and an interview he had been appointed as a cabin attendant at SAA. But after he tested HIV-positive during pre-employment medical screening, that offer had been summarily withdrawn. He had not received counselling before or after the test: in fact, he had not even been aware that he had undergone an HIV test.

Fatima Hassan's injustice barometer went into red. We quickly agreed to act as A's attorneys. But if we were to argue the case before a court we needed an advocate. South Africa has what lawyers mysteriously call a split Bar. This practice, inherited from England, means simply that attorneys and advocates perform different functions in the legal process; attorneys (the Side Bar) do all kinds of legal work while advocates (the Bar) are specialist litigators. Although both attorneys and advocates may appear in the courts, an attorney will brief an advocate when specialist litigation is required.

So, in Fatima Hassan we had only half of what we needed to commence litigation on A's behalf. To plug the gap we approached Karel Tip, a Senior Counsel and a respected labour lawyer. He earned his pedigree using the law against apartheid. Tip's initial response was negative: he told us that litigating for the right of HIV-positive cabin attendants to work on aeroplanes was the worst place to start a legal battle against HIV-related discrimination. He argued that such a case would play into the deeply held prejudices of the public as well as, probably, of the judiciary. Fatima Hassan and I disagreed. For us unfair discrimination was unfair discrimination. So the first step in this first case involved running a day-long workshop to educate our own legal team about HIV and to disabuse them of their own misunderstandings and prejudices. By the end of the day we were all on the same side.

In the late 1980s the prejudices against people with HIV ran deep. Discrimination was particularly prevalent in the employment setting. Some people feared to work with people with 'AIDS'. Pre-employment HIV testing was considered to be a legitimate way of weeding people with HIV out of the workplace. It was argued, even by respectable analysts who should have known better, that people with HIV were a bad investment and should not be trained or promoted because they would die before returns could be yielded.

Science is a great converter. After we had used it to educate our counsel, the ALP constructed A's case around a careful exposition of the best medical evidence and opinion available. We needed to prove to the court that people with HIV were as capable of working as anyone else, that they posed no threat to those they worked with or for. This meant busting prejudices and stigma. To do this we had to reach out to the scientific community. Seven experts were enlisted, covering the disciplines of occupational health, epidemiology, the basic science of HIV and its psycho-social effects. With the magnificent seven we threw the encyclopaedia of HIV medicine at SAA and the court.

Our founding affidavit annexed to it the most up-to-date knowledge about HIV available. An affidavit on the basic science of HIV and its transmission was provided by Dr Malcolm Steinberg. Respected virologist Dr Des Martin was brought in to counter SAA's claim that a yellow fever vaccination was an inherent requirement of the job because some of their planes flew to West Africa and that vaccination with a live but attenuated virus was contraindicated for people with HIV.

And so it was that on 8 May 2000 I found myself in the dim oak-walled sanctuary of the Johannesburg Labour Court. I was about to use the Constitution for the first time in my life to test the difference between right and wrong. To be in a court was my measure of real law. It was a coming of age. This was the point that I had imagined since taking over the ALP.

But it was not to be. Ishmael Semenya SC appeared for SAA. Once they had heard our opening argument, an assault by science against prejudice, they must have understood that they were going to lose the case. After a lot of toing and froing they tendered an unconditional settlement offer of R100 000 in open court, admitting that A's exclusion from employment solely on the grounds of his HIV status was unjustified.

Lesson for human rights lawyers: in the world where prejudice makes people blind, science is king!

The case was over before it started. That's part of the game of chess called law. You can put hours and hours of preparation and thought into a case which you want to set a precedent that will benefit many others, but the individual's interests are paramount. To a young man from a poor background R100 000 was a great deal of money. The ALP may have wanted to reject the offer, for the case to continue in order to establish a legally binding precedent, but A's decision was what counted.

Lesson for human rights lawyers: whenever possible, include an institutional applicant to represent the public interest!

Fortunately for us, however, another case also involving an HIV-related dismissal by SAA was working its way through the courts. The ALP had shadowed this case, which had started before A's. The applicant, Jacques Hoffmann, had lost his application for reinstatement by SAA in the Johannesburg High Court in a judgment that was bad for people with HIV generally. His lawyers, the Legal Resources Centre (LRC), decided the case was important enough to appeal it directly to the Constitutional Court.

This was to be my first engagement with the practice, now commonly used in constitutional litigation, of the amicus curiae, or friend of the court. Although disguised in Latin, the concept is simple to explain: it involves a non-party to a legal dispute offering to provide relevant evidence or legal argument that it believes will help a court to reach a resolution of a matter, literally being a friend to the court. The weakness of the LRC's case on behalf of Hoffmann had been that it had not marshalled the scientific evidence that we had gathered in A's case. The ALP thus decided to make an application to be an amicus before the Constitutional Court in the case of *Hoffmann v South African Airways*.[65]

For me this was real law of an even higher order. We had managed to reach the pinnacle of the legal system.

In September 2000 the Constitutional Court's unanimous judgment in *Hoffmann* was delivered by the future Chief Justice, Sandile Ngcobo. In the meantime the Treatment Action Campaign (TAC) had been gathering momentum and that day the Constitutional Court had its first experience of a phalanx of anxious activists, all dressed in 'HIV Positive' T-shirts, signalling their solidarity with Hoffmann, A and others like them.

The Court was unambiguous in its rejection of prejudice. Drawing on the ALP's evidence, it set out at length the science of HIV and its impact on human wellness. For the first time it invoked the notion of the African philosophy of Ubuntu and its relevance to non-discrimination and equality. It declared that people with HIV should not be condemned to 'economic death' and ordered that SAA offer Hoffmann employment

In its judgment the Court thanked the ALP for its evidence, saying: 'We are indebted to the ALP and counsel for their assistance in this matter.' The Court said that the medical evidence introduced by the ALP had 'altered the course of argument on appeal'.

We had won! Patience had paid off. A had received compensation and Hoffmann his job offer – and the Constitutional Court had spoken for the first time on HIV. But in those same moments something we came to call AIDS denialism was taking a grip on our government.

5

Saving lives – time for TAC

I n November 1997 Zackie Achmat and I visited Edwin Cameron at his home in Brixton, Johannesburg. Cameron was gaunt and unwell. He had AIDS. In the opening chapter of his book *Witness to AIDS*[66] he bravely recounts his descent into ill health after years of HIV infection. His story was the story of tens of thousands of others. So was his fear of impending death, which he described as 'fetid, frightening, intrusive, oppressive'. But unlike Cameron, most others were silent witnesses to their own collapsing bodies and dreams. They were also unable to afford ARV treatment. Unlike Cameron they did not escape death.

So, over a cup of afternoon tea, I watched as Cameron swallowed several pills and hoped for the best. In those days, there was still much uncertainty about the medicines, a worry about their side effects and a 'what-if-they-don't-work' fear. I could feel it in the room. It was certainly in my mind. But it was unspoken. Nearly twenty years later Justice Edwin Cameron of the Constitutional Court is alive and well. He has had his wished-for second chance and used it to make a massive contribution to law, democracy and the response to the AIDS epidemic globally. He has lived and loved his life. And continues to do so.

The medicines Cameron swallowed in front of Zackie and me are called antiretrovirals (ARVs). Some of these drugs had been around for some time, but in 1996 clinical trials had established that if a person with HIV took three antiretroviral drugs at the same time they would suppress the replication of HIV and thus prevent the depletion of the immune system and the onset of AIDS. This became known as combination therapy.

In 1999 the first results of a clinical trial carried out in Uganda of a single pill of the drug nevirapine (NVP) given to an HIV-infected pregnant woman during her labour, plus a single spoon of syrup to the child after birth, had shown dramatic efficacy: it reduced the rate of mother-to-child HIV transmission by up to 50%.

Soon after these results were announced a confirmatory trial was started in South Africa under the name of SAINT, the South African Intrapartum Nevirapine Trial. The objective was to verify the Ugandan results under local conditions. The initial results of SAINT had been announced at the International AIDS Conference held in Durban in July 2000, and from then on miraculous stories began to circulate of what people termed 'the Lazarus effect': people at death's door returning to health and well-being. The era of treatment had commenced.

Edwin Cameron's return to health bore witness to one of these miracles, but in those days, as he himself never shied away from saying, these drugs were not for the poor.

First of all, they were hugely expensive. Pharmaceutical companies massively inflated their prices knowing that people with AIDS would find a way to pay for the guarantors of their lives. Secondly, they were considered too complex to be made accessible via the broken public-health systems of developing countries. The HAART (Highly Active Antiretroviral Therapy) programme involved taking multiple pills at set times of the day and required monitoring and health-system support. The prevailing 'wisdom' considered Africans too illiterate to follow a complex 'first world' treatment regimen. In 2001 Andrew Natsios, the powerful Director of USAID, notoriously told members of the United States House of Representatives:

> If we had [HIV medicines for Africa] today, we could not distribute them. We could not administer the program because we do not have the doctors, we do not have the roads, we do not have the cold chain . . . [Africans] do not know what watches and clocks are. They do not use western means for telling time. They use the sun. These drugs have to be administered during a certain sequence of time during the day and when you say take it at 10:00, people will say what do you mean by 10:00?[67]

This, according to him, was good reason for not providing treatment at a time when ARVs still had to be taken at carefully spaced intervals during the day.

However, even after you discounted Natsios's racism, treatment remained unaffordable.

In South Africa HIV had broken out of its cage in the early 1990s. Within years it spread from its initial locus among people whose lives made them more vulnerable to HIV infection, migrant mineworkers far from family and gay men, to the population as a whole. For the rest of the decade there was a frightening increase in new HIV infections with the numbers of infected people rising from under a million in 1990 to three million at the end of the decade. By 2000 the annual antenatal survey of

HIV prevalence recorded that 25% of pregnant women presenting in public healthcare were HIV-infected.

However, HIV infection has a long asymptomatic period – often up to ten years. During all of this time the virus and the human immune system do battle with each other, a battle in which HIV invariably triumphs if its replication is not suppressed with ARVs. The lag between infection and the onset of what we came to know as 'opportunistic infections' meant that the explosion of HIV-related diseases such as TB, followed by death, began to be noticed in South Africa only in the late 1990s. Up until then the belief held by many that the scale of the HIV epidemic was being exaggerated could be sustained, because the war was a largely invisible one going on within tens of thousands of bodies.

But at about the same time as Edwin started his medicines in 1997, South Africa crossed the threshold into an AIDS epidemic. ARVs changed the course of AIDS in the developed world. People stopped dying. But in our world the death rate began to speed up. It was as if this medical breakthrough had taken place on another planet.

The time of death and dying had started.

We knew from the epidemiological modelling that a tidal wave of death was approaching, but until 1998 I had not personally known anyone who died of AIDS. That was a world ago.

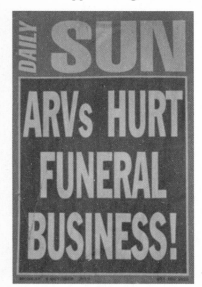

Famous newspaper poster: this one was very true.

Two deaths in particular catalysed the formation of the Treatment Action Campaign (TAC). One was 'natural' and one was a murder.

Simon Nkoli was an unusual man, to put it mildly. He was a respected political leader in the ANC and had been tried for treason in 1985 alongside two well-known leaders of the United Democratic Front, Popo Molefe and Terror Lekota. He was eventually acquitted in 1988. What made Simon different from his comrades, though, is that he was also flamboyantly queer, a founder of the Township AIDS Project and one of only two or three people in the whole of South Africa brave enough to live openly with HIV. Simon died of AIDS on 30 November 1998. Speaking off the cuff at Simon's funeral, Zackie called for a 'partnership that will save lives' and told mourners to 'cry, rage, mobilise, don't only mourn'.

That moment is captured in Jack Lewis's film *Taking HAART*. TAC was born 'astride of a grave'.

On 17 December 1998, two weeks later, Gugu Dlamini, a 37-year-old mother from KwaMashu township in Durban, was murdered after she had declared in an interview on a local radio station that she was HIV-positive, as part of raising awareness around World AIDS Day, 1 December. According to her daughter, Mandisa, young men in the community were bitter that Gugu, a woman and single mother, occupied a government-owned house. Her HIV disclosure turned their bitterness into a murderous rage. At a party a group of men 'beat her with anything they could find'. When they were done, they pushed her down a cliff and they told her neighbour: 'Come and fetch the dog, we are done with it.' Her death was testimony to the depth of stigma and shame surrounding HIV. Her picture was on the back of TAC's first 'HIV Positive' T-shirt. The murderous thugs snuffed out a life. Little did they know their violence would also spark a global movement inspired in part by her death.

The first demonstration by TAC, the announcement of its birth, followed a few days later: a small demonstration took place on the steps of St George's Cathedral in central Cape Town to demand access to ARV treatment. It involved Zackie and a group of comrades mostly drawn from the former ranks of the MWT.

I was not one of them. I was away in New York attending a United Nations conference that was ostensibly much more auspicious and important, the launch of the African Partnership Against AIDS. I was one of a small group of people who had been selected to speak on behalf of civil society. However, as with so many conferences organised under the auspices of one UN agency or another, it was expensive, pompous and ultimately insignificant. It turned out to be the little group of individuals in Cape Town who started something that changed the face of the African AIDS epidemic.

I had not been party to any discussions with Zackie about his plans for a new campaign, but I recognised its importance from afar. There was something in the moment that made TAC the necessary and right thing to do. But in addition, my work at the ALP had made me aware that the course of the AIDS epidemic would not be changed by HIV-negative middle-class do-gooders like me working in NGOs like the ALP. It didn't matter how well intentioned we were. AIDS needed a social movement and that movement needed to be political and mirror the demographics of the AIDS epidemic in terms of gender and race. It also needed to be led by people who had everything to lose from AIDS – people with AIDS themselves.

In January 1999 a meeting took place at the offices of the South African NGO Coalition (SANGOCO) in the same building in Braamfontein where the MWT had once had its office. This meeting really marks the beginning of TAC as an organisation. A small group of activists gathered to try to work out how to give wings to an idea: Zackie Achmat, Peter Busse, Edwin Cameron, Morna Cornell, Sharon Ekambaram, Mercy Makhalemele, Phumi Mtetwa, Colwyn Poole, Fatima Hassan and me. We agreed to formalise a treatment action campaign as *the* Treatment Action Campaign, initially as a wing of the National Association of People Living with HIV and AIDS (NAPWA).

That day we made plans to launch two campaigns. The first campaign would be to demand a programme to prevent mother-to-child HIV transmission, taking advantage of new knowledge reported from clinical trials in Thailand that had revealed that a short course of the antiretroviral drug AZT, taken by an HIV-positive pregnant woman in the third trimester of her pregnancy, could dramatically reduce the risk of an infant being born with HIV.[68] The PMTCT campaign would be driven by the TAC and its first stage would culminate with a 'Fast to Save Lives' and a demonstration on Sharpeville Day, 21 March, Human Rights Day and a public holiday in South Africa.

Parallel to this, NAPWA would lead a campaign to promote openness about and acceptance of HIV, aimed at destigmatising HIV.

The small group of people gathered round the table at the SANGOCO office were political activists, not AIDS activists. Half of us were émigrés from the MWT of the ANC. We knew how to organise campaigns, we understood politics, we could pontificate about 'the class character of the ANC' and 'the lessons of the Russian Revolution'. But most of us knew nothing about HIV, the deadly virus that had brought us back together again.

There was no model of AIDS activism in Africa that we could copy, so we began to look to the activist movement in the United States for ideas.

Stored somewhere in our memories we found TV images of AIDS activists in the US who, in the late 1980s and early 1990s, had organised die-ins, loudly demanding action and investment in research into new medicines. As we set about forming TAC, suddenly we spotted them at it again. This time they were disrupting the political rallies of US Democratic presidential candidate Al Gore – protesting about the Clinton/Gore government's support of the multinational pharmaceutical companies that were trying to stop South Africa's reformed Medicines Act. Once more they were blocking streets, brazenly disrupting rallies and sitting in at government offices.

Most inspiring was the New York-based AIDS Coalition to Unleash Power, ACT UP. During the presidency of Ronald Reagan their confrontational tactics had first forced AIDS onto the political agenda. To its eternal credit ACT UP's demonstration accelerated research into medicines to treat HIV. The screams of activists like playwright Larry Kramer were so loud that they could be heard as far away as South Africa. During my thirsty research into the history of the AIDS movement, seeking inspiration and ideas, I was jolted awake by the anger in an open letter Kramer had written and titled 'What Are You Doing to Save My Fucking Life?' [69]

(There you are: that word 'fuck' again, and how appropriate the anger it conveys.)

However, the social circumstances of the South African and United States AIDS epidemics were vastly different. Robin Gorna, a contemporary of mine at Oxford, but someone who had graduated straight into AIDS activism, told me that in the early days, when HIV used to be called Gay-Related Immune Deficiency (GRID), people talked about its links with the '4Hs': homosexuals, Haitians, heroin addicts and haemophiliacs. She said each group was marginalised, stigmatised and discriminated against in its own way. But the loudest voices came from men with HIV who were mostly white, middle-class, educated and gay. They were also people with some power. Their anger was ignited because middle-class white men were not supposed to die in their twenties and thirties. AIDS suddenly changed this and they got angry and assertive about their human rights to life and non-discrimination.

This was in sharp contrast to our South Africa and even more so across Africa. In our world the people who were infected with HIV were mainly black and poor, especially black and female. HIV took hold among people who had grown up anticipating the possibility of premature death in childbirth or from one disease or another, among people for whom the notion of 'human rights' was strange and unfamiliar. And even if you did know your rights, you could forget about standing up for them in dictatorships like Uganda, Malawi and Zimbabwe.

TAC could have got stuck at that point. But as we looked for ideas we discovered from the American activists that a key to unleashing people's power lay in their acquiring understanding of the science of HIV, the way the antiretroviral and other medicines worked, the human immune system and elementary virology. The Americans called this 'treatment literacy'.

So, to start to rectify our knowledge deficit, in 2000 TAC held its first workshop on virology, HIV, AIDS and its treatment. A small group of activists from ACT UP and the Treatment Action Group (TAG) flew in from the United States to teach us. They included young men with HIV who had already become veterans of the American struggle: Mark Harrington, Gregg Gonsalves and Michael Marco. Little did we know that this would also be the first step in a decades-long relationship.

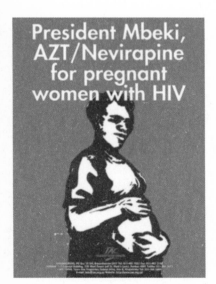

The postcard that TAC produced to send to the President demanding a programme to prevent mother-to-child-HIV transmission.

TAC's birth was not easy or uncontroversial. Our first few years of life were lonely and involved a hard swim against the stream. We were angry. We were unapologetic. We were demanding. Zackie was frequently rude to the people he considered obstacles to an effective response to AIDS. We were not popular. We were not liked.

We were the new punks on the block.

Polite society doesn't like punks and in those days the South African AIDS scene was très polite. Within months tensions developed between NAPWA and us. The tensions were political. We didn't tell people that one of the aims of TAC was to break the inertia and complacency that had developed in large sections of civil society, and NAPWA's leaders epitomised this inertia. The epidemic was black and poor but NAPWA was white and comfortably middle class. Its Director, Peter Busse, was a lovely, warm, thoughtful individual – but he was not a visionary leader. Like many others he seemed content to attend overseas conferences and multiple workshops while remaining detached from the needs and lives of the vast majority of people living with and beginning to die from HIV. He was unable to spit truth at power.

Busse should not be blamed for this. Complacency and comfort have been and are a blight on the whole 'AIDS industry'. Vast amounts of money and much wasted time are spent in conferences and workshops that have grand aspirations and titles but do little other than line the pockets of their participants with per diems and provide the chance to visit exotic locations.

TAC organised hard. We demonstrated, confronted, challenged and demanded. This was not the style of Busse and others at NAPWA. As a result a bitter conflict developed over the failure of the NAPWA leaders to mobilise for the 'Fast to Save Lives' or to ensure a proper police investigation and inquest into the death of Gugu Dlamini. Accusatory emails took to the air, burning the inboxes of the then fairly small circle of

An early photo of TAC activists. Left to right, Jonathan Berger, myself, Sharon Ekambaram, Zackie Achmat, and my first son, Ciaran.

members of the AIDS Consortium. People whispered that we were bastards. Later some suggested the conflict had hastened Peter's death in
2006. It soon became clear that it was no longer business as usual and
that a rupture was imminent in the community.

Sharon, too, had transitioned from the MWT to TAC. She was TAC's
first Gauteng co-ordinator. One day we woke up to find the NAPWA office,
from which she and TAC had been operating, empty. All that was left
was a lone chair and a disconnected telephone. NAPWA had relocated to
the safety of the grandly named Centre for the Study of AIDS at Pretoria
University. There Mary Crewe, the chair of the NAPWA board, could
protect it. This she did until the time she handed it over to two men until
then largely unknown, Nkululeko Nxesi and Thanduxolo Doro.

In the years that followed, this dishonest duo did many strange things.
They aligned an organisation of people living with HIV with people who
denied the existence of AIDS; they allied themselves with politically
aligned traditional healers and a German vitamin salesman who punted
'cures' for AIDS; and they repeatedly supported Manto Tshabalala-
Msimang, the increasingly errant Minister of Health.

But I will come to that.

Challenging big pharma

When we met in January 1999 at the SANGOCO offices we imagined
that TAC's main focus would be to campaign to reduce the price of antiretrovirals as well as other medicines required to treat the opportunistic
infections that seize advantage over a weakened immune system. We
believed that the excessive price of these medicines, a result of the patents that cloaked them, was the main barrier preventing people with
AIDS in Africa from getting the same life-saving benefits of medicine as
their brothers and sisters in developed countries.

In 1997 one of the first legislative reforms that had been undertaken
by South Africa's democratic government had been to amend the Medicines and Related Substances Act with the objective of creating competition in the medicines market and thereby reducing the prices of
essential medicines. The amended law allowed the government to engage in parallel importation and made generic substitution of off-patents
medicines mandatory. This was permissible in terms of international law
and, we believed, mandated by the Constitution.

But Mandela's government was naïve about the good intentions of the
capitalist world. They amended the law at a time when gung-ho multi-

national pharmaceutical companies were flexing their muscles to confront governments that threatened what they considered their intellectual property. 'Big pharma' (as activists call it) had been emboldened by the 1994 World Trade Organisation (WTO) Agreement on Trade-Related Aspects of Intellectual Property Rights (TRIPS), an agreement whose passage has been directly linked to lobbying by pharmaceutical companies. In the new neoliberal world, TRIPS aimed to set a uniformly high standard for global intellectual property protection.

This was the context in which in February 1998 the Pharmaceutical Manufacturers Association (PMA), an umbrella body for 41 multinational pharmaceutical companies operating in South Africa, initiated litigation to halt the implementation of the amendments. The President – Nelson Mandela – was listed as the first respondent.

Litigation is more often tortoise than hare. It can be threat, feint and bluster. The PMA probably initiated the litigation as a stick to keep the Mandela government immobile. At the same time it commissioned its allies in the Clinton government to put South Africa on a trade 'Watch List'. But this tactic backfired . . .

Long before we joined the battle in South Africa a small group of activists and academics had taken up the cudgels in the United States. Led by people like Jamie Love and the Consumer Project on Technology, they took on both the companies and the US government.

By the time we woke up the litigation had been grinding on for two years and had reached stalemate. In November 2000 the matter was set down to be heard in the Pretoria High Court in March the following year. One morning in early January 2001 Zackie Achmat phoned me. He insisted that we meet urgently with Gilbert Marcus, a senior advocate at the Johannesburg Bar with a proud record of human rights litigation. We met Marcus at his home and decided to seek the court's leave for TAC to intervene as an amicus curiae. We intended to provide evidence as to how the amended law would improve the affordability of medicines for HIV and argue that the government was acting on a constitutional duty to fulfil the right of access to healthcare services mandated in section 27 of the Constitution.[70]

TAC framed the legal dispute as essentially a moral one between rich, hugely profitable pharmaceutical companies and poor people in life-or-death need of essential medicines; between rich companies wielding great economic and legal power (as well as their influence over the

United States government and the WTO) and a newly democratic state seeking to keep a constitutional promise to protect the health of its people in the midst of the AIDS epidemic.

To be admitted as an amicus you have first to obtain the consent of the warring parties. We wrote to the PMA and they refused consent. This was a huge tactical blunder. Their refusal kicked off what lawyers with their love of Latin call an in limine dispute, effectively a trial within a trial to decide whether TAC's arguments had merit and should be heard by the court. A fast, furious and intense two months followed.

TAC reached out to the international community and – without so much as stepping outside the borders of the country – launched an international campaign around the court case, drawing on and reinforcing campaigns that had already been launched by Médecins Sans Frontières (MSF), ACT UP and others. We tied the date of the court hearing to an international mobilisation for treatment access, advancing the idea that access to medicines is a human right.

TAC called for a Global Day of Action Against Drug Company Profiteering on 5 March 2001. As the weeks passed, TAC's support grew far beyond its initial allies and the PMA's assault backfired as pricing of essential medicines became an issue of international concern, perhaps the first globally co-ordinated human rights campaign of the 21st century.

On 5 March the world seemed to rise to our appeal. Demonstrations against the pharma companies were held in 30 countries worldwide, including Brazil, the Philippines, Thailand, Kenya, England, Germany and France. Activists carried pairs of shoes to company offices, dumping them at their gates to signify lives lost as a result of the high price of medicines. The European Union and the Dutch government passed resolutions calling on the companies to withdraw their case. The famed writer of spy-thrillers, John Le Carré (whose novel *The Constant Gardener*, published that same year, was about the shenanigans of big pharma), signed TAC's petition and handwrote a message of support. So did the British pop singer Annie Lennox and Bono, the lead singer of U2.

On our side of the Limpopo, when the big day dawned the court was packed to capacity with activists in TAC's 'HIV Positive' T-shirts. The night before, 500 people had camped outside the court, and the court proceedings were preceded by a 5 000-strong march through Pretoria to the US Embassy.

This was now a political trial with a difference. Forty years earlier Nelson Mandela and his co-accused had been charged with sabotage in this same court. In 1963 Mandela was the first defendant. This time he was the first respondent. But once again the tables were turned on the accusers. The multinational companies had started this litigation but in the court of public opinion it was now they who were on trial. The world watched with almost as much rapt attention as fifteen years later it would watch the murder trial of Oscar Pistorius. TAC's message was spread far and wide through interviews with the BBC and CNN. For several months Sky News showed footage of our legal team entering the court as a filler in the lead-up to its hourly news.

Some say that judges may consider only what is presented to them on the papers and in argument inside the courtroom, but it is a fact that they cannot isolate themselves from intense public debates taking place in the world outside. On 6 March 2001, when Judge Bernard Ngoepe handed down a ruling that admitted TAC as an amicus, he stated: 'I am aware that the entire nation is interested and many people beyond our boundaries.' However grey and hoary they sometimes appear, judges remain human beings. They are not immune to public concern. Advocacy to generate this concern, to get an issue into the air, marches and media are an essential component of social justice litigation.

TAC's involvement meant the pressure on the companies became too great. On 18 April 2001 the case resumed after several weeks' postponement. Immediately the PMA's lawyers requested an adjournment. A day later they announced that they were unconditionally withdrawing from the case.

First blood! Celebrating TAC's victory over the PMA in April 2001. Zwelinzima Vavi, the General Secretary of COSATU, together with Zackie Achmat, Prudence Mabele and myself on the cover of *The Shopsteward*.

Big pharma had been defeated by a little David called TAC. Within months the prices of ARVs began to fall dramatically. Access to life-saving medicine had become affordable for millions of people living in developing countries.

The international AIDS activist movement had scored a goal of global significance.

The 'prevailing wisdom' that ARV treatment was too expensive would soon lie shattered on the floor.

Activists had tasted power and we had appetite for more.

Supper with the Santanas

In 2003 Mexican guitarist Carlos Santana and his wife donated the profits of his summer gigs in the USA to aid children and families affected by AIDS in South Africa. They set up the Amandla AIDS Fund, a trust to disburse the money. In October 2006 they came to South Africa and visited projects benefiting from the donation. By some happenstance I was asked to accompany him on a tour of some of the worst-affected villages in the rural areas of eastern KwaZulu-Natal.

I was asked to meet Santana at what was then known as Johannesburg International Airport. Having encountered U2 lead singer Bono on a similar mission, I expected pop-star arrogance. I looked for someone with a train of porters and protectors, media and ego-massagers. He was nowhere to be found. Instead a man in a skullcap arrived with Deborah, his wife, and two of their children. We checked in on a flight to Durban and he took his seat in economy class along with other mortals.

Later that evening, after a journey on a luxury bus on which I gave a talk about TAC and the AIDS crisis – much like a tour guide pointing out the surrounding geography – I sat down to supper with the Santana family in a lodge deep in the KwaZulu-Natal bush. It was as ordinary as an ordinary family gathering. Afterwards Santana and I sat at the bar and he showed me a video of his spectacular performance at the Montreux Jazz Festival earlier that year. He hummed and drummed his hands on the bar in accompaniment.

The next day our different currents of life took us off in different directions again.

I wondered about those invisible currents and how they had converged fleetingly to place me next to him 30 years after I had first listened to his records. We had played Santana's LPs on a record player in my two-bunk four-bed fifth-form dormitory in Manor House at St Peter's School. I can still picture the cover of his double album Moonflower, I can still hear the wailing poetry of his guitar, talking a language we could feel but not understand. For 48 hours the real Carlos

Santana had climbed off the album cover into the space where I was living my life.

As awareness of the AIDS epidemic spanned the citadels of privilege and prosperity, other global celebrities, including U2 front man Bono and Annie Lennox, lent their support (and a little of their money) to our cause. But none were as down to earth and unpretentious as Santana.

In my memory music is deeply entangled with places and times. Sound and song get enmeshed with lost smells, emotions, longings. Songs like 'Black Magic Woman' will forever be part of my experience of growing up.

In every struggle for political or human rights I have encountered the most heroic, engaging, self-sacrificing, lovable human beings. In the midst of enormous stress, even fear, there is humour. And there is always imagination and creativity. It brings out the best in the human being. That is what the human rights struggle requires. AIDS was no exception. Poets, comics and a choir called the Generics were to be found in TAC.

The converging and diverging of streams of life is unpredictable and continuous. What pulls people together and what pulls them apart is as arbitrary and unpredictable as the rolling of flotsam and jetsam on the great oceans. Or so it seems.

Challenging bad government

In early 2001 I was phoned by Dr Haroon Saloojee, a paediatrician involved in treating children at Coronation Hospital in Johannesburg. Haroon was aware of TAC's campaign to prevent mother-to-child HIV transmission and invited me to meet him at the hospital. A few days later Zackie Achmat and I were escorted through wards where we saw dying children: we were told their names and saw some of the suffering they endured.

By 2001 South Africa had crossed the boundary from an HIV epidemic, with a frightening number of new infections, to an AIDS epidemic, with a frightening number of deaths. Doctors like Haroon who worked in the public health system were beginning to report being overwhelmed by people sick and dying of AIDS.[71]

What we saw that day was the tip of the iceberg. By 2000, birth followed by rapid death was the lot of 70 000 children a year, a huge hidden pain that blighted what should have been a time of joy for many families and couples. Most of these children lived painful little lives and died within a few years. Their loss was being experienced by 70 000 mothers, 70 000 fathers and countless siblings, aunts, uncles, grandparents . . . This terrible loss was being felt mostly by the dispensable poor, and as a result their suffering and screams went unnoticed in the larger society.

Haroon's decision to approach TAC and the ALP was a brave and difficult one. He comes from ANC stock. He had grown up in Ferreirasdorp, the oldest part of inner-city Johannesburg. His family were closely associated with the ANC leaders Essop and Aziz Pahad, brothers who were close friends and advisers of Thabo Mbeki. Essop Pahad espoused AIDS denialism. But despite this, Haroon chose to speak truth to power rather than succumb to it. So, together with two other principled paediatricians, Dr Ashraf Coovadia and Dr Peter Cooper, he had formed a loose campaign called Save Our Babies. They started a petition among doctors calling for access to antiretrovirals for pregnant women with HIV. At the time I met him the petition had 273 signatures.

By the time of our walk through the death wards of Coronation Hospital, TAC had already been campaigning on this issue for a number of years. In lawyers' language we would say that we had created a long 'paper trail' of correspondence stretching all the way back to 1997. Since that time the evidence of the efficacy of these drugs had become ever more compelling. The SAINT results also cleared away excuses made by government about the prohibitive cost of AZT; NVP required only one pill and one dose of syrup and its manufacturer, the German-based pharmaceutical company Boehringer Ingelheim, had anyway offered to provide it free to the South African government for five years. There was also no doubt about the ability of the health system to administer the drug. Providing one pill in labour and a spoonful of syrup after delivery was no more complex than a vaccination – and nobody argues against vaccinating children.

By early 2001 the only argument left to the government was that the Medicines Control Council (MCC) had not registered ARVs (and the drug nevirapine in particular) specifically for preventing mother-to-child HIV transmission. So for a period this was our demand. On 18 April 2001 nevirapine was registered. There was no good reason left on earth for the government not to provide it. The fact that it continued with excuses as to why these medicines could not be provided set the stage for another test of how law and medicine could join forces against an irrational policy.

TAC could no longer justify further delay in resorting to the courts. Thus in mid-2001 the TAC National Council took the difficult decision to launch litigation seeking as relief an order that the government develop a plan to provide health services to prevent mother-to-child HIV transmission in the public health sector. The clock was now ticking and TAC leaders had set a timeframe for the launch of litigation. We too had no good reason left to delay.

Joe Slovo praised 'the hurly-burly of legal practice' as 'satisfying and politically useful'.[72] 'The adversary system of court confrontation, with its contest of tactics and competing styles of forensic performance, allowed for creativity and some scope for self-expression,' he said. Slovo was right. Law is a wonderful discipline. But most of its practitioners that I've encountered remain conservative and hidebound. Law can be as much a straitjacket as a technicolor dreamcoat. Its practices have withstood the test of time. Charles Dickens's description of 'wigged gentlemen' lawyers in 1780 in *A Tale of Two Cities* seems not too distant from the practice of South African courts more than 200 years later.

'Speak well of the law. Take care of your chest and voice, my good friend, and leave the law to take care of itself.'[73]

Slovo described the Bar as 'basically a posh trade union' and many of its traditions as 'something guild-like'. He saw a trial as 'a battleground on whose terrain small and temporary social victories could be won'. But he warned that 'the honesty and integrity of many of the old-style judges, which made possible the occasional redress of grievance even against white authority, also helped maintain the illusion that equal social justice for all might eventually be attained through the existing framework'.

Law remains a great protector of inequality. Most of the people who practise law do so on behalf of clients whose aim is to maintain the status quo, not to challenge it. I discovered that a large part of legal practice seems to be about what you cannot do, what a lawyer says is 'settled' in law. The daily practice of law and litigation operates within that settled space, framed by centuries of precedent.

In this context, if it is to be effective human rights and political lawyering has to challenge the established boundaries. The starting point is *not* to accept, rather than accept. It is to disrupt. This instinct to disrupt established and complacent orders is something I learnt from punk rock, but very few lawyers that I know have had the good fortune to make the acquaintance of Johnny Rotten.

When it came to the point of taking that first step that launches litigation, the person who was the ALP's head of litigation at that time proved

to be of the conservative type. The growing urgency TAC felt, created by
the knowledge that a simple intervention existed that could save many
infants' lives, was not enough to overcome her innate 'can't-do' conservatism. Day after day, the ALP's legal team was unable to draft a letter of
demand, the crucial first letter that sets the process of litigation in
motion. This caused a split between lawyers at the ALP that would rattle
on for a further five years. One day, as frustration mounted among TAC
activists waiting for us to get our act together, I confronted our lawyers
and asked them point-blank, 'Do you wish to be in or out of this case?'

They opted out.

That same afternoon I drove to the other side of Johannesburg to the
downtown offices of the highly respected Legal Resources Centre. There
I met with Geoff Budlender, then an attorney and head of the Constitutional Litigation Unit at the LRC. He needed no persuading.

He opted in.

In recent years we have become accustomed to 'law-fare' over socio-
economic and other rights in the Constitution. It is amazing how much
political dispute goes through the courts, something that causes great
chagrin to the ANC leaders, who frequently cite it as being evidence of
the 'counter-revolutionary and anti-majoritarian' nature of the litigants
and the courts. But in the early 2000s launching litigation against the
ANC government involved taking a very difficult decision. The ANC was
still young in government, Nelson Mandela – although no longer President – was still a giant on the political stage, and any sort of action that
appeared to be against the ANC could be misrepresented as unpatriotic
or worse. A great deal had to be done to persuade even the activist
members of TAC that litigation was a democratically mandated and not
treasonous road to follow.

But that is part of the process of the maturing of a democracy and its
citizens.

After meeting with Budlender we set to work in earnest. We began to
collect the evidence that would tell a court the story of the unnecessary
pain and suffering being caused by the irrational decision not to implement a PMTCT health programme. This evidence was recorded in affidavits, which, in human rights litigation, are repositories for the stories of
individuals affected by human rights violations. These stories help to
win the empathy and understanding not only of the court but of the
wider public generally.

Thus it was that one afternoon I drove to Sharpeville, famously the scene of the 1960 Sharpeville massacre, to meet with a young woman called Sarah Hlalele and ask her if she would support the case and tell her story in an affidavit. I drove into the dusty township and found the little matchbox house where she was staying on one of its bleak treeless streets. Met at the door by a member of the family, I asked to see Sarah. She pointed to a withered young woman sitting on the floor in a corner of the house eating soup directly from a saucepan.

Sarah had HIV. Sarah had AIDS. Sarah had been denied access to ARV treatment and was ill with various HIV-linked opportunistic infections. Her brother had driven her from her own home so she was staying with relatives. She was eating from a saucepan because her relatives were afraid of her and would not let her use the household knives, forks, spoons or cups. Sarah was drinking soup because she had candidiasis (fungal thrush) in her mouth and throat, which made ordinary eating and swallowing painful. She was a pitiful sight of lost dignity.

As we talked Sarah wept and unfolded her tale. She had learnt that she had HIV when she was still at school. When she became pregnant she travelled 60 kms away to Chris Hani Baragwanath (CHB) hospital for care, rather than to the nearby Sebokeng hospital because of fear of being recognised and stigmatised.

Sarah was a member of an HIV support group and had been advised to go to CHB because it was home to the Perinatal HIV Research Unit (PHRU). For a number of years, under the leadership of clinicians Dr Glenda Gray and Dr James McIntyre, the PHRU had been a site for clinical trials investigating the use of ARVs for PMTCT. Gray and McIntyre were activist doctors: I had known them both since the early days of the AIDS Consortium. When TAC held its first demonstration outside the gates of CHB on 21 March 1999 they were both there. It was a few weeks before South Africa's second democratic elections and Gray provocatively chanted, 'No AZT, no vote!'

By the time Sarah had arrived at the PHRU, the SAINT trial was up and running. Sarah told me that because she lived so far away from CHB she had been given a single nevirapine tablet to take when she went into labour. But on 18 July 2001 she went into labour prematurely. In her own words:

> Because I did not know that I was in labour when the ambulance took me from home I did not bring my Nevirapine tablet with me. At Sebokeng Hospital I told the doctor I was HIV positive. But they could not give me

Nevirapine because it was not available. I was very tired as my recent illness had made me very weak. I gave birth to a boy. They took my baby away because he was very small. I still wanted my baby to have Nevirapine after he was born, but because he was so small they could not take him to CHB. I asked for an ambulance, but found out that the hospital had arranged a bus to transport my premature baby to CHB. I felt that this was not safe so he did not receive the medicine. Now it is too late.[74]

Sarah's son was named Kgotso. That day, as she told me her tale, her body was racked by bursts of sobbing. This made her appear even more pathetic and tragic. But by giving her story and becoming one of the first brave women to trust the Constitution, she began her own process of recovery and empowerment. That afternoon she took the first steps on a journey towards reclaiming her dignity.

One of the strengths of TAC was our media profile. One of the weaknesses of our media profile was that most reporting focused on Zackie Achmat and me. As a result the real heroes of the TAC struggle are still largely unknown. The stories we told second-hand should have been sought from and told by women like Sarah, Vuyiseka Dubula, Busisiwe Maqongo, Hazel Tau, Joanna Ncala, Portia Serote, Linda Mafu, Portia Ncgaba and many, many others. Each will have a different personal story with common themes. It's not too late.

In Cape Town Vuyiseka Dubula was one of the activists at the forefront of the TAC campaign. She pioneered TAC's community treatment-literacy campaigns and in 2010 was elected our General Secretary. Later she started to study again. One of her objectives was to find her own voice. She can tell her own story. It should be introduced with the famous five words uttered by Jimmy Page that preface Led Zeppelin's famed rendition of 'Stairway to Heaven': 'This is a song of hope.'

Over to you, Vuyiseka:

I'm a young woman living with HIV, I came to the knowledge of my status in April 2001.

I was born in the Eastern Cape but came to Cape Town when I was 15. I lived with my father and stepmother in Philippi. We had only two rooms in our house, shared between more than six people and we relied solely on my father's income. My father felt the pressure and as a result was very abusive to my stepmother and us children.

As the first born I had a lot of responsibility, not only to look after my younger siblings but also to look after the house and do chores like the washing. There was never any free time. I found three different after-school jobs to try and save some money or get money for clothes since my father was only willing to pay for school uniforms. Although I was not interested in boys there was also pressure on me to find a boyfriend, both as a source of income but also as a means of escape from a very difficult home environment.

Still, I was young and enjoying life like any other young person, not expecting this news.

At the time I had completed a college course in Human Resources but I couldn't find a job in that field so I was working at McDonald's in Sea Point. One day, just out of curiosity I went to the clinic in Green Point. I walked into that clinic with confidence. The test took 20 minutes and lasted an eternity. When I heard the news that I was HIV positive I was completely dumbfounded. I walked home in a daze and the only thing I could think was: this means death. In my mind I was going to die almost immediately and I kept thinking about how I hadn't done anything yet and that five people, my family, relied on me.

I went into a deep depression. I moved back in with my mom because I thought it would be better to die at home and although I didn't show anyone, I cried every day. I was 22 years old.

Now I consider myself lucky in a way because I tested while I was still healthy, not sick at all, but was just curious to know. But I also consider myself unfortunate. It was unfortunate that this happened at the time when treatment was a dream for a poor Philippi girl because I had to rely on my small nutrition booklet as my guide to Positive Living. Only in Khayelitsha were ARVs starting to be available.

After being diagnosed HIV positive I then decided, I'm going to start a new life. A life of internal isolation, guilt and some denial. My mother and my sisters were very supportive although they could not believe that their dearest sister, who is still healthy, had a virus in her blood.

The expectation was for me to cry when breaking the news. I could not cry because I wanted them to see me strong. We were a poor family and relied on income from my parents' informal employment. My father was a taxi driver, my mother was a domestic worker, my great-mother was a plantation farm worker.

My life changed when I met a young woman who was the same age as myself who was feeling a similar pinch in her shoes as me. Nomandla

Yako was an Educator at Site B clinic and she took me to the TAC offices. Nomandla was a woman like me, the same age, HIV positive and with an HIV positive child. Yet she wasn't feeling sorry for herself, she was doing something. She knew everything she needed to know about the disease; I knew nothing.

She introduced me to TAC and from that day on I went every day, religiously, because I wanted to learn. I started to learn more about HIV and what role being a woman played in me getting the disease. I was able to put my history in perspective. I also realised how important it is to keep busy, to think 'What can I do, what can I contribute?'

That was the day my life changed.

I joined the TAC in June 2001 and that day I became part of a bigger family of young women and men living with HIV. They were empowered by naming the symptoms of Opportunistic Infections and what is needed to treat them.

I wanted to be like them. I was so hungry for knowledge that I studied day and night, every book that was available, so I mastered the science very quickly. Soon I became an educator and I worked to open branches of TAC in the Klipfontein area. My life and burden became lighter by the day. I decided to come to the office on as many days as I could. We started a TAC branch in Samora as a support system for other people. I felt I needed to share with other people who were feeling lonely and had lost hope.

I am now part of a bigger struggle. The struggle is not one. There are many struggles within the bigger struggle. Reducing women's and children's vulnerability to HIV is one of the struggles that has become ongoing. After TAC won at the Constitutional Court I was only half-happy with the Department of Health's new Guidelines because of the ongoing separation of the child from the mother – by thinking it best to prevent infection to children – forgetting that the good health of the mother is also important in a child's life.

I changed my life totally in 2004. I grew my dreadlocks. Shaved my relaxed hair, and went back to school.

Since I was telling people to start treatment I realised I must lead by example. I started antiretrovirals because I was planning to have a child in 2006 because I know that a healthy mother results in a healthy child. I am very healthy. My child is HIV negative. I became a staff member for TAC in 2002 till currently. I have moved from being a receptionist to a national position.

Vuyiseka Dubula with me at the finish line of the Comrades Marathon in 2012. Other than Vuyiseka, I helped coach six TAC activists who all reached the finishing line. A moment of joy and pride.

In the years after Vuyiseka wrote this her daughter, Nina, was born – HIV-negative. In 2013 she ran and completed the 89 km Comrades Marathon. We crossed the finishing line together, hand in hand, in 10 hours and 53 minutes. In 2014 her son, Azania, was born – HIV-negative.

In 2017 she will complete her PhD.

If Sarah had lived, the story she would have told would have been similar but different. That's life. We are all variations on a theme. Sarah's story would also have been of how she came to terms with her HIV status, about the birth of her son, how she struggled with her fears, why she became a TAC activist.

Sarah would have told of her own growth, the power she acquired through learning the science of the virus that inhabited her body, the solidarity she felt by meeting other people living with HIV who had cast off victimhood and become activists. She would have told of her love for her HIV-negative daughter, Puleng, and her HIV-positive son, Kgotso.

Sarah would have told of the first day she put on TAC's 'HIV Positive' T-shirt with a sense of both trepidation and freedom.

Sarah would have told of the day when she decided to be open about her HIV infection and to become a public spokesperson for the campaign to prevent mother-to-child HIV transmission – openly HIV-positive, openly defending her rights, a citizen of the new South Africa testing the meaning of her rights before the courts.

Sarah would have told of the demonstrations she joined with other HIV-positive people, how she felt on 18 December 2001, the day when Judge Chris Botha of the Pretoria High Court pronounced in favour of TAC, and of how she felt when a callous denialist government announced its intention to appeal, thereby suspending the court order and condemning thousands more children to preventable HIV infection.

Over the nearly two years that I knew Sarah I witnessed the unfolding petals of a new personality. The person I first encountered as a shrivelled human wreck came back to life. A citizen with pride and potential was there for all to see. There were many other activists like Sarah and it was a privilege to get to know them through this and other campaigns. With access to knowledge and medicine we were able to treat her thrush and around August 2001 she started taking antiretroviral medicines.

Tragically, however, after almost a year on ARVs and a marked improvement in her health, Sarah fell prey to lactic acidosis, one of the rarer and more dangerous side effects of stavudine (d4T), one of the three ARV drugs she was taking. If not diagnosed and managed early enough, lactic acidosis starts a fatal chain reaction of acid build-up that is extremely difficult to reverse. When Sarah started to feel ill she did not seek medical attention. She told me that she was aware and fearful of the side effects of ARVs, but she did not want to seem to be living evidence in support of powerful public figures, such as ANC Youth League leader Peter Mokaba, who were campaigning against ARVs, calling them 'poison'. By the time we got her to Sister Sue Roberts and she was hospitalised, it was too late.

The wonderful Sarah Hlalele

Sarah Sebongile Hlalele

Born 08/05/71 – Died 14/04/2002

Hamba Kahle, Sarah Hlalele

You will remain a symbol of hope for us.

died on 14 April 2002. She did not live to see the victory her affidavit helped bring about in the Constitutional Court.

I will be in debt to her for all the days of my life. You should consider yourself in the same position.

On 9 June that same year Peter Mokaba, too, died of AIDS. The shame of AIDS denialism will forever hover around his memory.

In some ways it was fortuitous that the ALP's attorneys dilly-dallied and that we passed the ball to Geoff Budlender, one of South Africa's finest human rights lawyers. His skills as a human rights attorney were honed at the LRC, which he'd helped Arthur Chaskalson establish in the years before the end of apartheid. The TAC case was a hothouse. Budlender had had experience of bitter political trials, which made it interesting when he told me several times that the TAC case 'was one of the most bitter cases I've been involved in' – there was so much political animosity that it felt like one of the high-stakes political trials he had been involved in in the late 1980s. He described it as 'the second death-penalty case in a way'. But he wasn't fazed, laughing about it with a wry irony.

Budlender's other strength was that he had been inside the mind of government. From 1996 to 2000 he served the new government as Director-General of the Department of Land Affairs, but – like quite a few other activists – found himself strangled by its bureaucracy. He returned to lawyering.

Public impact litigation often stretches out over a number of years. This was pressure-cooker litigation. The case was fast and furious. TAC's letter of demand was sent to the Minister of Health and each of the nine provincial MECs on 17 July 2001. I learnt a lot about public impact litigation from working with Budlender. As the government's defence continually shifted ground, our case remained firm. In this context, Budlender explained to me the importance of precision in the letter of demand, how legal craftsmanship to ensure precise formulations can shape the whole further direction of a case. It certainly did in this case.

The first court hearing was in late November 2001. The night before, TAC again erected a marquee in Church Square outside the High Court and in the morning we marched carrying little white crosses which we left outside the office of the Minister of Health. Judge Chris Botha handed down judgment in our favour on 14 December. The government appealed this judgment in the Constitutional Court early in May the following year. Again we marched to the court, this time with nearly 5 000 people.

5 July 2002. Midwinter in South Africa. Midsummer in Barcelona where I was attending the 14th International AIDS Conference. That morning I was a speaker at a session on prevention of mother-to-child HIV trans-mission along with the highly regarded American health and human rights activist Dr Paul Farmer. The whole global AIDS community was aware of the battle against AIDS denialism in South Africa (an issue I will unravel fully in the next chapter) and of the importance of this case. That morning the Constitutional Court had handed down its unani-mous judgment. I stood before 500 people and broke the news of the Court order that an effective programme for the combating of mother-to-child transmission of HIV be progressively rolled out. The standing ovation my presentation evoked was not for me, but for all those who had fought, lived and died in the struggle we had waged for the simple right to a medicine. At that moment, as I stood there, I held of some of them in my thoughts: Vuyiseka Dubula, Sara Hlalele, Jack Lewis, Mandla Majola, Sister Mpumi Mantangana, Busi Maqungo, Pholokgolo Ramo-thwala, Dr Hermann Reuter, Hazel Tau . . .

In the court building itself, dozens of TAC activists had waited anxiously until the judges filed in. After they were assembled the order was read out by another legend of the legal fraternity, Chief Justice Arthur Chas-kalson. As the Court found in favour of TAC and ordered the roll-out of NVP, it kicked a gaping hole in the wall of AIDS denialism. Tears were wept on both sides of the court. Albie Sachs, one of the judges that day, wrote: 'Once again, after the judgment was delivered there was total silence. We filed out of the court and stood together for a moment in the passage. Then, once more, cheering broke out. And, once again, I cried.'[75]

6

Civil society versus uncivil government – the horror of AIDS denialism

If you had asked me to define AIDS denialism in 1998 when we formed TAC, you would have had me stumped. That little band that set up TAC envisaged a largely co-operative relationship with our government. Nobody anticipated the arrival of 'AIDS denialism', not just as some oddity lapping harmlessly against South Africa's shores, but as a deadly virus that found its way into the body politic of the ANC and the government. Nobody anticipated that the President's response to TAC's postcard asking for 'AZT for pregnant women' would be aggressive forays launched from the twin towers of the Union Buildings to attack scientists and activists.

In fact, initially the government was sympathetic to TAC's cause. In early 1999 Nkosazana Dlamini-Zuma, the Minister of Health, met with TAC to discuss our demand that AZT be prescribed to pregnant women with HIV. She said that the main barrier to rolling out the medicine was the drug's cost. In June 1999, almost immediately after her appointment as Minister of Health, Dr Manto Tshabalala-Msimang held a two-day peace meeting with civil society organisations, many of which had been alienated from the government as a result of its involvement in the Sarafina 2 and Virodene scandals. She and her Director-General, Dr Ayanda Ntsaluba, sat there and listened throughout. I was impressed.

For most of the next year I was Manto's confidant: at times I was even her unofficial assistant. We spoke regularly on the phone. She sought my advice, consulted me on AIDS and human rights, and appointed me to a committee to oversee Pfizer's $75 million donation of Diflucan, an antifungal drug, to the public sector.

There seemed to be promise and possibility in the air. Then disaster struck.

In late 1999, as Manto and I were building trust, Mike Cherry, a professor of Zoology at the University of Stellenbosch, wrote a short article in the prestigious international journal *Nature* about President Mbeki's surprise questioning of the safety of AZT in a speech to the National Council of Provinces. He followed it with a second article titled 'AZT critics "swayed South African president"', which raised suspicions about the link between Mbeki and a splinter group of scientists who vociferously attacked the scientific consensus on HIV and AIDS – most of them even denying that such a virus existed.[76]

South Africa says AIDS drug 'toxic'

Cape Town

South Africa's president Thabo Mbeki last week said the country would not take the "irresponsible" step of supplying AZT (zidovudine) to HIV and AIDS sufferers until the drug's safety was established.

The statement is being seen as an attempt to justify the government's tardiness in making AZT available in state hospitals, even to rape victims and pregnant women.

Mbeki claimed that legal cases were pending in South Africa, the United States and Britain against the use of AZT on the grounds that it was harmful.

But this has been strongly denied by Peter Moore, medical director for sub-Saharan Africa for Glaxo Wellcome, the

drug's suppliers, who have requested a meeting with Mbeki to clarify the issue. The company has been negotiating with the government for the past three years over the price of supplying the drug to state hospitals.

Mbeki's statement was made in his first address to the National Council of Provinces since he became president in June. He argued that a large body of scientific literature claimed that AZT is so toxic as to be a health hazard. He had asked national health minister Manto Tshabala-Msimang to investigate this, but said that, until her investigation was complete, it would be irresponsible for the government to ignore researchers' warnings.   Michael Cherry

Coincidentally Cherry was a friend of mine; we had both studied at Balliol, he a diligent post-graduate, I an unfocused young Militant. He always found me amusing. From time to time we had met to talk about our far-away South Africa. But it was years since we had seen or heard of each other.

One of the major pillars of AIDS denialism is the hysterical denunciation of the drug AZT, 'poison' they called it. This happened to be the same medicine TAC was demanding for pregnant women with HIV. Unbeknown to TAC, these 'scientists' had managed to make contact with President Mbeki and use their half-cooked and selective science to persuade him to instigate an investigation into the drug by the Medicines Control Council (MCC). The result of this was a new set of frustrations to delay the finalisation of a policy concerning the use of AZT.

In January 2000 Cherry wrote an op-ed article in Business Day insisting on the drug's safety in its use to prevent mother-to-child HIV transmission. The very next day a fierce hand-delivered letter arrived from Mbeki challenging Cherry to re-examine the science behind his arguments and defending the President's use of the internet to source the information on which he had based his decision to request an investigation into the safety of AZT.[77] Thus began the crisis of AIDS denialism.[78]

For me its advent meant being pitched into an exhausting and emotional battle against an assembly of cranks, cronies and bit-players. Normally such flat-earth eccentrics live peacefully out of sight, shouting at the shadows of their imagination. But in our case they were blown larger than life by the attention and resources that were given to them by the ANC and the President.

Confronting AIDS denialism meant taking arms against a sea of irrational arguments. They were rarely openly advanced by Mbeki, but they underlay his decision not to provide antiretroviral treatment to people with HIV. As he was President of both the ANC and the country, he was in a position to force his views on his Health Minister, the ANC and public servants. For example, although it was nowhere expressly admitted in the thousands of pages of the government's answering affidavits in the TAC case, we knew that AIDS denialism motivated the government's opposition to providing nevirapine to pregnant women with HIV.

That was the end of my budding friendship with the Minister. I found it particularly tragic that leading public servants, people of distinction, people I had befriended and whose contributions to our society I admired, notably the then Director-General of the Health Department, Dr Ayanda Ntsaluba, and Dr Nono Simelela, the head of the AIDS Directorate, could perjure themselves by signing affidavits they clearly did not believe in. Years later Simelela reflected in an interview: 'What affected me personally was being a gynae, understanding the science and believing in the science and writing things that really I knew were really stupid, were not making sense. But because of the position I was in, the portfolio I was holding, I couldn't say "no, I'm not going to do this".'[79]

AIDS denialism took us into another world.

Fortunately we survived it. Today the Constitutional Court judgment in the TAC case and TAC itself are widely celebrated. HIV transmission from mother to child has been reduced to under 2% of pregnancies. Fewer than 5 000 babies are infected each year. Billboards encourage women to test for HIV and to seek immediate treatment if they are pregnant. TAC even got a commendation in South Africa's National Development Plan, adopted by the Cabinet in 2014, as an example of civic activism.

But it will never be possible to forget the strain and pain of those years. TAC's decision to confront the ANC and the government was not made easily. It had a price for us personally. As a result of our refusal to be cajoled into following the party line, the denialists and the ANC sought to stigmatise us both organisationally and individually. Some of it was laughable. One denialist wrote about me as 'the cause-hopping Oxbridge Fabian' who 'struts about like a bantam rooster at marches and on television, playing populist crusader' and serving the 'valuable role of loyal opposition to the pharmaceutical conglomerates, just like bantustan leaders during apartheid'.[80]

The ANC claimed that TAC was funded by pharmaceutical companies. In a particularly nasty speech given at Fort Hare University in October 2001, Thabo Mbeki imputed the motive of racism to people like myself:

> And thus it does happen that others who consider themselves to be our leaders take to the streets carrying their placards, to demand that because we are germ carriers, and human beings of a lower order that cannot subject its passions to reason, we must perforce adopt strange opinions, to save a depraved and diseased people from perishing from self-inflicted disease.[81]

AIDS denialism destroyed the effort of the Minister to rebuild a partnership with civil society and it turned us into enemies. To begin with I pleaded for sanity. In one meeting with a dozen other activists I broke down in tears as I tried to describe the pain of losing a child from my own experience. But she wasn't listening. She and the President had entered a world in which we were the enemy. The insults reached their nadir in 2003, at a function organised by the Department of Health to welcome to South Africa Dr Richard Feachem, the Executive Director of the Global Fund to Fight AIDS, TB and Malaria (GFATM). It was in the middle of the civil disobedience campaign and I was in the audience. Manto Tshabalala-Msimang looked at me and then departed from her prepared speech. She said that white people with hidden agendas were manipulating ignorant black people and using them as rent-a-crowd for demonstrations against the government. In her own words that night, 'They ... wait for the white man to tell them what to do. Our Africans say: "Let us wait here for a white man to deploy us ... to say to us ... you must toyi-toyi here."'[82] I stood up and shouted back that she was lying.

The threats and insults were hard to endure, but they did not make us give up. Backing us were friends and comrades dying of AIDS. Investing their hopes in us were a string of heroic doctors. Below is my roll-call of some of the men and women who were vilified and intimidated for adhering to the Hippocratic Oath and providing treatment to those that they could:

Dr Mark Blaylock and Dr Colin Pfaff, from Manguzi hospital in Kwa-Zulu-Natal, who commenced a programme to prevent mother-to-child transmission of HIV despite official warnings not to do so. At one point Blaylock was suspended from his post.

Dr Costa Gazi, an East London doctor who was disciplined and dismissed after he accused the Minister of culpable homicide.

Barbara Kenyon, the organiser of GRIP, a project in Nelspruit that provided ARVs for rape survivors. She was evicted from Rob Ferreira Hospital in Nelspruit, on the orders of MEC Sibongile Manana.

Dr Malcolm Naude, who supported GRIP and dispensed ARVs, and was suspended as a result.

Dr Thys von Mollendorff, who started a treatment programme at Tintswalo Hospital. I had the privilege of driving to his hospital with a consignment of ARVs before they became available in the public sector.

These and others ought to be given national honours. Perhaps one day they will be?

As I have said, the July 2002 Constitutional Court ruling in the TAC case created a breach in the wall of AIDS denialism. Four years after TAC had started its campaign, the government was ordered to provide the simple regimen of drugs needed to reduce the risk of mother-to-child HIV transmission, but even after the court's ruling resistance continued in several provinces. The roll-out began in Gauteng because the Health MEC, Dr Gwen Ramokgopa, was a genuine doctor, but in Mpumalanga and Kwa-Zulu-Natal, Health MECs Sibongile Manana and Peggy Nkonyeni did all they could to slow it down.

The victory gave an enormous boost to TAC, but it also meant that the campaign to provide ARVs as life-saving treatment rather than life-saving HIV prevention had to begin in earnest.

Around the same time as the judgment, TAC had put me in charge of another process to try to get a plan on treatment. In mid-2002 TAC began approaching the National Economic Development and Labour

Council (Nedlac), a statutory bargaining council incorporating labour, government, business and civil society, with requests that it be the forum for negotiating a National Treatment Plan. Our campaign was carefully choreographed. In July a National Treatment Congress took place in Durban and its resolutions were forwarded to Nedlac. Then TAC staged several sit-ins at Nedlac to demand its attention to the issue of AIDS, claiming rightly that HIV was an issue with grave socio-economic implications and was far bigger than just a health issue.

Our main reason for going through Nedlac was to take the power over AIDS policy away from AIDS-denialist gatekeepers at the Department of Health. We were also trying to enlist the support of business and labour for the call for a treatment plan. Behind the scenes I had held discussions with Nedlac's Executive Director at that time, Phillip Dexter, who was well aware of the trap we were setting.

The Nedlac process was painstaking but thorough. Then General Secretary of the Southern African Clothing and Textile Workers' Union (and future Minister of Economic Development), Ebrahim Patel, negotiated on behalf of the labour movement. Patel, in those days a close ally, we knew was fully in support of TAC's strategy. Raymond Parsons and Vic van Vuuren led on behalf of the business sector. I reinvented myself as one of the representatives of the Nedlac community sector.

As the discussions gained momentum the government negotiators, Dr Ayanda Ntsaluba and Rams Ramashia, the Directors-General of the Health and Labour Departments respectively, found themselves party to writing a 'framework agreement on the prevention and treatment of HIV/AIDS' in spite of themselves. More than ten meetings took place in October and November 2002. Discussions ran long into the night and began to have a weight of seriousness and possibility. As a comprehensive set of principles for the provision of ARV treatment found their way onto paper, I started to feel that this might be the historic breakthrough TAC had fought for.

By 28 November a plan had been agreed. On Sunday, 1 December, World AIDS Day 2002, the Sunday Independent published a front-page story heralding the breakthrough, one which it said 'shall result in government rolling out the supply of antiretrovirals in all public hospitals'.

Later the same day a statement by the government contradicted the story.

Clearly President Mbeki had put the brakes on the process. After that the government negotiators stopped attending meetings. Business got cold feet. The train halted, never to leave the station, at least not through Nedlac.

So began 2003. Another year. South Africa was now deep into the epidemic of death and dying, and the need for the provision of treatment was growing more and more acute. TAC was a movement on the rise. It had succeeded in drawing to itself thousands of committed activists whose lives literally depended on the success of our campaign.

This was 'a new struggle'. The difference from the old struggle was that activists were being killed not by apartheid's bullets or the hangman's noose but by a virus that had become treatable. And people were dying in greater and greater numbers. The Mbeki government was hiding the statistics but we had evidence that by 2003 up to 600 people a day were dying of AIDS.

With progress through Nedlac deadlocked, the TAC National Council decided it had no options other than to up the ante. We resolved on a programme of action, starting with a massive march at the opening of Parliament in Cape Town and the President's annual State of the Nation address on 14 February. Assuming that the marchers' demands would once more be ignored, we also resolved to start a civil disobedience campaign the following month.

Given the weight we attached to the 'Stand Up for Our Lives' march, we decided to transport activists from Gauteng and other provinces to Cape Town. We hired what we billed as a Treatment Train and over a thousand activists, many of them ill with AIDS, took to the rails between Johannesburg and Cape Town. It's a slow train that pushes onward into and through the night, but the mood was ebullient and determined. On board we ran classes on civil disobedience and held choir practices and workshops on treatment literacy. At Beaufort West, in the middle of the empty Karoo, the train stopped for an hour. The town's residents looked shocked at the sight of black activists in 'HIV Positive' T-shirts trooping to the town's once-upon-a-time-not-so-long-ago 'whites only' public swimming pool. We took a quick and welcome dip after a grimy night on the railway.

The march was TAC's biggest so far. Well over 5 000 people attended and rallied at the gates of the parliamentary precinct. There was a grim but festival atmosphere. On the same day we placed a full-page advertisement in *Business Day* carrying the Nedlac treatment plan. But, once more, the South African government (and the President) was not listening to its citizens.

The time of dying

2003 was the year in which I began to encounter the deaths of people close to me, people with a life force and vitality that I could never have imagined being quenched.

One of them was the TAC poet Edward Mabunda. Edward had grown up in Soweto but in the 1980s moved to the wretched poverty-stricken township of Winterveld. At that time Winterveld had been at the heart of a bitter and violent uprising against the puppet Lucas Mangope's Bantustan government of Bophuthatswana. Edward was a heroic ANC member who had been part of that struggle. Now he found himself battling the party he had fought for and was intensely loyal to, over its refusal to provide medicines for AIDS, a position that would deny him his life.

Edward Mabunda, performing in Cape Town at the 'Stand Up for Our Lives!' march, February 2003.

Edward lived openly with HIV. He translated his passion and anger into oral poetry that he recited at every TAC march and meeting. The last time he took the stage was at the start of the 'Stand Up for Our Lives' march. In Jack Lewis's 2012 film *Taking HAART* the wonderful, vibrant Edward gives a rendition of his poem 'How can I sing a love song when my sweetheart is dying?':

> How can I sing a love song when my mother is dying?
> How can I sing a love song when my brother is dying?[83]

By this time Edward was already struggling with AIDS, his legs were swollen and he had been in pain on the Treatment Train travelling from Johannesburg to Cape Town. But there is no sign of his physical pain in his performance.

Almost immediately after showing the march, the film cuts to an interview with Edward incapacitated in a bed at the Johannesburg General

Hospital, his body stiff and mummified, explaining why civil disobedience was necessary. 'We are prepared to die for this National Treatment
Plan.'[84]

Several days before his death I visited Edward in hospital. I was accompanied by Willie Madisha, then the President of COSATU, and Zwelinzima Vavi, its General Secretary. I wanted them to stare death in the
face. I wanted them to see AIDS so as to cement their support for our
struggle. From his deathbed and in a candida-choked voice Edward made
a heartfelt appeal to the ANC to change its policy on AIDS, failing which
he called for an escalation in the campaign of civil disobedience against
the party he loved. He died on 9 April 2003.

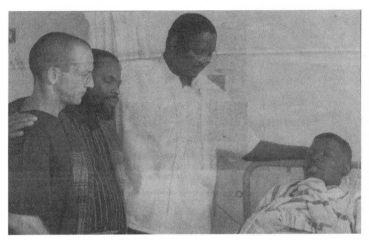

The *Sowetan* carried a photo of Zwelinzima Vavi, Willie Madisha and myself
with Edward Mabunda, his body prostrate in his hospital bed.
That was the last time I saw him alive. (Len Kumalo, *The Sowetan*)[85]

Edward's funeral took place ten days later. It was attended by hundreds
of people. Because Edward had lived openly with AIDS, we chose to bury
him openly with AIDS. This was very unusual. At the time people were
dying like flies, but very few people's deaths were openly attributed to
AIDS. The funeral of a TAC leader who had lived openly with HIV provided
an opportunity to destigmatise HIV, to show communities that AIDS could
be a cause for pride and honour, not just shame. To break the silence.

Edward's funeral made manifest all the contradictions and conflicts
caused at the grassroots of the ANC by its embrace of AIDS denialism.
The mourners were divided between TAC activists in their 'HIV Positive'

T-shirts and ANC branch members wearing ANC regalia. In the wake of
TAC's civil disobedience campaign, a palpable tension between the two
groups hung in the air. There were fears that the TAC activists, most of us
from outside the township, might be attacked by members of the ANC
Youth League. I asked Sharon to recall her memories of the day. Here's
her story.

> I remember that TAC activists had to stand up to ANC leaders in the
> community to ensure that Edward was buried as an activist who fought
> against the ANC's denialism. This fighting took place in the days pre-
> paring for the funeral. The ANC members wanted to bury him as an
> ANC member and cover up his AIDS activism. The TAC members defied
> the ANC to ensure that he was buried as a leader of TAC. The Gauteng
> TAC office produced posters of Edward and Charlene [Wilson, whose
> funeral was held in Pretoria that same day] which were put up all over
> the community in honour of both comrades. It was the 'HIV Positive'
> T-shirts that were prominent when Edward's coffin was lifted and car-
> ried to his grave, just as was the case with Charlene and Sarah Hlalele.
> We always covered the coffin with a T-shirt which was left on the coffin
> when it went down. The entire funeral proceeding, while deeply reli-
> gious, was interspersed with beautiful singing and dancing by TAC
> activists in 'HIV Positive' T-shirts, worn prominently as a mark of respect
> and dignity to honour the person who was brave enough to say that they
> had AIDS.
>
> This was in a period when people were buried in procession like a
> conveyor belt but with no reason being given for their premature deaths.
> I just remember walking around noticing the large number of mud
> mounds, freshly-made little graves marking the burial places of babies.
> I remember strict time slots and you had one hour to finish your busi-
> ness as the next burial needed the burial tools to lower the next coffin,
> [along] with the tent and chairs that came with the hiring of equip-
> ment for a funeral. And the graveyard was like a market with hundreds
> of people. Often because the place was so busy, family members could
> not find the funeral of their loved ones: they got lost in cemeteries
> teeming with people attending literally hundreds of funerals.[86]

I attended two funerals that day.
Before driving to Winterveld I had spent the morning on the other
side of Pretoria in the coloured township of Eersterus at the funeral of
Charlene Wilson. Hers was another open funeral. Charlene had asked to

be buried in her 'HIV Positive' T-shirt. As I looked at her in her coffin I could still sense her pride. It was hard to comprehend her stillness in death. In life Charlene had been a raucous, loud, humorous, vibrant coloured woman.

The racial demographic of TAC's membership reflected the racial epidemiology of the AIDS epidemic. Although the new South Africa eschewed the apartheid classifications, and although everybody rightly rejects them as a basis for privilege, sadly race and identities – real and imagined, imposed and inherent – have been internalised and remain very much a part of many people's sense of self and community. It used to be said that 'HIV does not discriminate' on the basis of race. But it does take full advantage of inequality and class. Because of our history, class and poverty overlap with race. And there is, thus far, little solidarity between people across class, or at least little solidarity between rich and poor. As a result, coloured, Indian and white people have always made up a minority of the activists in TAC.

Charlene made up for her minority status with a loudness that drew attention to herself. She was fully supported in her activism by her wonderful mother, Louisa Hobson, as well as by her sister and brother. To be open about HIV infection in a coloured community, where many people regarded HIV as an African disease, was even more unusual. But Charlene and her family were as open as open could be! It was hard to imagine someone more alive than Charlene. I remember watching her give a talk about AIDS to students at Wits University and thinking: 'This woman is so alive that she cannot die.'

But she did. In March 2003 she developed lactic acidosis, the rare but aggressive side effect of the antiretroviral drug stavudine (d4T) that had felled Sarah Hlalele a year earlier. She was quickly hospitalised. We organised for her to be placed under the care of the wonderful nurse-activist Sue Roberts, but it was too late. I was with her at the moment she died. I thought that I saw a single tear gather in the corner of one eye a minute before her death, as if she was consciously surrendering her life. As soon as she died I left the hospital to go to a meeting at the TAC office in Braamfontein and tell her comrades of her death. The news was met not with silence but with howls of pain and grief.

Everlasting death

In my life's journeys I have experienced more than my fair share of death, particularly the deaths of fellow activists on the journey into AIDS activism. I think of Peter Busse, Sarah Hlalele, Charlene Wilson, Edward Mabunda, Fana 'Khab-zela' Khaba, Ronald Louw, Thabo Cele, Wakhe Phangalele, Kebareng Moeketsi, Winstone Zulu . . . to name but a few.

I have also known people who lived bravely with AIDS-related illnesses that placed them in the shadow of death but who defeated death because they started taking medicines in time. 2003 was a year of dying. There was so much death around us that I wondered about my own ability to move from death to death, to compress grief into an afternoon and get up the next morning and go back to work on our campaign. I worried that I was becoming desensitised to one of the most profound of human experiences, 'The undiscover'd country from whose bourn / No traveller returns'.

Death needs thinking about.

On 19 March 1995 and on 7 April 1996 my first two children, the boy Joe and then the girl Caitlin, were born and died in almost the same instant. They never had any time.

My father, Alan Heywood, died in New York on 1 October 2015. I wrote that sentence a few days beforehand, leaving the date blank, and typed in the date the day after he died. But I knew he was dying. Cancer was eating him up. Chemotherapy had eaten him up. He lay in a bed that faced out over his garden, gaunt, emaciated and alert. I think he knew he was dying but he wouldn't admit it. In a rare confidence shared with me, the son he could not talk to, he said he didn't want to die. As I watched my father's decline I was troubled. This death was more personal, my unformed feelings were invasive, like a medical scope of the soul. I was witnessing the life's end of someone I was biologically connected to, someone whose thoughts I would never be privy to, a man who had given me my life's beginning. But I didn't know him.

That was not new. I had always known I had never known him. But now time was running out. There would soon be no time left to fill this gaping hole. I knew the outline of his life, I knew the parts of his character that I had collided with, but that was it. I didn't know the person although I am sure there was a person in there. I only knew the shell, 'the brute / Brute heart of a brute like you' that I had rebelled against, the person whom I thought I identified in Sylvia Plath's bitter poem 'Daddy'. It pained me that I didn't know his parents' names, why they had died at such early ages, what his experience was as an orphan – that's the first time I have ever described him in that way – from an impoverished Mancunian background.

I felt sorry for him. It was autumn. His bed looked out over rocks and trees. His field of vision was now limited to the little square of hillside the house was attached to. I tried to put myself in his head, imagine what he was seeing, but I couldn't. Once again I realised the importance of time, the impermanence of being, my need to make a mark on the world.

A few days later, the morning after he was admitted to a hospice, I flew back from New York to Johannesburg to participate in the #UniteAgainstCorruption march to the Union Buildings. I made it off the plane, time enough for a shower and then on to Pretoria. We marchers made our mark.

Early the next morning I got a phonecall from my mother: he had died a few hours earlier. Unlike with Charlene Wilson, I wasn't there for the moment of his death. The book of conversations we still needed to have slammed shut. I know so little of the man who gave me life. What remains are memories of the fights we had. I still have bad dreams about them. But I've decided he wasn't Daddy.

In the days after he died, everyone I informed, from the taxi driver to friends, asked how old he was. When I replied 76, they reacted, 'So he's still young.' That made me realise that a person I had thought of as old wasn't really. The inequalities of life and death are the types of things that continually unsettle me. In South Africa at the worst point in the AIDS epidemic, life expectancy dropped to 48, but thanks to access to ARVs it climbed back to over 60. On any given day I can fly from South Africa where life expectancy is 60, to the USA where life expectancy is 78.8, in 16 hours.

At my father's memorial service a few days later I read Brian Patten's poem 'So Many Different Lengths of Time'. The poem said a lot, but it didn't say it all. My sisters had forbidden me to express my deeper thoughts and to tell the mourners at the memorial service that day of desire to reconcile with the person who had so quickly been reduced to a box of ashes.

There was a lot of pain back in those days.

The terrible physical pain and emotional puzzlement as to why treatment for AIDS would be withheld from activists like Edward Mabunda and Christopher Moraka and tens of thousands of others are not understood or felt by the apologists for AIDS denialism. AIDS was clothed in stigma and fear, so many did not see its terrible human toll. You had to be with me on the frontline to witness the pain. Members of TAC, particularly its leadership, observed so many deaths we might as well have been living through a war. I was witness to the carnage; I remember walking through graveyards after burying another TAC member, looking at freshly dug mound after freshly dug mound, mostly of young people and infants, the cemetery no sooner vacated by one group of mourners than it was filled by another. Traffic jams to bury the dead.

This is not something understood by those who, like the Rev. Frank

Chikane, wish to reinvent President Thabo Mbeki as a global statesman. In fact, it's not just that it's not understood: it's overlooked or forgiven. Mbeki may be urbane, intelligent and suave. But the fact remains he has got off scot-free. A peer-reviewed article published in the *Journal of Acquired Immune Deficiency Syndrome* has recorded the cost of his embrace of AIDS denialism:

> More than 330,000 lives or approximately 2.2 million person-years were lost because a feasible and timely ARV treatment program was not implemented in South Africa. Thirty-five thousand babies were born with HIV resulting in 1.6 million person-years lost by not implementing a mother-to-child transmission prophylaxis program using nevirapine. The total lost benefits of ARVs are at least 3.8 million person-years for the period 2000–2005.[87]

That record cannot be expunged. It will be there until the end of time. It must never be forgotten or forgiven.

Why civil disobedience was necessary

I run therefore I am. As I run I think. One day, while running on the dirt roads of my village, Gerhardsville, the words of 'Bring on the Lucie (Freda Peeple)', a John Lennon song, found their way into my thoughts. Lennon sings it with intensity and anger. In my mind its chorus 'Free the People Now!' became *Treat the People Now!* As soon as my run was over, I sent an email to this effect. *Treat the People Now!* became TAC's slogan for 2002 and 2003. It appeared on posters of Nelson Mandela wearing TAC's 'HIV Positive' T-shirt alongside a call rallying people to 'Stand Up for Our Lives'. Although uncontroversial now, our use of Mandela's picture on a TAC poster endorsing TAC's campaign infuriated some in the ANC leadership.

We didn't care. The growing number of deaths fuelled our anger. They underlay the decision taken by the TAC National Council in early 2003 to announce a civil disobedience campaign against the ANC government if our demand for a national treatment plan was not acceded to.

The decision to launch a civil disobedience campaign was a very difficult one, both politically and emotionally. In those days the ANC was still hugely popular and the idea of a campaign against it was almost heretical. COSATU, for example, was one of TAC's strongest allies, but they were not prepared to support the campaign publicly – although privately leaders such as Zwelinzima Vavi were briefed, and were supportive and encouraging. But TAC stood on principle and pushed the boundaries as far as we could. In the eyes of ANC leaders we were already the enemy.

It was now a question of who would blink first.

We had decided to launch the campaign on 21 March, Sharpeville Day, a public holiday, Human Rights Day, a day laden with the political symbolism of the 1960 Sharpeville massacre in which 69 people had been shot dead by apartheid police and hundreds wounded. The month before we produced our most provocative posters yet. The poster carried photo portraits of the Minister of Health, Manto Tshabalala-Msimang, and the Minister of Trade and Industry, Alec Erwin.

The contentious 'Wanted' poster

Zackie and I had had a rare fight over the content of that poster. Zackie had wanted it to declare 'Wanted for Murder'. I thought that was pushing it too far and risked alienating TAC's supporters, especially those already struggling with dual loyalty to TAC and the ANC. I won, but only after threatening to resign from my position as TAC's national secretary.

This was just one instance where Zackie was prepared to go further than me in poking at power and inviting a backlash: I'm generally more conservative and conciliatory. Somehow, during those years, we were able to find a middle ground and accommodate each other.

To start the civil disobedience campaign, TAC planned to march to police stations in Sharpeville, Cape Town and Durban to formally lay charges against the two ministers, and then refuse to leave the police stations until the ministers were arrested – thereby compelling our arrest.

In their 2002 TAC study, Steven Friedman and Shauna Mottiar argue that one of TAC's greatest strengths was to make AIDS a moral issue and to be able to define and then occupy the moral high ground.[88] This could prove just as effective a strategic approach to social justice for other social movements entangled in confronting inequalities, such as around food, basic education or housing. In the eyes of many, the moral strength of TAC's demands justified its tactics of confrontation. In 2001 and 2002,

for example, ordinary law-abiding citizens would phone into radio stations to express support for TAC's campaign of breaking patent laws on
exorbitantly priced essential drugs such as Pfizer's antifungal Diflucan
(fluconazole). But despite this the civil disobedience campaign involved
a gamble with public opinion. Was this a campaign too far, one that would
rebound on us?

On 21 March 2003 I was one of the leaders of the protest in Sharpeville. Zackie and Mandla Majola were leading the demonstration in Durban. Sipho Mthathi was in Cape Town. In Cape Town and Durban marches
proceeded to police stations, charges of culpable homicide were formally
laid and confrontations took place with the police that led to over 100
arrests. In Sharpeville our action started with a dignified church service
presided over by the Methodist bishop Paul Verryn. Then there was a
short march to the police station to lay charges against the ministers.
No arrests took place. I confess that this was in part due to my own conservatism. I was nervous of being arrested and losing my permanent
resident status in South Africa.

Kebareng Moeketsi on the
first day of TAC's civil disobedience
campaign, 2003.

The memory that remains with me
of that day in Sharpeville is of a
33-year-old TAC member from Alexandra, Kebareng Moeketsi. There is a
photograph of her seated in church,
dignified and thoughtful, the WANTED
poster resting on her knees.

Six days later she died of AIDS.

The evening of that Human Rights
Day, TAC once again led the TV news
with its protests. In the following days
and weeks other demonstrations took
place. They were not easy. Sometimes
matters got personal. For example, a
confrontation took place between Zackie
and the Minister of Health as TAC dis-
rupted a conference that she was due
to speak at in Cape Town. Zackie made
a poor-taste comment about her wig, a
comment he later apologised for. Then two weeks later the Minister laid
into me at the high-profile event with the GFATM Executive Director. This

was when she pointed me out in the audience and accused me of being 'a white man' manipulating black people and I shouted back that she was a liar.

After their deaths in the middle of the campaign, posters were produced with pictures of Edward Mabunda and Charlene Wilson carrying the words 'Why Civil Disobedience Is Necessary'.

Although it was a gamble, the civil disobedience campaign saw public support for TAC swell to such a size that even the great ANC risked being knocked over by it. Jacob Zuma was the Deputy President of South Africa and chairperson of the South African National AIDS Council (SANAC). SANAC had been established at the end of 1999 as a body to co-ordinate government and civil society responses to HIV. Its formation was announced by Thabo Mbeki. At the time we had welcomed the idea, but questioned whether government would allow it to really lead the response. Our suspicions, unfortunately, were justified. During this time Mbeki was the back-seat driver of SANAC. He made sure it didn't have any petrol! Zuma was officially at the wheel but behaving as if he didn't know how to drive – or was it that he knew how to drive but party loyalty, not public health or people's lives, provided the map? Whatever it was, in late April we were contacted by Zuma's political adviser, Lakela Kaunda, to request a meeting. The ANC wanted a peace treaty. A delegation from TAC met with Zuma and were told that the government would consider implementing a national treatment plan if TAC suspended the civil disobedience campaign.

Once again, this was not an easy decision to make. TAC's internal democracy is something that has never been appreciated or understood by either our friends or our foes. Ordinary members own TAC. They entrust their lives to it. They take its internal democracy seriously. TAC's rank-and-file membership, not leaders like Zackie Achmat and me, were in charge of decision-making. Thus the decision on whether or not to suspend civil disobedience could not be made without a series of intense consultations with TAC members. The one I attended took place in the Council Chamber of the Johannesburg Metropolitan Council. Several hundred TAC activists were present. There was deep anger and distrust of the ANC, with many people expressing suspicion of their motives. The discussion was difficult and emotionally charged. Nonetheless, TAC leadership were able to persuade members to suspend civil disobedience. This cast a shadow of suspicion that we had compromised. As I told one interviewer a few years later, 'People were so angry and felt that we'd sold

them out. I remember one person who said, "You can suspend civil disobedience, but you can't suspend the fact that I'm dying. You can't suspend the fact that I'm in pain."[89]

But despite such suspicions we clearly understood that this was a suspension and that the clock was already ticking.

As we waited for the ANC and Cabinet to work out how to do a dance
around Mbeki, HIV did not suspend its murderous rampage through people's bodies. Dying continued. As we approached TAC's second National
Congress in August 2003, calls for a resumption of the civil disobedience
campaign grew. Desperation was in the air. We produced a poster listing
the names of over 200 TAC activists who had died in 2003. There was a
sense of betrayal and anger.

Senior ANC leader Zweli Mkhize, then the Health MEC in KwaZulu-
Natal, was summoned to our Congress. But his excuses and evasions
didn't wash. Congress resolved to resume the civil disobedience campaign.

It seems that this was what it took to restore a sense of urgency to the
government. In the following days we were told that Cabinet would 'soon'
discuss a plan to provide ARV treatment.

On the afternoon of Thursday, 7 August 2003, I was driving through the
suburb of Fourways. My phone rang and looking down I saw the call was
from Nono Simelela, the director of the government's HIV programme in
the Department of Health.

Simelela was a friend, but AIDS denialism had placed our friendship
under a lot of strain. She had been the first black woman in South Africa
to qualify as a gynaecologist. She had become the head of the AIDS
directorate on 1 December 1996, not knowing that within a few years she
would find herself in the vortex of AIDS denialism, having to answer
questions sent to her by the President about AIDS. As I have already
mentioned, Simelela was the deponent in affidavits filed by the Department of Health in the TAC case, affidavits that she cannot have agreed
with. Sadly, for reasons best known to herself, Simelela did not rebel
against the President, although it harmed her integrity and sense of self-
worth. During these difficult years I had maintained my relationship
with her. Zackie, on the other hand, had famously made her cry as he
accused her of treachery in a seminar.

She was crying again when she phoned. But this time the tears were
of relief. She told me that that afternoon Cabinet had agreed to a national

treatment plan and that Joel Netshitenzhe would announce it the next day.

I wanted to cry too. We had taken a stand and won. The battle was over. Or was it?

AIDS turned Winstone Zulu's world upside down. In 1989 he was the first Zambian to publicly disclose his HIV status. His four brothers died from TB. I first met Winstone in 2002 when he attended TAC's National Treatment Congress. Winstone had suffered from polio as a child and was in a wheelchair. He had stopped taking ARVs some months before. He admitted to me that loneliness and his respect for Thabo Mbeki as an African leader had made him prey to AIDS denialism. But in TAC he found a new brother/sisterhood which he embraced. He restarted treatment and this, together with the renewed hope and the solidarity he found in the struggle for treatment, gave him another ten years of energy. In those years he became respected worldwide as an African AIDS activist. He died on 12 October 2011.[90] He was 47. He had been born the same year as me.

I miss him.

Writing about these times remains painful. Knowing now that the battle was not over and that I have another whole journey to recount fills me with a sense of dread. For although the tale that I could unroll is of a heroic activist movement that refused to let go, and continued to press its claims on the streets and through the courts, its dark side is that it is also a tale of government deceit, abuse of power, obfuscation and death.

The parasite that was AIDS denialism in the Presidency, the Ministry of Health and the ANC took a terribly long time to dislodge. Its ardent promoters in the government included the Director-General of Health, Thami Mseleku, and at various times several provincial MECs for Health, such as Sibongile Manana in Mpumalanga and Peggy Nkonyeni in Kwa-Zulu-Natal. Many such reprobates remain in government to this day.

As Nono had promised, Cabinet did make an announcement. But then it took until 19 November for a government-appointed task team – a team from which TAC was excluded – to publish the actual Operational plan for comprehensive HIV and AIDS care, management and treatment for South Africa. Then TAC had to fight for the treatment plan to actually commence, something that happened only in April 2004. Once it did

start, TAC was forced to counter a new phenomenon, the emergence of
a number of state-sponsored quacks who all offered 'alternative' treat-
ments and propagated the deadly falsity that HIV did not cause AIDS.
There was a deliberate effort to stigmatise ARV treatment and inject
fear about its side effects into people with HIV.

More litigation, more protests, more pain, 600 deaths a day, 600 x 365
x 3 more years, lots more death.

Addressing the International AIDS Conference in Toronto, Canada,
in 2006, where I called on Manto Tshabalala-Msimang to resign.
She was sitting in the front row.

For me, my part in the war against AIDS denialism reached its peak on
15 August 2006 at the International AIDS Conference in Toronto. A few
days before, 'MM', a prisoner the ALP and TAC were representing in litigation to demand that prisoners should have access to ARV treatment,
had died. At the conference Tshabalala-Msimang had made a mockery
of us by using the official South African government stand to promote
her garlic and beetroot 'remedies' for AIDS. In response TAC had trashed
the stand. Passions were inflamed.

I was due to speak at a plenary before 5 000 people. Zackie had phoned
me the night before and said that I should call on Manto Tshabalala-
Msimang to resign or be fired. The next morning I saw Manto sitting a
few feet away from me in the front row. Personal confrontation is not
something that comes easily to me and where possible I sidestep it. But

I had no choice. Sometimes you just have to take a stand. I stood before her and explained why she was not fit for her political office. I said she should resign. As soon as the words were out I tried to swallow them back. I looked at her. She did not flinch and instead chortled and grinned back at me.

Lost in activism

During the TAC years I lost touch with my soul. The struggle around HIV was all-consuming. We were in a race to learn, a race to act, a race to organise, a race to save lives. One campaign led to another. One crest gave way to another. The deaths of close friends and comrades dulled my senses. The intensity of our frenetic activism is borne out by the scale of what a few activists accomplished in such a short time.

Paradoxically it was a time rich in jagged emotion but with a personal cost. I stopped reading literature, writing poetry or working on my PhD. Artistic work requires quiet time and reflection, a different pattern of thinking.

Almost the only time I protected in those years was for running; the beauty of running is that you can expend physical energy and reflect at the same time. Running was a place where I could plan without planning. It was in these years that I began to notch up my Comrades Marathon finishes. In fact, from 2000 I have run it every year.

To numb some of the pain I became what some of my closer friends described as a 'functional alcoholic'. For some reason drinking alcohol, beer in particular, has become a rite of passage in many countries, and British private school and Oxford had taught me the messy art of heavy drinking. Days of penury when I returned to South Africa broke that habit. But now I could make light of my ability to knock back large quantities of whisky and still be able to run a marathon or attend a meeting at 6 am the next morning.

In 2007 a friendship flowered and brought my soul back to life. That year I began a long poem that was a harbinger of all the themes in this book. Writing 'Dawn at Kalk Bay'[91] helped me reel my soul back in. I started to anchor myself to literature, mine and others', once more.

Inside government: reluctant leader of SANAC

On the last day of the Toronto International AIDS Conference Stephen Lewis, the UN Secretary General's Special Envoy for HIV/AIDS in Africa, used his plenary speech to enormous effect. He called our government 'obtuse, dilatory and negligent about rolling out treatment. It is the only country in Africa whose government continues to propound theories more worthy of a lunatic fringe than of a concerned and compassionate state.'[92]

This and our protests at the conference got such a bad press at home that members of Cabinet rebelled. It was reported at the time that the Minister of Social Development, Zola Skweyiya, who had attended the conference, was so embarrassed and incensed by Tshabalala-Msimang's behaviour that on his return home he demanded that Cabinet take action and rein her in. Conveniently, around this time she fell ill with alcohol-related sclerosis of the liver. During her illness the Deputy Minister of Health, Nozizwe Madlala-Routledge, acted in her place. This was to prove a boon.

Suddenly – for the first time since the civil disobedience campaign – a hand was extended to TAC to talk peace.

Thus it was that a few weeks later a delegation made up of Zackie Achmat, Sipho Mthathi, me and several others was invited to Tuynhuys, the Cape Town office of the President, to meet the Deputy President, Phumzile Mlambo-Ngcuka. It's impossible to know what kind of fire-breathers the government officials expected to meet. We had been demonised by President Mbeki, his Minister of Health and parts of the ANC. Yet they probably found us human and humble.

We took our seats around a great oak table in an ancient boardroom and rose politely as the 'DP' (as Deputy Presidents are called by their colleagues here) entered the room. Mlambo-Ngcuka is gracious and warm; we soon dropped our guard. We explained that we were most willing to work together and had only two conditions. First, we asked to be closely involved in the writing of the 2007–2011 National Strategic Plan (NSP) on HIV/AIDS, TB and Sexually Transmitted Infections. Secondly, we called for the restructuring of the National AIDS Council (SANAC), so as to make it a genuine forum for discussion and debate between government and civil society. We requested that both these processes be complete by the coming World AIDS Day, 1 December 2006.

The Deputy President agreed.

Frenetic weeks followed. The Deputy President's Special Adviser, Zolile Magugu, acted as the contact man and fixer. He was a former South African Ambassador to the Netherlands and to Australia and is the definition of a gentle patriot. He and I developed a respectful working relationship. He shielded me from information about the divisions that still existed within the Presidency regarding the TAC. Interestingly, one of the most vocal opponents of working with TAC was the Rev. Frank Chikane, rather than Mbeki himself. According to Magugu the talks with TAC had Mbeki's direct backing.

The writing of the NSP involved an egg dance. The 2000–2005 NSP had been an anaemic document. No-one, least of all the government, paid it any attention. When its timeframe lapsed no-one noticed – a process to develop a new plan did not commence for almost two years. This meant that at the peak of new HIV infections and deaths there was no official plan. Thank you, Thabo Mbeki.

In September 2006, when TAC became involved, however, a new draft NSP was already at an advanced stage. It had been developed by the then head of the AIDS directorate, Dr Nomonde Xundu, under the supervision of Tshabalala-Msimang. Xundu is a proud and prickly pear. She was very defensive of her draft. Magugu's advice, so as to help Xundu save face and not unduly antagonise her, was to write a new plan within the shell of the existing draft!

This was easier said than done. The draft that we took over was incoherent. Predictably it made no commitments or targets for ARV treatment. As we set about work it was evident that we had agreed to an impossible task. Rushing to finish the NSP by 1 December 2006 would have meant accepting a weak and confusing plan. Yet the Department of Health was intending to do just that.

TAC leaders decided that launching a poorly conceived and empty plan was a deal-breaker. I phoned Magugu and told him to put the brakes on. He agreed and instead we decided to focus on the shape and powers of a new National AIDS Council.

In the run-up to World AIDS Day Magugu and I put in long hours in the west wing of the Union Buildings, the official seat of the Presidency, to try to reach an agreement. During this time we never once encountered the denialist who had caused all the trouble. He too walked the corridors of the Union Buildings but he was invisible, a ghost who had finally surrendered his power to subvert the AIDS response – neither disapproving nor sanctioning what we were doing.

In early 2007 an intense process began around drafting a new NSP. It was not easy. Manto Tshabalala-Msimang, despite being on sick leave, maintained her spies and lackeys. One in particular was a deceitful man named Nkululeko Nxesi, whom I've already mentioned. As National Director of NAPWA, Nxesi and friends had tried to sabotage TAC's efforts

from the early days. They had made allies of various denialist charla-
tans, including Dr Matthias Rath, the German AIDS denialist and vitamin salesman. Now they were hard at work again, attempting to block
the setting of ARV treatment targets.

The NAPWA gang did not stand for anything. They were a malicious
negative presence. For example, in late 2006 carefully structured clinical
trials had demonstrated conclusively that circumcision could reduce a
man's risk of being infected with HIV. Yet Nxesi and crew did all they
could to prevent the inclusion of a commitment to promote voluntary
medical male circumcision in the NSP. They opposed it as an HIV prevention strategy because, they argued, it undermined African culture and
was an 'imperialist plot' against African men. A common symptom of any
form of denialism is blind-eyeism. Thus they conveniently disregarded
the fact that circumcision as part of initiation into manhood is a traditional practice among several of South Africa's major ethnic groups,
including the Xhosa people.

Another of Tshabalala-Msimang's bouncers was her Director-General,
Thami Mseleku, a vast bulk of a man. He also exhibited symptoms of
being an ardent AIDS denialist. One day he and I had a screaming match
on the sidelines of the SANAC as he raved about how antiretroviral treatment was poisonous and toxic. He argued for unproven traditional medicines in their place.

But TAC had learnt to be persistent in this life-and-death game. Once
again we corralled the best clinicians and researchers to work on both the
treatment and prevention parts of the plan. Principles were established
and ambitious but realistic targets set.

One of the things I have seen repeatedly is that it is impossible to
write a plan by mass meeting. In a planning process with too many
cooks, strategy is sacrificed to self-interest; people have to see their own
pet projects and convictions reflected. So, in the final days, the NSP was
extensively rewritten by Professor Helen Rees, Dr Nomonde Xundu and
me. On 4 May 2007 it was approved by Cabinet and then officially un-
veiled at a press conference a few days later.

When Cabinet announced that it had approved the 2007–2011 NSP we
knew that AIDS denialism had finally been defeated. An official policy
now existed which set a target of enrolling 2.5 million people on ARV
treatment by 2011. There was no going back. From this point onwards it
was only downhill for Tshabalala-Msimang and her cronies.

In early May 2007 a meeting of the new SANAC civil society sectors was held. I was elected as the new Deputy Chairperson. In this role I was tasked with steering the national AIDS response hand in hand with the Deputy President of South Africa, whose duties include acting as the Chairperson of SANAC.

I phoned Zolile Magugu to tell him the bad news: they were stuck with me for another five years, I warned. He said he was delighted!

I worked as Deputy Chair of SANAC in a voluntary capacity, without remuneration, using the time afforded by my job at the ALP to try my best to turn this institution into an effective and legitimate co-ordinating mechanism for the HIV response. For the first year I was deputy to Phumzile Mlambo-Ngcuka, who was warm, thoughtful and dedicated to the task. Then, after the overthrow of Thabo Mbeki in September 2008, the indifferent Baleka Mbete became Deputy President and SANAC Chair. When Kgalema Motlanthe became Deputy President in May 2009, he replaced her.

Motlanthe is urbane, intellectual and accessible, but always careful to be proper. He carries a feeling of wholeness about him. You feel Integrity with a capital I in his carefully chosen words. He is Patience with a capital P, a characteristic that was chiselled out of the decade he spent as a prisoner on Robben Island, followed by a decade as general secretary of the National Union of Mineworkers. One day he should write his own story. He was a stable patriarch for SANAC, but at the same time an arch-prevaricator. In my view his biggest weakness was that he was unwilling to deal with the Nxesi clique, constantly trying to reconcile the irreconcilable. That is a design fault in a senior politician.

Nonetheless we became confidants. I could sit easily with Motlanthe and, over a cup of afternoon tea in the Deputy President's official residence, open up about the difficulties we were facing with his comrades in the ANC as we tried to fix broken health and education systems. Motlanthe's view was the opposite of what we would encounter on the streets. He told me that civil society played a necessary role and that the ANC ought to see us as allies, even if what we told them hurt. He supported me when I explained why litigation had become necessary.

Occasional interactions with Motlanthe prevented me from thinking that all senior politicians had been corrupted. He is an inspiring man. Overall my tenure as Deputy Chairperson of SANAC was five years of immense frustration. Between May 2007 and September 2008 an ailing

Manto Tshabalala-Msimang and her noxious Director-General did what they could through their NAPWA proxies to prevent progress. SANAC transferred the war on the streets to a war around the conference table. It became the site of a series of battles over policies we needed or programmes we saw were not being implemented properly.

But we had an advantage. The position of Deputy Chair gave me some official power and sway in the media and the ability to contradict the country line on AIDS when it was untruthful. With Vuyiseka Dubula and several others battling on the inside and TAC and ALP activists demonstrating on the outside, we nailed down the key parts of the NSP, particularly its commitment to getting large numbers of people on treatment. TAC's activism was unceasing. We made sure the NSP was not going to be just another policy that lay on the shelf, a quintessentially South African blight.

By the time I resigned as Deputy Chair in November 2012 the NSP was still the focus and centre of the South African AIDS response. It still is.

I have to admit there is something very satisfying about sharing public platforms with the President, being photographed in the media with ministers. It's comforting, it's like being in a warm living-room with a glowing fire that you would rather not leave for the chilly exterior of the real world. It makes you self-important and complacent.

Paradoxically, though, the warmth can chill you. You become reluctant to be the spoiler, to speak truth to a power that you are now part of.

I learnt a lot from that experience. Perhaps the most important thing was that proximity to political power is a risk that at best immobilises activists and at worst corrupts them.

I can't say that I didn't experience these temptations but I can say that I avoided entrapment. The key to maintaining independence for any activist is accepting the duty of accountability. I was not propelled into this position for myself but on behalf of TAC activists who still inhabited the real world of AIDS, who had expectations of me and to whom I had to account.

Those years also provided an invaluable insight into government. Long before I became Deputy Chair, I recall Jacob Zuma, who chaired SANAC between 1999 and 2005, sleeping through meetings, the shower-head famously given to him by cartoonist Zapiro occasionally jolting to attention from some dream or other. AIDS meetings seemed good places to take a rest from the ANC's factional politics.

From another ringside seat I saw why, on so many levels, government does not work. I attended meetings and meetings and meetings and meetings. I watched officials sit through meetings and meetings and meetings with no apparent purpose other than that they were expected to meet meet meet. Many of them do the job of government with about as much enthusiasm as a factory worker – but for much greater material reward.

My VIP seat also offered me an insight into the AIDS industry, with its endless succession of conferences, hotels, lunches and discussions that go round and round and round – but do nothing to justify their cost.

Being elected as civil society's chief shepherd taught me some first-hand truths about this much-romanticised fifth estate and its often degenerate nature. People love a feast. Thus at SANAC you would find religious 'leaders' whose prime religion seemed self-service, trade union leaders who had forgotten what a factory worker looks like and certainly never reported back to their unions, individuals who claimed to be the representatives of six million people living with HIV but communicated with no-one other than themselves.

Things changed when Dr Aaron Motsoaledi was appointed Minister of Health in May 2009: he out-activisted the activists with his passion and determination to defeat AIDS. SANAC remained important, but the

World AIDS day 2009 in Pretoria. From left to right, Michel Sidibé, Executive Director of UNAIDS, Dr Aaron Motsoaledi, Minister of Health, President Jacob Zuma, Deputy President Kgalema Motlanthe, myself and the Mayor of Tshwane, Dr Gwen Ramokgopa. I was wearing a neck-brace after a serious mountain-bike accident.

presence within it of self-servers meant it became increasingly irrelevant. Motlanthe's reconciliatory style had meant AIDS policy was frequently established at the lowest common level between opposing sides. The civil society meetings were tedious, a jockeying for prime position at the table of state. That is a recipe for paralysis.

AIDS activists internationally have forced governments to accept and implement a principle that should be important in all social justice struggles: 'nothing about us without us'. In the case of AIDS this principle was even given an acronym: GIPA, the Greater Involvement of People with AIDS.

The growing recognition of civil society as a stakeholder in global and national negotiations is a late-twentieth-century phenomenon The potential power of civil society has been actualised incrementally over the last century. Its political significance is an issue people have been grappling with for a long time. In his 2007 book *Blessed Unrest*, the environmental activist Paul Hawken makes a well-worth-reading (if somewhat rose-tinted) contribution to this discussion.[93]

I believe organised pro-change, pro-poor civil society is essential for achieving social justice, but if it is to realise its latent power it too must thoroughly clean out its own stables. It should be seen to live by the same standards of accountability and transparency that it demands of government and private power.

Civil society is riddled with contradictions too numerous to describe here. The Indian writer and activist Arundhati Roy points out in characteristically fierce terms that the 'NGO-isation of politics threatens to turn resistance into a well-mannered, reasonable, salaried, 9-to-5 job. With a few perks thrown in. Real resistance has real consequences. And no salary.'[94]

Roy is not wrong. The professional activist is frequently an impediment to social justice. Many of our colleagues have jumped on the gravy plane. Their inert presence at the table allows governments and the United Nations to be able to pretend there is community involvement. But we know that frequently they do next to nothing to really fight for the poor they claim to represent.

The phenomenon of co-option is not unique to the AIDS movement, but this should not obscure what accountable civil society organisations – one of which is TAC – can achieve. Co-governance forums such as SANAC are potentially very important and in theory SANAC offers a model that could be employed for other social issues. Activism is never just protest – activists must also be prepared to share responsibility. But when you go into the boardroom it is essential that you take the mandate of the streets with you.

By 2012 I had been Deputy Chair for five years. My detractors were mobilising against me, some of them cynically using my race to question whether I should occupy a position of such responsibility. At the same time I could see that the cost-benefit ratio of hours and hours spent in meetings was clearly tipped towards greater cost and less benefit. New and real challenges were emerging in the AIDS epidemic, such as multidrug-resistant TB, drug stock-outs and corruption in the health system. Back on the streets with TAC seemed like a better place to exercise power.

I think the Nxesis and others thought they had won on the day when I announced that I was stepping down as Deputy Chair. But the next few years, in which I retrained my activist vocal chords, would prove that I could outlast them. I like to remind myself of a phlegm-drenched Johnny Rotten at the Sex Pistols' last-ever concert in January 1978 famously telling the audience over the last bars of the song 'No Fun':

'A ha, haaaaaa . . . ever get the feeling you've been cheated?'[95]

Defying 'prevailing wisdoms' –
AIDS Activistes Sans Frontières

*If the cure for AIDS were a glass of water, more than 90% of the world's popula-
tion would not have access to it.*
Joseph Decosas, 1996

I n his memoir *No Time to Lose,* Peter Piot recalls a part of his life in 1976
as a relatively inexperienced virologist at an underresourced lab at the
Institute of Tropical Medicine in Belgium. The laboratory had been provided with fragments of liver from a nun in Kinshasa who had died of a
haemorrhagic virus. After receiving news from another laboratory that
this was a completely new virus, the Belgian government suddenly woke
up and demanded action. Piot was called by his boss, Professor Stefaan
Pattyn, and told to pack immediately for Kinshasa because identifying the
virus had become a political priority: 'Belgian expatriates in Kinshasa
had begun panicking, sending their children to Europe because of the epidemic.' As Piot recalled, 'I thought: So, that's how it goes. Unless something is a political priority, figuring out how to save lives is not a big issue.'[96]

In the 1970s, when Piot started his journey hunting down new viruses,
he says 'we didn't even have fax machines – only the phone and the
telex'. Twenty-five years later Piot's world was gone. Piot himself was still
around, by then Director of UNAIDS. But our world was unrecognisable
and changing fast. The unfolding communications revolution suddenly
made conversations across borders immediate and affordable. We became connected by email. We could organise through the internet.

The emergence of TAC and of a global activist movement around HIV
coincided with this revolution.

From the earliest days of the AIDS epidemic, activism was always the
engine of the response to HIV. Without edgy, rude, challenging activism
the quality of the response to HIV would in all likelihood have settled
back to the level of response to all other diseases of the poor. Those who
doubt that the revolution I am about to describe was linked to activism
need only look at the lack of progress with other diseases or causes of

ill health and death, tuberculosis, Ebola and Zika being the most obvious. Once TB was no longer a threat to developed countries, the havoc it wreaked in the poor people's world was its own business. In 1976 Peter Piot's trip to the Congo led to the identification of a new and largely fatal haemorrhagic virus, Ebola. However, there was little interest in research around treatment or vaccines for Ebola until it became a political priority in 2014/15. After a sluggardly World Health Organization (WHO) declared the Ebola outbreak a public health emergency, a candidate vaccine was developed and licensed at unheard-of speed. In the august words of the BBC: 'Progress is now being made on an unprecedented scale. Trials, which would normally take years and decades, are being fast-tracked on a timescale of weeks and months.'[97]

It requires activism to make a health issue – indeed any issue – a political priority. Activism is a social determinant of health.

TAC learnt its baby-steps in AIDS activism from the United States. There is a wonderful 2012 documentary on the rise of the American AIDS activist movement called *How to Survive a Plague*.[98] This film follows the confrontations between ACT UP and researchers in the 1980s and shows how a ground-breaking alliance came into being between activists and some medical researchers. This alliance between science and social mobilisation is a key to understanding the successes of the AIDS movement. Activists studied and understood the science of HIV, they became what we call 'treatment literate', they tracked research in basic and clinical science. A virtuous circle was formed. Researchers became educators and advocates. Activists became researchers.

TAC plagiarised from ACT UP. We grafted their methods onto our own struggle traditions and created a hybrid. From South Africa we took the toyi-toyi. Old freedom songs were reworded to be about TAC and ARVs. Song was used to mobilise people. A choir called The Generics was formed. The iconic 'HIV Positive' T-shirt was born. Zackie Achmat and I threw our knowledge of politics and campaign strategy into the broth.

International AIDS activism was loosely co-ordinated between meetings, spread across a myriad of AIDS conferences, held over email and the internet. There was constant learning from, monitoring of and engagement with science. The movement's strength lay in its lack of structure and bureaucracy. Its actions were often spontaneous. Its energy was drawn from the vision we held of achieving universal access to ARV treatment and our conviction that this was possible.

We were greatly assisted by another by-product of globalisation: the huge growth in passenger airline transport facilitated international conferences. The first International AIDS Conference had taken place in Atlanta in 1985. In 2000 Durban hosted the 13th International AIDS Conference – the first time it took place in a developing country

Conferences were often held in exotic places which seemed to have more to do with tourism than the lives of people with AIDS. The first regional conference I attended was in Lilongwe, inside the palace of the former Malawian dictator Hastings Banda. A conference on AIDS in the mining industry, an industry that was a vector for the rapid spread of HIV throughout the region, took place in a comfortable hotel at Victoria Falls. The first plenary speech I gave was in Abidjan in Côte d'Ivoire.

On one level AIDS conferences were a gross waste of money. But they helped transmit activism: we met, put faces on emails, mobilised and demonstrated. We targeted UNAIDS, challenging it to set global norms on AIDS. When it did we used its authority to advance our vision that healthcare and access to medicines are human rights.

As a result of the relationships we struck up at these conferences, new networks were conceived and established. In 2002 we formed the AIDS and Rights Alliance for Southern Africa (ARASA) to focus broadly on human rights issues. This was followed in August 2002 by the formation of the Pan-African Treatment Access Movement (PATAM), narrowing the human rights focus to the right to treatment while broadening the reach of the network to the whole of Africa. A year later, in 2003, the International Treatment Preparedness Coalition (ITPC) was formed during an activist summit in Cape Town.

These networks were not the first. Organisations such as the International Council of AIDS Service Organizations (ICASO), the International Community of Women Living with HIV (ICW) and the Global Network of People Living with HIV (GNP+) preceded them. But the new networks globalised activism and shifted its centre to the South. People were suddenly plotting and planning from Cape to Cairo, Russia to China, Nigeria to Venezuela, Brazil to Nepal, Australia to India.

Some of these networks have survived. Some shrivelled. Some died. But in the 2000s they were all part of a burgeoning movement which seized the advantages of the time. The struggle for access to ARV treatment for people with HIV succeeded the anti-apartheid movement as the first international human rights movement of the twenty-first century. Activists imagined and innovated and, by doing so, managed to capture the world's imagination.

By the time we had finished, at least fifteen million people were receiving ARV treatment worldwide.

Little China Girl

Some of life is part accident and part improvisation. Some of our journeys are planned, some commence in the most random and arbitrary of ways.

In November 2004 I visited the Austrian town of Salzburg. It was freezing, with snow on the ground. That was not enough to deter me from running along both banks of the Salzach River, marking my path between two ancient bridges.

I was in Salzburg to attend another big meeting that in the overall scheme of things achieved very little. There I met Scott Burris, a thoughtful US legal academic who at the time was doing some work on health and human rights in China. After a presentation I delivered about AIDS and human rights in South Africa, Scott invited me to visit Beijing in 2005 to do some teaching for activists on human rights and AIDS.

Six months later I landed in Beijing. On that first visit I spent most of my time closeted in a prison-like concrete conference centre on the edge of the vast Beijing sprawl, suffocated under Beijing's notorious grey skies. In between bouts of karaoke, Qi Cui, an attractive young Chinese woman unpacked her society for me. If we had been given a few more days we might have fallen in love. On the last day we journeyed together to the city centre. As I marvelled my way across the vast Tiananmen Square, into the Forbidden City and out through the hutong (alley), I felt the heave of this society; its past welled up into the present and future.

Brave old world

With half my life half lived I realised I had only half understood half the world up to that point. Despite everything I had seen, read, heard, felt, despite all my journeys, when I set foot in China I felt as if I had never heard the beat of one of humankind's greatest civilisations. What was worse, I didn't even know I was missing it. A vast country opened up, one whose cultures, artefacts, architectures and peoples reveal the creative power and potential of the human imagination.

Somewhere during that walk through the Forbidden City, China slipped into my soul. So did its people, particularly those who were taking personal risks to draw attention to China's growing AIDS crisis.

Sadly, as China rises as a global power once again, the artefacts of ancient China, the keys to the soul of its civilisation, are being enveloped in a brash, crass, boastful modernity. Swaggering skyscrapers are eclipsing the hutongs, the traditional neighbourhoods, which are becoming an endangered species of architecture.

But that's not my campaign.

In 2006 UNAIDS was predicting a dire epidemic for China, one that might rapidly outgrow even the South African epidemic. UNAIDS projected that up to ten million Chinese people would be infected by 2010. But what they didn't say in plain English was that controlling this epidemic was difficult because many of the people most at risk of HIV infection were stigmatised and criminalised. Sex workers, injection drug users and gay men were top of the pops.

Complicating matters was the Chinese Communist Party (CCP), which was in denial about AIDS, refusing access to information about the real scale of the blood-selling scandal that had allowed HIV to run riot in rural villages, particularly in Henan Province.

From my studies in Marxism I knew about the CCP and Mao Zedong, the Cultural Revolution and the famines it induced. Today the CCP is not what it used to be: today it is the handmaiden of a rampant and unforgiving capitalism. Beijing is not the grey uniformity of the departed Soviet Union, a grey that eventually made its citizens willing to gyrate under the flashing strobe lights of capitalism. The CCP learnt from the 1989 student occupation of Tiananmen Square and the subsequent massacre that the best way to prevent another mass uprising is to co-opt modernity.

Beijing has all the hallmarks of a bustling, fashionable, liberal, modern city. It feels free. It buzzes. It beats. As I wandered through the new city it took an activist to give me an analogy that helped me understand what I was *not* seeing: he likened the CCP's control over the new burghers of Beijing to invisible electric cattle-fences. As long as you stay on the right side of the electric fence and don't get too close you can munch freely at the green grass. But should you dare to push up close against it, or cross it, you are in for a sharp and immediate shock. And the CCP is good at shock treatment. The Orwellian bureaucracy of the CCP has resulted in a state whose methods of control would have overwhelmed even the imagination of Orwell himself. It is still all-seeing and all-powerful. Its control over one billion people is low-key and appears to be unintrusive. It is not a ham(mer)-fisted dictatorship à la North Korea.

This way the Chinese government can suppress dissent with impunity. Because the continent is so vast and most of China's million towns and villages so distant from the media, popular uprisings are brutally put down without notice. Within the cities a massive army of spies is at work noting any sign of independent organisation and then nipping it in the bud. If you don't believe me, pop in on Chinese Human Rights Defenders, an exile organisation quartered on the internet, which documents the ways in which lawyers and human rights activists are targeted for intimidation.[99]

On that first visit people trod cautiously around me. An elder academic, known to be a spy, was always in the meeting room. But from the lips of Qi Cui I heard the names of a few activists; Wan Yanhai and Hu Jia came into my firmament. These are people who were being persecuted or in prison for their efforts to bring truth and justice to the Henan blood-sales scandal. I also heard mention of another young man, Li Dan.

In China, civil society as we know it does not exist. The CCP works tirelessly to keep it that way. In the stead of NGOs you have what are called GONGOs, government NGOs! After fifty years of Maoist dictatorship, citizens who want to strive for social justice have no memory of alternative political traditions to build upon. As usual in the world, it falls on a few brave individuals to take a stand. Through their efforts an independent civil society is labouring into life.

These thoughts and impressions, as well as the kiss that Ci Qui later agreed she would have accepted, are what I took from that first visit.

A year later I was on the other side of the world attending the International AIDS Conference in Toronto. China was still in my heart and its fire was still burning in my belly. So I decided to use a plenary speech to put a spotlight on the persecution of Chinese activists and the dangers of a massive and unchecked epidemic in China.

My presentation was titled 'The Price of Political (In)action'. In it I drew parallels between AIDS denialism in South Africa and in China. I spoke about the centrality of human rights for effective HIV prevention and care. Directing my words to UNAIDS and other powers, I said that 'The tragedy for people vulnerable to, or living with, HIV is that the political response to AIDS is directly influenced by geopolitics and rules of "diplomacy" which disallow truth-telling'.

When the session was over, two small queues of Chinese people formed at the podium. One queue was made up of government officials, at their head the urbane scientist Professor Wu Zunyou. Wu is head of the Chinese Centre for Disease Control and Prevention (CDC); he was anxious to rebut my allegations of human rights violations.

He invited me to visit China to see for myself that I was wrong. I agreed to do so only on condition that I would have unfettered access to civil society activists. He was caught in a catch-22. Refuse and my complaint was proved. Accept and risk giving airtime to the critics of the Chinese AIDS programme. He agreed. So I agreed.

The other queue was made up of several activists who thanked me for speaking out in their defence.

One of them was a young man named Li Dan.

In 2007 I was back in China. This time I landed in Wuhan in central China, Hubei Province. Getting off the plane in what felt like the middle of the earth was strangely reminiscent of returning to South Africa in 1989. I worried that I might be detained and sent packing. I passed nervously through immigration control sensing (rightly or wrongly) that I was being scrutinised. I felt expected. The immigration official disappeared with my passport. After a few minutes it was returned – and my journeys inside China began again.

The CDC had approved my visit, but activists were my hosts. This way I came to know Li Dan and Shen Tingting, the two activists who were running the Dongjen Centre for Human Rights Education and Action and its offshoot, the Korekata AIDS Law Centre, from their offices in the Beijing Hutong. I would also get to meet Wan Yanhai, the more confrontational and abrasive leader of the Aizhixing Institute of Health Education. The Chinese characters for 'Aizhixing' 愛知行 represent love, knowledge and action; they are also a play on the Chinese word for AIDS. Not surprisingly, Wan Yanhai is now in exile.

Li Dan is a man to fall in love with, gangly and slightly clumsy, good-looking but nervous. He had been an active member of the CCP Youth League and his ambition was to be an astrophysicist. However, on hearing of the suffering of peasants and AIDS orphans in Henan Province, he quit his doctorate in solar physics at the Chinese Academy of Sciences and travelled to Henan. Once there he established an orphanage. This well-intentioned but naïve initiative brought the full force of the CCP down on him. He was threatened, beaten and warned off. In 2006 he was kidnapped for several days. Then a conference he had planned in southern China was prohibited when the university involved suddenly got cold feet.[100]

Travels in China. With Li Dan and Shen Tingting. An unusual meeting of
activists and authorities in Beijing in 2010.

Shen Tingting is a small, vibrant young woman from Beihai in Guangxi.
She fell into human rights work without any grand plan. In her own words
she 'grew up in a common family, my parents are normal citizens that
struggled to make a living. They rarely talked about politics. I was a "good"
student at school. I believed in everything the school taught me, including party propaganda. But with the work in Dongjen, I have access to a
new world that tells another side of the story.'[101]

Of such unlikely people are activists made the world over. Activism is
in our human nature, but it is the restoration of conscience that brings
it into being.

I visited China three more times in the years that followed. My experiences there helped me to understand how important legal protection is
for civil and political rights as the foundation for organising struggles for
social justice. In China there is no human rights law for citizens to shel-
ter behind for protection and there are no independent media to run to.
No duty of justification or accountability to the citizenry falls upon the
government. Activists are immensely vulnerable.[102]

I came to know one 'enemy of the state' personally. Tian Xi is a scrawny
young man, clumsy of manner, shy and bespectacled. He was nine years
old when he was infected with HIV during a blood transfusion at People's

No. 1 Hospital in Xincai County, Henan, in 1996. He did not discover his HIV infection until 2004. What made Tian Xi unusual was that he refused to shut up. He told me that 'in order to seek for judicial fairness and rights of being an AIDS patient I went to Beijing to petition with other local HIV affected people'.[103] Thus commenced his solo quest for compensation for himself and possibly as many as a million other people who had also been infected through selling or receiving blood.

Tian Xi is little of stature but big of inconvenience. His voice irritated the mighty Chinese state. As his one-man campaign gathered steam he travelled from the sticks in Henan to Beijing and beyond, bearing witness to his and others' infection. He was put under house arrest and harassed. In 2011 he was lured back to the People's No. 1 Hospital with the carrot of compensation held out by its director. When he spotted the ruse he lost his temper, banged his fist on the table and broke a few teacups. For this he was put on trial, found guilty and sentenced to a year in prison.

During his imprisonment SECTION27, the organisation we founded in 2010 as a successor to the ALP, organised campaigns for his release. When he came out he remained unrepentant. His conclusion: 'The whole matter showed that the local government lack basic knowledge of law. They don't know what is equal before the law. The jail is a school of "how to be grateful to our government".'

When I last heard from him Tian Xi was still unbowed, although disoriented by his experiences at the hands of the Chinese state. The last email I received from him was subject-lined 'I am very sorry for the faults because of my youth'.

I am glad to say that my visits were about more than my own awakening. I think I was able to push both UNAIDS and the Chinese government to open up a little more space for human rights and civil society in the AIDS response. Because I chaired the UNAIDS Reference Group on HIV and Human Rights they had to take my visits to China seriously.

I had to walk a fine line. The authorities knew I was in town. They were never visible but there was evidence that they were monitoring my movements. On one occasion an activist I had arranged to meet just twelve hours earlier was contacted and warned against meeting me. I took advantage of my official UNAIDS position to give both me and the people I met with a little 'diplomatic' protection. Wearing that hat, I spoke out on human rights to university students, ran a workshop with a commune of former heroin-users in a far-flung village and made official visits to clinics and hospitals. I even wrote an official report for the CDC on my assessment of their human rights policies.

At times I found myself in the odd position of being an intermediary between the Chinese government and a number of the civil society organisations it regarded as a threat. One of the reforms I assisted in wringing out of Wu Zunyou and the Chinese Health Department was the setting up of a forum for discussion on human rights issues, discreetly named the China Red Ribbon Beijing Forum. In 2010 I spoke at its launch and used my speech to try politely to push the boundaries a little. I pointed to the value of collaboration with civil society organisations, rather than their suppression, advising that:

> Organisations . . . like Aizhixing, Dongjen and Yirenping are an asset to China. Individuals like Wan Yanhai, Li Xige, Tian Xi, Zhu Longwei and others are vital for accountability and effectiveness in the AIDS response. If harassment continues, it will make it difficult to build trust and an effective partnership. Some have already said that this Forum is a sham. It is not sufficient for us to say that they are wrong, I think we should prove them wrong.[104]

That evening I was invited to a supper with the former Deputy Minister of Health, Hao Yang. Hao was a genteel communist. He told me the story of how Manto Tshabalala-Msimang, our notorious Minister of Health, had once been stopped at security at Beijing International Airport. Bottles of wine that she had removed from her hotel room were discovered in her luggage.

I have not visited China since 2012 but I am told by activists that the Forum continues to exist. It is anaemic and far from what we would accept in South Africa. But it's as good as you can get in China at this point, a flimsy bridge across some of the troubled waters.

The fruits of activism

Activism drove the response to AIDS for 30 years. Activists forced their way into decision-making forums. By their own efforts, not as a result of charity, people with HIV were a recognised stakeholder and included in decision-making at a national and international level. The barriers to treatment were toppled. Priorities for scientific research, policy-making and agenda-setting were reset.

AIDS activism also influenced politics and government. In some coun-

Newspaper headlines.
TAC's lawfare with the government started in 2002 when we
approached the Pretoria High Court to challenge its MTCT policy.
Despite victories for TAC and premature announcements
of peace it only really ended in late 2009.

tries it drove democratic law reform. It led to wider recognition of human
rights and an acceptance of difference. Early in the epidemic Professor
Jonathan Mann, for some years the head of the WHO Global Programme
on AIDS, had insisted that protecting human rights was crucial to effective HIV prevention. This contradicted the prevailing wisdom that epidemics always justified breaches of human rights. Building on this idea,
the Australian judge Michael Kirby coined the idea of the 'AIDS paradox'.
Kirby argued that in order to prevent people being infected with HIV you
have to protect those who are infected (or at higher risk of infection) from
stigma, unfair discrimination and criminalisation. Respecting people's
human rights assists them with disclosure and encourages them to test
for HIV and seek care – in that way protecting others.

Mann's efforts in the boardrooms combined with activists' efforts on
the streets meant that attention began to turn to the human rights of sex
workers, gay men, prisoners and people who inject illegal drugs such as
heroin. In 1996 recognition of the AIDS paradox had led me on the first
of many visits to Geneva to help to draw up the UNAIDS/OHCHR *International Guidelines on HIV/AIDS and Human Rights*. After that, with every passing year new resolutions were taken to protect the rights of people with

HIV. In some countries, for the first time ever, laws were introduced to decriminalise or protect these groups of people. China, for example, was very proud of its methadone programme.

Civic space opened up. Respect for difference and diversity deepened. Or so we thought.

AIDS activism also had a positive effect on the right to health more broadly. During the first decade of the twenty-first century, over 70 states incorporated a right to health into their constitutions. The recognition that there exist both state *and* corporate duties to respect, protect, promote and fulfil this right marked a great leap forward. AIDS activism was able to push back against attempts by corporate powers to erode this right. The best example of this was the Doha Declaration on the TRIPS Agreement and Public Health adopted by the 2001 WTO Ministerial Conference. This declaration affirmed the sovereign right of states to override patents and license cheaper generic medicines in cases of public health emergency. It came in the wake of the global focus on the abuse of patents and intellectual property for profiteering that had resulted from the PMA's thwarted litigation against the South African government.

As a result of activism, the noughties were a decade of advance, innovation and increased accountability in governance systems for health and AIDS. In 2001 the UN General Assembly convened its first Special Session on HIV/AIDS (UNGASS), which resulted in a ground-breaking Declaration of Commitment on HIV/AIDS. Thereafter UNGASS continued to convene every two years for the rest of the decade and introduced a reporting requirement for states on progress towards achieving targets. Three further UNGASS declarations followed in 2006, 2011 and 2016. These special sessions, or high-level meetings as they are now called, became a rallying place for civil society, another space to lobby and cajole, to demonstrate and demand more serious targets and resources.

Perhaps the most important institutional innovation was the establishment of the Global Fund to Fight AIDS, TB and Malaria (GFATM – 'The Global Fund'). At UNGASS 2001 the Secretary General, Kofi Annan, had called for a 'war chest' for AIDS. The Global Fund became this chest. It was set up as a financing mechanism and not an implementing agent. At the insistence of activists and some donors, it recognised that AIDS programmes should be country-led, not designed in Geneva or Washington.

The Global Fund was demanded by us. When it was set up activists inveigled their way onto its staff and further entrenched civil society by making our involvement mandatory in national-level Country Coordinating Mechanisms (CCMs), the bodies tasked with preparing country funding proposals. The new normal was that activists, sex workers and gay men, people still stigmatised and criminalised by many governments, were included in governance arrangements for the response to HIV. Besuited gentlemen found themselves at the table with bedecked drag queens and bedraggled drug-users!

Then in 2003, hot on the heels of the Global Fund, and in part in reaction to its early flaws, a right-wing Republican President, George Bush, melded his own conservative agenda with the clamour of activists to support treatment initiatives outside the USA. Congress approved an Act creating the President's Emergency Plan for AIDS Relief (PEPFAR) – a targeted initiative with a strong focus on treatment.

Activist pressure led to other innovations in global health institutions whose sole aim was to increase access to treatment. Thus we saw the birth of UNITAID, a global health initiative largely financed by a levy on airline tickets, and the Medicines Patent Pool (MPP). Bold new campaigns – such as setting a target of three million people on treatment by 2005 (popularly known as the '3 by 5 initiative') – were launched by usually inert bodies such as the WHO.

And the money flowed like never before. In 1996 global expenditure on AIDS was only $300m per annum. By 2001 this had risen to $1.3bn. In 2015 the Global Fund alone disbursed an estimated $27bn. During its first decade PEPFAR has directed over $50bn to AIDS programmes across the world. And allow me a quick word here to the naysayers of 'AIDS exceptionalism': health as a whole has benefited from the massive injection of cash into AIDS. According to Professor Larry Gostin, a foremost expert on global health, between 2000 and 2010 governments in sub-Saharan Africa nearly trebled annual per capita spending on health from $15 to $43. In roughly the same period international health assistance increased from less than $6bn annually to $26.9bn.[105] Funding for health from governments and foundations grew by 180%. Of course, the anarchic nature of this funding is the subject for another book.

And above all we saved lives. Millions of them.

Activism got the money. Money permitted the research. And when scientific breakthroughs came – and there were many – because of activism, new medicines and preventative technologies could be rapidly deployed to the communities that most needed them.

The noughties were a decade of discovery; new understandings of HIV and new medicines to treat it tumbled out of the cupboard. In the pages that follow I will run through some of the breakthroughs – just in case you think I am prone to exaggeration. If you are impatient, read it as an HIV treatment literacy lesson, an introduction to the lexicon of the treatment activist.

During the first decade of this century there was a continuous improvement in the technologies of testing for and measuring HIV, especially in resource-poor settings.

When I first heard of HIV, in the dark age of the 1990s, the only way to test for it was by testing a sample of blood in a laboratory for the antibodies generated by the immune system whenever a virus or bacteria enter the blood. There was a notorious six-week 'window period' between the time of infection and the time a test could detect the immune response. The need to send blood specimens to the nearest laboratory, which were often only in the cities, caused delay. Sometimes weeks elapsed between the HIV test and its result. In this fear-filled lapse of time many people would decide not to return for their test results.

We contributed to sustained pressure to make testing easier and more accessible, while at the same time putting in place laws and policies to prevent the abuse of HIV testing. A decade later a rapid HIV test, which could be administered with only a finger prick, yielded a result in minutes. It has allowed HIV testing to be taken out of laboratories and clinics and into the most remote villages. It has also meant that HIV testing could be made accessible to categories whose criminalisation, stigmatisation or marginalisation causes them to fear and avoid public health services.

In 1997 scientists tailored the polymerase chain reaction (PCR) test, at first used on infants, to allow testing to seek out HIV directly. Antibodies take time to develop, so the PCR test was especially important to test whether new-borns had been infected by their mothers. A vital peace of mind for new mums and dads. Or not.

HIV targets the CD4 cells, an indispensable part of the immune system. A high CD4 count indicates an intact immune system; a CD4 count below 200 points to life-threatening damage. As our knowledge of the workings of HIV grew it was understood that the art of phlebotomy is not only important for diagnosis, but also for measuring and monitoring the virus in an infected person. The CD4 count, for example, is a measure of the health of the immune system. This test, too, preceded AIDS, but its use on people with HIV made it possible to measure the stage of HIV's attack on the immune system. For a period the CD4 count guided doctors on when to start ARV treatment.

At the start of 2000 CD4 testing was exorbitantly expensive, cumbersome and not often available outside developed countries. But as scientists experimented it became ever more affordable and available. According to Professor Wendy Stevens, South Africa's leading scientist in molecular diagnostics, between 2010 and 2015 25 million CD4 tests were conducted in South Africa on people with HIV.

Finally, the 'viral load'. This is a test which measures the quantity of HIV in a millilitre of blood. This, too, underwent a revolution in price and accessibility. It became available in 2010 and it is now the most widely used indicator of whether ARV treatment is succeeding in suppressing HIV. In 2015 alone, South Africa's National Health Laboratory Service (NHLS) conducted four million viral load tests.

Revolution, what revolution?!

Medical innovation in approaches to treating AIDS and then HIV materialised just as fast. The breakthrough came in 1996 when it was reported that antiretroviral drugs used in 'combination' therapy were succeeding in halting a person's progression to AIDS. After this the use of the drugs was continuously tested and refined, including in the populations that needed them most. In the early 2000s it was learnt that HIV, rather than being dormant for the 'asymptomatic period', in fact remains in a constant, intense and destructive duel with the immune system, replicating itself billions of times a day until it eventually overwhelms the highly effective human immune system. As a result the prevailing wisdom about when to initiate a person on ARVs was subjected to fresh scrutiny. This led to changes to the WHO treatment guidelines such as raising the CD4 count threshold for starting treatment from 350 to 500 and, by 2015, to the understanding that treatment should ideally be initiated immediately if an individual tests HIV-positive.

ARV treatment itself became simpler, with fewer side effects and a smaller pill burden. Whereas at the time of the 2000 Durban AIDS conference someone with AIDS had to take up to 20 pills a day, at precise times in the day, since 2012 the Fixed Dose Combination (FDC), a single pill containing three different drugs taken once a day, has become the standard drug regimen.

At the time we had marched to the opening of the Durban conference in 2000 there were no more than a few thousand poor people accessing antiretroviral medicines in developing countries. When we marched again in July 2016 this number had grown to seventeen million. Most of them were in Africa.

Looking back on the 23 years of my involvement in AIDS, the activist movement seems almost unreal in its ambition and achievement. AIDS activists bucked the trend. AIDS activists shattered prevailing wisdoms. At the height of the period of neoliberal economics AIDS activism expanded people's rights, insisted on the sovereignty of nations and their duty to protect the rights of their people and pushed back multinational companies which were becoming used to having their own way. In a world increasingly characterised by growing inequality, AIDS activism won and then enforced the principle of universal access to AIDS drugs.

The AIDS movement wasn't really planned. It didn't have a successful model to copy. In fact it occurred after decades of failing to rein in the alcohol or tobacco multinationals, companies whose cynical disregard of the disability and death that are caused by their 'products' remains challenged only by a few heroic activists – but not by effective social movements.

There is a great deal for social justice activists of all stripes to learn from studying the AIDS movement. HIV was a non-traditional post-colonial liberation struggle. It was and is a globalised struggle for individual liberation, not only from HIV itself, but also from stigma, prejudice, ignorance and outmoded Victorian laws that criminalise sexual choice and love.

For me, AIDS activism marked a point where I graduated from advocacy for an impossible socialism to a recognition of the transformative power of mobilising with people for their and others' human rights. If people get organised and act to express their power, then socialism, or something based on the ethics of socialism, may follow. The AIDS movement made me appreciate the liberating power of the idea of social justice.

For a few dollars more

In 2012 the International AIDS Conference was held in Vienna. I attended with Adila Hassim and others from TAC and SECTION27. At this conference, for the first time there was an official human rights march, organised by the conference. We paraded through the streets of Vienna in a carnival that felt more like a funeral. There was nothing edgy or dangerous. Instead the human rights movement felt co-opted. Adila and I fled, opting for sightseeing in Melk, an ancient village on the Danube with a beautiful abbey.

For me that march signalled that we were well and truly in a recession in the global AIDS activist movement. Millions of people were still not on treatment, kept powerless and voiceless – women, children, illegal migrants, drug-users, sex workers. But the anger had gone.

The intense focus on AIDS that dominated the 1990s and 2000s was sometimes pejoratively described as 'AIDS exceptionalism'. But that was absolutely necessary in order to get up the speed needed to get the plane in the air. The challenge now is how to keep the plane there.

Flying isn't easy.

Now it's 2017. The recession in the AIDS activist movement has been a long one.[106] We are only just coming out of it. There were a variety of reasons for this: funding was disappearing after the 2008 financial crisis. Activists were tired. The decade of victories had led to a loss of vision. And as a result political commitment began to wane.

But we must also shoulder some of the responsibility. During the advance of movements like TAC little thought was given to the possibility that, if we won, there might come a time when millions of people would be on ARV treatment, but millions of people would still not be. Once we had got the plane in the air, where would we fly to? What if there was a fuel shortage before we reached our destination? That is the place in which we now find ourselves.

But one thing the recession was not was an indication that the challenges of the AIDS epidemic had been overcome.

Far from it. There is still a global AIDS epidemic and South Africa remains its epicentre. In 2016 over 400 people were still dying of HIV-related illnesses every day in South Africa, mostly of tuberculosis. They died experiencing the same pain felt by those who died in the early days of our struggle. They did not die because of President Mbeki's AIDS denialism but because the public health system has failed to provide them with appropriate care.

On each day in 2016 nearly 800 people were newly infected with HIV. They are predominantly young people. Most of them are girls and young women.[107] They were not infected because President Mbeki questioned the link between HIV and AIDS but because of very poor-quality schooling and social fragmentation. These two factors conspire to cause a huge drop-out rate in the last two years of school. Thereafter it's perpetual unemployment, economic dependence on men and – in the context of permanent mass unemployment which renders labour power redundant – at worst selling the only other marketable commodity you were born with, sex. It's inequality, stupid.

In recent years a dangerous complacency has developed around HIV.

Internationally, political commitment has receded from the whole of the United Nations to UNAIDS alone. In South Africa it has receded from a whole government to a lone minister, the Minister of Health, Dr Aaron Motsoaledi. HIV is just one among many pressing social crises that afflict our country. There is instability and suffering in almost every area of social life: housing, employment, food security, economic stability, basic education. The walls are crumbling and the politicians are bumbling.

In this period, sustaining the momentum to ensure both the treatment and prevention of HIV is more complex. It is more intimately tied up with the pursuit of social justice.

'There is nothing in this whole AIDS mess that is not political!' wrote US playwright and gay activist Larry Kramer as early as 1989. There can be no truer nor more concise statement. Because of the clamour of activists AIDS was briefly a political priority. But as Lenin is reputed to have said, 'Politics is concentrated economics.'

Politics, economics and financial flows have become ever more fickle, fragile or elite-centred. In the early 2000s the world was awash with funny money, aided by millennium financial scams and sub-prime mortgages that created the illusion of a financial bubble. The belief that the developed countries had money to spare coincided with the moment in which activism had catalysed a deeper but ultimately short-lived political commitment to the control of HIV.

But after the global financial crisis in 2008, different political priorities emerged. Funding for AIDS flatlined. Funding for such civil society organisations as TAC declined substantially. By 2014 TAC had been forced to cut its budget by a third for want of a few dollars.

Without money activism was stymied and the recession in activism ushered in a recession in political accountability. Civil society space began to close and, as it did, the old shit rose to the surface once more. In countries such as Uganda and Malawi there has been a resurgence of state-supported homophobia. The retreat of the activists from spaces like UNAIDS permitted new discourses and depictions of AIDS to take shape. The hard-won language of human rights gave way to locating the AIDS response within 'investment frameworks'. Giant multinational accountancy firms such as KPMG and PricewaterhouseCoopers were brought in to call the shots on who lives and dies, crunching names back into numbers, inventing mathematical formulae that could demonstrate to donors their 'investment returns'.

In the post-2008 environment the leaders of the global response at UNAIDS tried for a while to depoliticise AIDS. In 2009 Peter Piot was succeeded by Michel Sidibé, a UN career diplomat from Mali. At about the same time UNAIDS started telling the world that 'the end of AIDS' was in sight. Senior officials at UNAIDS told me privately that this was their strategy 'for retaining donor interest in a resource-constrained global financial environment'. They hoped that donors would be persuaded that with one final push it would be possible to reap the rewards of the first two decades of their 'investment'.

However, the idea of 'the end of AIDS', much as we may wish it, wrong-foots the global response and fundamentally mischaracterises the AIDS epidemic. HIV is more than a virus. It reflects the inequality and violence that predominate in our world.

So here we are back at the bottom of the hill again. The air in which the plane flies has not changed. At its core HIV is still a transmittable virus. The routes of its transmission are inextricably tied to inequalities, gender inequality especially.

But unlike twenty years ago, HIV is now a medically manageable, treatable and theoretically curable virus. Just as TB has been for 50 years. But whether people live with or die from HIV depends on whether they have access to functional health systems. Just like TB. In other words, equality and inequality are the main determinants of HIV. Put another way, social justice or social injustice.

As the 2000s gave way to the 2010s our experience at SECTION27 and TAC made this clearer and clearer to us. We were drawn into campaigns to challenge the adequacy of budgets for health services and the sufficiency of health workers. The word 'stock-out' entered our lexicon. The consequences of unbridled corruption loomed much larger. Inevitably, it was to the quality of public healthcare systems and the social and economic determinants of HIV infection that we had to turn our fire. That is why, in South Africa and internationally, the next phase of AIDS activism must become part of a wider quest for social justice.

8
Crossing borders

Life is what happens to you when you're busy making other plans.
John Lennon, 'Watching the Wheels'[108]

Journeys simply don't end. Journeys don't simply end. Journeys don't end simply. A destination is a starting point. An arrivals hall becomes a new place of departure. AIDS will not end in my lifetime. Even if a 'cure' is developed, the inequalities that spread HIV to every corner of the earth will remain. Humans may develop mastery over the virus, but we have still to overthrow the inequalities that cut its path in the first place.

Because the journey of an activist is so complex, on each new foray it is important not only to set your compass but to keep checking it. You must know where you are on the map, change tack when necessary, strengthen certain strategies, abandon others.

I had never planned to be an AIDS activist, yet by 2008 I found I had been head of the ALP for just over a decade. My vision of a dynamic human-rights law firm had slowly gained flesh. The ALP had established a successful record of countering unfair discrimination and saving lives.

One thing I had learned is that it takes time and teams to make change happen. For many years the ALP was just a clutch of individuals. I used to tell Phumi Mtetwa, once the ALP's manager, that despite its appearance of strength the organisation 'rested on chicken legs'. Individuals, however committed or clever, are insufficient to bring about lasting change. Teamwork made the ALP. Over the course of half a decade we had slowly grown a team of driven, dedicated, professional lawyers and activists who were united by the same ethic and vision.

Two people in particular had added enormously to the capability of the ALP. Jonathan Berger had joined in 2000, recruited to develop our understanding of and expertise in the field of law in relation to access to medicines and intellectual property. Jonathan had first qualified as an architect before studying law and very deliberately embarking on a journey into human rights law. He had started his journey as a protégé of the charismatic Zackie Achmat, inspired by Zackie's work in forming the National Coalition for Gay and Lesbian Equality (NCGLE).

Jonathan became the chief architect of several important cases run by TAC and the ALP, most notably the complaint TAC submitted to the Competition Commission in late 2002. In this novel complaint we alleged that unlawful profiteering and excessive pricing by two multinational pharmaceutical companies, GlaxoSmithKline and Boehringer Ingelheim, were violating the right to health for people with AIDS. We submitted evidence that they were charging excessive prices on three of their patented antiretroviral medicines – AZT, 3TC and nevirapine. Rob Petersen, returning to my life, now in the guise of a respected Senior Counsel, led our team. His understanding of economics and politics was vital to the ultimate success of our strategy.

After a year-long investigation the Competition Commission agreed with us and was prepared to refer our complaint to the Competition Tribunal, effectively a court. The companies took scared and opened settlement negotiations. This was the case that broke the pharma companies' resistance. Negotiations led to the issuing of voluntary licences on all three medicines, dramatically reducing their prices and making them immediately affordable to millions more people.[109]

Dr Adila Hassim joined the ALP four years after Jonathan. Jonathan and I had interviewed Adila over the phone while she was finishing her PhD at the University of Notre Dame in the United States. Her infant child yawled in the background. Adila and I had literally crossed paths several years earlier when she had been a clerk at the Constitutional Court: much later I would notice her name lurking among the TAC activists in a file recording the handing-down of the famous 2002 nevirapine Constitutional Court judgment in favour of TAC.

Adila, bright and articulate, had joined the Bar in 2003. Her PhD was on socio-economic rights in the South African Constitution and she needed a playground to test out her beliefs. She had already been offered a higher-paying job at the Open Society Foundation, but accepted our invitation to join the ALP as a senior researcher.

In early June 2004, on my return from my seventh Comrades Marathon, I bumped into her again. This time it was in the dim corridor at the ALP. It would take a few years for us to fully discover each other but over time we became close confidants, collaborators, comrades and friends.

Adila crosses all my boxes. She is the youngest daughter of the great

South African writer Aziz Hassim, whose historical novel about a family of Indian people in South Africa, *The Lotus People* is a sadly neglected classic – a text as important and neglected as *Ingqumbo Yeminyanya*.

She is one of the new school of post-apartheid social justice lawyers who seek to connect the Constitution with the great tradition of using the law to advance civil and political rights, established under apartheid by such human rights lawyers as Bram Fischer, Nelson Mandela, George Bizos, Arthur Chaskalson and Pius Langa. With the freedoms they and others fought for now guaranteed by our supreme law, the new legal frontier is to test the ability of the law to meaningfully advance such socioeconomic rights as access to food, health, housing and education.

By the time I bumped into her Adila had already clerked at the Constitutional Court: in the late '90s for the then Deputy President of the Court and later Chief Justice, Pius Langa, and then for Edwin Cameron when he held a brief acting appointment at the Court. Through working with these two legal giants in the early days of the Court she had acquired invaluable knowledge and experience.

Adila's head holds heady memories of those heady days. Some evenings we would excavate her recollections. I would lap up tales of important moments of legal history such as the preparation of the judgment certifying that the final Constitution abided by the 34 Constitutional Principles that had been agreed by political parties in the CODESA negotiations. The fact that Adila had also clerked for Justice Cameron tied another knot with our work. Her cumulative knowledge and intuitive feel and instinct for constitutional law became a great asset to Team ALP and later for SECTION27, the new organisation that we would carve out of the ALP.

In the early 2000s I had been insufficiently attentive to managing the ALP. I had subsumed the ALP into building TAC, directing human and financial resources to what – at that point – I considered the greater responsibility. The ALP's agenda of fighting for nondiscrimination became secondary for a while to the great task of building a social movement powerful enough to ensure access to ARV treatment for all people with HIV.

Consequently, when Adila arrived in 2004 the ALP's legal work and cases were stuck in the mud. Several important matters had stalled.

One against the South African National Defence Force (SANDF) had been so badly managed that an HIV-positive soldier's claim of unfair discrimination had prescribed – a cardinal sin in law.

In 2006 the ALP separated from Wits University and set itself up as an independent organisation. Adila is not confrontational but she is persistent and plain-speaking and does not tolerate any type of fool, and this was when she took over as head of ALP litigation. Over the next two years she cleaned up our litigation unit, put legal work back on a professional footing, and took over and led on all of our most important cases, notably the case challenging discrimination against soldiers with HIV in the SANDF.

This case had started twenty years earlier with a letter I had sent to Joe Modise, the Minister of Defence, challenging the policy of testing all soldiers for HIV and weeding out those who were positive. I received a reply from his Deputy, Ronnie Kasrils. Adila and I picked this up again in 2007 on a visit to a man called Sipho Mthethwa, a former soldier in the ANC's guerrilla army, Umkhonto we Sizwe. Because he had HIV, Sipho found himself in the anomalous position of training soldiers but not being allowed to accompany them on deployment abroad. Another of our clients had had the offer of employment as a trumpeter in the Air Force band withdrawn once he'd been tested. We eventually won that case in 2014, ending twenty years of litigation. The SANDF's defence was a tale told by a small army of useful idiots, often full of sound and fury, but ultimately signifying nothing. Nonetheless, in their expensive defence of the indefensible they succeeded in obfuscating, stigmatising, wasting taxpayers' money on expensive and inept lawyers, and harming quite a few innocent men and women.[110]

With Jonathan Berger and Adila Hassim we had at last developed the backbone of a winning team. But that was no reason for complacency.

Rethinking activism

2008 was a watershed year. On 20 September the ANC National Executive Committee rebelled against President Thabo Mbeki and, in ANC-speak, 'recalled' him from his 'deployment' to the highest office in the land. Given Mbeki's despicable role in AIDS denialism, TAC was not about to protest. The Deputy President, Kgalema Motlanthe, became interim President and within days of the palace coup he appointed a new Minister of Health.

Barbara Hogan has a long record of taking a stand for justice. She had joined the ANC as a young woman and worked in the ANC underground. In 1982 she had been the first woman to be found guilty of high treason by the apartheid state and served the next eight years in prison. She had been a Member of Parliament since 1994.

But, unlike ANC leaders who became dizzied or drunk with power or who made compromises that steadily ate away at their integrity until there was not enough left to worry about, she kept hers intact. She had been a silent supporter of TAC through the years of AIDS denialism. Immediately after her appointment a delegation of TAC leaders led by Zackie Achmat visited her home in Cape Town to congratulate her.

Hogan's mandate from a part-cleansed ANC was to bury AIDS denialism. Suddenly, after nearly a decade, TAC and the ALP were brought in from the cold. I met with Hogan to discuss what we thought should be her priorities. Given that the Ministry of Health was riddled with AIDS denialists, most prominently its larger-than-life Director-General, Thami Mseleku, she needed a staff that she could trust. Fatima Hassan, who for many years had been a pillar of the ALP, was appointed as special adviser to the new minister. Adila Hassim and Jonathan Berger found themselves on various quickly established ministerial advisory committees – although we were told that Hogan met internal resistance within the ANC to some of these appointments. Then on 1 December 2008, World AIDS Day, I found myself no longer the angry activist shouting from the stands but instead sharing the stage with Motlanthe and Hogan at the Kingsmead Stadium in Durban, as we tried to ring in a new era in the response to the HIV epidemic.

The Times headline the next day declared, 'AIDS activists and government bury the hatchet – after 330 000 die needlessly. "The war is over".'

But paradoxically a time of healing was soon to become a time of rupture, for this was the year in which the 'rainbow nation' started to feed off itself. In May 2008 murderous xenophobic violence was ignited in Alexandra and then swept the country, taking nearly sixty lives, causing fear and dislocation.

The tensions unleashed by the xenophobia spilled over into our relationship with Barbara Hogan. She was angered by an article I wrote during her brief but crucial tenure as Minister of Health in which I described the Free State province as 'killing fields' where 'the death penalty had been reintroduced'. Although placing the blame for the Free State ARV crisis squarely with the province, I criticised Hogan for reportedly saying that its moratorium on ARV delivery was because the province government were 'victims of their own success' and not because of bad management.[111]

In Cape Town the TAC and ALP response to the xenophobia was hailed as exemplary.[112] Zackie Achmat and Fatima Hassan worked tirelessly to catalyse and lead a civil society response that showed solidarity with refugees and migrants, provided humanitarian relief and built a coalition of people who tried their best to stanch the bloodshed. They became exhausted witnesses to the barbarity that people can inflict on each other and to the pain and suffering that result. Their nascent Social Justice Coalition did everything from collecting and distributing sanitary pads and nappies to organising protests.

In Johannesburg, the ALP and TAC held back from full involvement and the civil society response was far more fragmented. I was concerned that throwing all TAC's human resources at the fight against xenophobia would lessen our capacity to maintain oversight of the response to HIV. This led to tensions between Zackie and me which spilled over into the ALP and TAC. It also became mixed up with personal and personality issues that had simmered over the years

In 2006 Zackie and I had talked half seriously about having a twenty-year anniversary party. In those days, after so many years of working with him, a breakup seemed inconceivable to me. I recalled witnessing the outbreak of war in 2007 between one-time close comrades Willie Madisha and Zwelinzima Vavi. Madisha had been the President of COSATU between 1999 and his expulsion in February 2008. We had worked closely with both him and Vavi and seen their positive interactions and their warm feelings for each other.

Zackie and I had been friends and comrades since meeting in London in 1986. We were co-authors of many campaigns. In early 2008 I remember thinking that a Vavi/Madisha type breakup could never happen between the two of us. It shouldn't have, but as much as the stress of battle can be a great unifier it can also be a great divider. In June 2008 during a board meeting of the ALP the tensions spilled out. You could have cut the atmosphere in the meeting with a knife. Outside the meeting we turned the knives on each other. Accusations were wielded like sticks, words thrown like stones, tears, then apologies. But the harm was done. Zackie and I have not worked together since.

A few months later the strain in relationships led to Zackie's resignation from the ALP board. In 2009 Fatima Hassan followed by resigning as a member of staff.

All I can say with hindsight is that human beings need to exercise great care in maintaining important friendships. We didn't have that much common sense.

In this fast-changing political and organisational context Adila Hassim began to pepper me with her questions about the future of the ALP. Brand ALP had become well established nationally and internationally though not, I feel compelled to point out, because of any expensive brand-consultant. In particular Adila asked that I think about why the ALP was increasingly being drawn into issues and cases that had little to do with HIV directly.

In 2008 and 2009, for example, we assisted the Legal Resources Centre and others to protect Zimbabwean refugees in Johannesburg. Many of them were staying at the Central Methodist Church (CMC) in downtown Johannesburg. On 8 January 2009 a mass police raid resulted in the unlawful arrest and police harassment of over 500 people. We had come to know the CMC because MSF had established a clinic there, particularly to provide treatment for HIV and TB. It was a sanctuary, the first place where refugees from other African countries would be received with some care and concern. But its living conditions were squalid. It sometimes accommodated up to 3 000 people, many sleeping on its pews, stairs and floors. But for desperate people fleeing tyrants like Robert Mugabe and seeking a better life it offered a community. For some, safety is a relative matter.[113]

It was a complex broth. The giving over of the church to accommodate the refugees was not supported by all its members. The presence of up to 300 children caused an outcry. Many of these little boys and some girls had left their parents and trekked alone from the economic devastation of Zimbabwe to try to find a safer life. When allegations of sexual abuse of children surfaced, they were used to tarnish and cast doubt on Bishop Paul Verryn, the CMC's pastor. There were threats to relocate or repatriate the children, something the children resisted. As a result, in January 2010 the ALP, in its own name, sought and obtained a court order appointing Dr Ann Skelton as curatrix to represent them and see to their best interests.

This was an important case, but it was hard to see its direct relevance to an AIDS Law Project.

In August 2009, in another example of an off-mission case, the ALP intervened as an amicus in a dispute before the Constitutional Court regarding the state's duty to pay court-awarded damages promptly and the right to seek an execution order that could attach state assets in the case of non-payment.

Nominally the case involved an unfortunate man by the name of Hendrik Nyathi. He had been horribly injured as a result of negligence in a state hospital. After he'd successfully sued for damages, the state failed to pay him. Mr Nyathi eventually died before ever receiving a cent in relief. Our involvement in the case arose after a long delay in payment of compensation to Dr Malcom Naude, a doctor who had been unfairly dismissed because of his insistence on treating rape survivors with ARVs at the Rob Ferreira Hospital in Nelspruit.

The relatively simple legal issues in the *Nyathi* case were clouded by lots of Latin. To the person in the street it all appeared befuddling and esoteric, but important principles regarding access to justice and the rule of law were at play. Assisted by the ALP and other amici, in the judgment the Constitutional Court ordered the government to amend legislation so as to allow for the seizure of its assets if it failed to pay damages awarded by the courts.

Importantly for the ALP, *Nyathi* was the first time Adila stood up and argued before the Constitutional Court.

The ALP's core work – the human rights of people with HIV – was also taking on a new shape. More and more of the campaigns we were involved in to ensure the sustainability and quality of the HIV response were morphing into bigger issues about the structure and quality of the public health system.

A decade earlier, when we had formed TAC and first demanded access

to ARVs, we had frequently been criticised by naysaying health profes-
sors who considered themselves experts. They talked down to us, arguing that the health system was not strong enough to support an ARV
programme. They claimed that our demands were reckless and would
break the health system. We ignored them. Our mission was first to save
lives and then to fix the health system. If we had done it the other way
round, many more people would have died.

But with the demise of AIDS denialism and more and more people now
being enrolled on ARV treatment, we had to ask ourselves whether the
frail and anaemic public health system would be strong enough to support the biggest medical programme in history. Eventually it would have
to supply medicines on a continuous basis to over six million people with
HIV. Was it robust enough to do so?

In late 2008 we received sobering evidence that these questions could
not be postponed any longer.

One day I received a phone call from a salt-of-the-earth woman called
Trudi Harrison. She informed us that in the Free State, one of South
Africa's poorest provinces, a moratorium had been imposed on new
enrolments for ARV treatment. Although there had been no official announcement, the apparent reason was that the provincial health budget
had run out.

On hearing this we scrambled the ALP, ordering our staff into the air
and onto the road, to try and find out what was happening. It was true.
In the remains of that year we produced reports, wrote media articles,
organised demonstrations. In particular we harassed Barbara Hogan, the
Minister of Health, to do *something* – sometimes antagonising this new
friend of TAC. I also raised the issue forcefully at the National AIDS
Council.

As a result of the outcry we generated, the moratorium was lifted
after two months. But during those sixty-something days, according to
Dr Francois Venter, President of the Southern African HIV Clinicians
Society, an additional 30 people a day died of AIDS. During the moratorium one of the people we became attached to was six-year-old Thapelo
Mlonyeni. His on-off access to medicines destroyed his already fragile
health and he died in October 2009.

As usual, it is the children who suffer most from the sins of the politicians.

9
Back into the unknown –
the birth and infancy of SECTION27

One of the works of art that I have treasured from when I first saw it in 1982 is the film *Reds*. This biopic set in the midst of the 1917 Russian Revolution, directed as a labour of love by Warren Beatty, is framed around the explosive comradeship of American writers and communists Jack Reed and Louise Bryant. When I watched *Reds* as a schoolboy I had hardly heard of Lenin and Trotsky and certainly had no idea that they would become major players in my life a few years later. It was the combination of love and idealism that I idolised, the romanticism and heroism of revolution, the poetry of revolutionaries.

I learnt the words of one especially moving scene by heart. A horrific civil war between the Reds and the Whites, financed by the West, followed the revolution and sapped the resources and morale of the world's first workers' state. A Red Train carrying Bolshevik leaders toured many of the war's frontlines, exhorting battle-weary troops and co-ordinating the Red Army's battle strategy. In this scene Reed is aboard the Red Train somewhere on the Asian steppes. He is seen challenging the Bolshevik leader Grigory Zinoviev, because he had changed the words 'class war' to 'holy war' in a speech Reed had written.

There follows a fight between the two men. Zinoviev justifies altering Reed's words in the interests of party propaganda and tells Reed that his problem is that he doesn't know what he wants from life:

> You haven't resolved what your life is dedicated to. You see yourself as an artist and at the same time a revolutionary. As a lover of your wife and as the spokesperson for the American Party.

The words Reed chooses to respond to Zinoviev seared their way into my soul:

> . . . if you don't think a man can be an individual and be true to the collective, or speak for his own country and the International at the same time, or love his wife and still be faithful to the revolution, then you don't have a self to give.

And then come the (for me) immortal lines:

> When you separate a man from what he loves the most, what you do is
> purge what's unique, and when you purge what's unique in him you
> purge dissent. And when you purge dissent, you kill the revolution.
> Revolution is dissent. You don't rewrite what I write!

At which point an artillery shell hits the train and explodes.

Twenty-five years later, what reminded me of *Reds* was that I felt Adila
Hassim and I had found a chemistry similar to Reed and Bryant. We were
comrades. We were each fiercely independent. We felt the same burning
desire to change the world.

Adila and I realised that the AIDS Law Project needed to change, but
we weren't sure how. We bounced ideas off each other, followed conversation trails into a thought-wilderness that we had not explored before.
Work planning became mixed up with discussions about poetry and literature. At the Ant, a pub in Johannesburg's Melville, ideas were conceived
and then coaxed into fully fledged life. During nights of intense discussion our thoughts formed in a flurry of words that were consolidated into
ideas, and eventually nailed down as concrete suggestions to our Board.

'The ALP is no longer fit for purpose; its name speaks to a mission that
has changed,' Adila argued.

'The ground has shifted, and though we were part of the shift, that's
all the more reason for a reconsideration of who we are and what we are
trying to achieve,' I agreed.

'There are now a million people on ARV treatment, but sustaining and
expanding that will require a much stronger health system and that
means invoking the duties arising from Section 27 of the Constitution
more forcefully,' Adila insisted.

'The formula that worked for AIDS advocacy depended on respect for
the Constitution and the rule of law, but the manner in which Jacob
Zuma has subverted the law in relation to the charges of corruption
against him poses a broader threat to the courts that could impact negatively on social justice. We have to develop capacity in this area.' We
both agreed.

'People are hungry and yet Section 27(1)(b) – the right to sufficient food and water – is completely ignored. What if we could mobilise people to demand the fulfilment of their right to sufficient food?'

'And what about the right to basic education? What barriers are there to catalysing a movement to claim this right, similar to the one TAC and the ALP built around HIV?'

And so on and on and on.

Meaning crystallised out of many days and nights of debates about questions like these. Somewhere in mid-2009 our minds were made up. We sounded out friends, comrades, lawyers and donors. Then on 23 September 2009, we went to the ALP Board of Directors to inform them that we thought the ALP should be closed down and a new organisation created. At that point the proposed organisation didn't have a name, but we had formed a clear idea of what it should do.

The Board was careful but unexpectedly receptive. That day a new journey into social justice commenced. SECTION27, named after the clause in the Bill of Rights that sets out the right of everyone to have access to healthcare services, sufficient food and water, as well as social assistance, was born nine months later. We expanded our mission to encompass the right to basic education as well as issues of rule of law and accountable government. We presumptuously called ourselves 'catalysts for social justice'.

That was the end of the ALP. A new journey was about to begin.

Pay-back time: the journey towards quality basic education

In my account of my first journeys in social justice I dwelt a little on my privileged education. From the age of eight to eighteen I had continuous education at a school that not only fed my emotional and intellectual needs, but helped me discover them. Teachers inspired rather than instructed me. In addition I was taught to play the trumpet, acted in school plays and had access to a swimming pool and rugby fields that ran down from the school to the River Ouse where, if you were so inclined, you could learn to row. In a protective environment I started to learn about relationships, love and sex. As a result of this education I consider myself proof of the proverbial pudding that, as the UN Committee on Economic, Social and Cultural Rights has declared, 'a well-educated, enlightened and active mind, able to wander freely and widely, is one of the joys and rewards of human existence'.

Education has always been a site of contest in South Africa, and it remains so today. It can free you or chain you. Because it had been used for the latter purpose for so long, the spirit of equality imbues the right to basic education in the South African Bill of Rights. Although the eight words used to describe the right may be bare and unemotional, behind them lies the iconic image of the schoolboy Hector Pieterson – shot on a protest march by school students on 16 June 1976 – being carried through the streets of Soweto, his young life bleeding away. Behind those words lies black people's revulsion against three centuries of inferior education, a misnomer for a system designed so that black people would not become more than 'hewers of wood and drawers of water'.

The privileged status of the right to basic education isn't clouded by any qualifications. You don't find such phrases as 'progressive realisation', 'reasonable legislative and other measures' or 'within available resources' in the text. The state's duty is unambiguous and simple: everyone has the right 'to a basic education, including adult basic education'.

By the time we launched SECTION27 in 2010, fourteen years had passed since the Constitution was signed into law by President Mandela – enough time for it to become clear that this was a duty which the government was failing abjectly to meet. Ninety-five per cent of schools remained segregated by geography and class and therefore also by race. The government huffed and puffed about its commitment to education. It frequently points out that the largest portion of the annual budget is spent on fulfilling the right. In 2016/17 this amount was R204 billion. But the government undermines its own good intentions by deploying unqualified political 'cadres' as school principals and overlooking managerial and policy failures, as well as deepening corruption. The South African Democratic Teachers' Union (SADTU), an influential component within the ANC's tripartite alliance, continually privileges the interests of its members over those of learners.

This has left schools and schoolchildren to fend for themselves. As a result standards have declined and teenage pregnancy increased, while pass rates are manipulated.

Ironically, in the past decade inferior education for the mass of black children has become as much of a marker of ANC rule as it was of the National Party.

One morning in February 2012 Adila walked into my office and showed me a report in the *Sowetan* that alleged that in South Africa's most northern province, Limpopo, school textbooks had not been delivered by the end of the first month of the new academic year. She was outraged. At her instigation I agreed we should find out if the report was true, so we immediately dispatched two young lawyers, Nikki Stein and Nthabi Pooe, to Limpopo, a province that to most of us at the time was a great unknown. They verified the reports.

As an aside, I should say that a sine qua non of activism is that you should still feel empathy and even outrage at what befalls other human beings. If you do, do you have the energy and belief to act on that outrage? Most of us succumb to acceptance of the unacceptable. The vast majority of the suffering citizenry, including you and me, have come to regard the abnormal as normal. In this violent, shocking world of ours few people would even notice a newspaper report, tucked away among other horror stories, about the denial of textbooks to an unknown number of children in an unknown province. It would not be a cause for anger. It would be just one more sad story in a barrage of sad stories. But when Adila Hassim noticed it, she moved SECTION27 into action.

The 'Limpopo textbook saga' (as it would be known) became one of the biggest news stories of 2012, as well as the butt of cartoonists and comics. It became synonymous with state dysfunction and corruption. For the two lawyers we dispatched to Limpopo it was itself an education, a voyage of self-discovery. Nikki Stein is a young white woman from a privileged background. Her life has been sheltered from deprivation and poverty. Nthabi Pooe is a young black woman, at the time just out of the University of the North West, the daughter of two teachers.

Nthabi and Nikki were our musketeers. They took numerous lengthy drives to Limpopo. In far-flung villages with names like Nowhere and My Darling they discovered brave school principals who were prepared to speak out. By contrast, in the sweltering face-brick offices of the local Department of Education they encountered arrogant and unconcerned officials who made fun of their femininity. In a meeting with Dr Karodia, the head of the national intervention team that had taken over the administration of the provincial education department in late 2011, they were told that the province 'is the wild wild west and everybody has a horse and a gun'. Karodia told them that he couldn't be expected 'to wipe every tear from every eye'.

Their travels made them witness to all aspects of the crisis in education. They carried back to our relatively sanitised offices their sense of shock and disbelief at the state of schools, toilets in particular. It was their sense of outrage that would propel the case forward.

We got to work. Over several months SECTION27 built up reams of correspondence with officials in the Department of Education. Some admitted the problem. Others vehemently denied it. But letters, meetings, promises and deadlines didn't bring books to the schools. Once more, resort to the courts became inevitable. Once more unto the Pretoria High Court, its neighbouring Church Square, always a good space for a gathering, and Vermeulen Street that runs beside it! Once more unto the unassuming red face-brick court buildings we had first entered in 2001 in litigation over PMTCT! Once more into panelled courtrooms where we had argued and won the right of soldiers with HIV to non-discrimination in the army!

We knew this place.

On 20 April 2012 the Centre for Applied Legal Studies, our attorneys in this case, sent the government our first letter of demand seeking delivery of the textbooks. But our demand went a little further. By then four months of school time had been lost. Delivery of the books would be great, but – Adila and I asked ourselves – what about the lost time? Could the courts do anything to remedy that? I remember the day we found the answer during a conversation in a car park: we added a demand for a catch-up plan for the learners denied textbooks.

As is always the case, the litigation was a small part of our overall efforts. But it was the public stage upon which the drama could be acted out.

15 May 2012. The beginning of winter and the day 'the textbooks case' had been set down to be heard before Judge Jody Kollapen. As is our method, we had planned a demonstration in the streets outside the court together with the National Association of School Governing Bodies (NASGB), an organisation that had agreed to come in as one of the applicants in the case. We gathered early that morning in a trade union office not far from the court. Sixty people jammed every corner, sitting, squatting, standing and having a lesson in our argument – about to be tested before the courts for the first time – of the duties created by the inclusion of the right to basic education in the Constitution.

We frequently sing the praises of the courts. But the truth is they are a bit of a lottery. Each day the Judge President of a court allocates cases to the available judges and a case may appear before an energetic judge or a lazy judge, a constitutionalist or a conservative. You may appear before one proudly keeping himself resilient against a Constitution he (for it is usually a he) would prefer had not been born. Or you may come across one like Judge Kollapen, formerly National Director of Lawyers for Human Rights and Chairperson of the South African Human Rights Commission – a man with a passion for justice.

The day we drew Judge Kollapen was the day we drew a winning number.

SECTION27 and Others v Minister of Education and Another was the first time an explanation of the exact duties created by Section 29 was requested from the courts: the legal question was whether the right to basic education, which the Constitutional Court had earlier held to be 'immediately realisable', meant that each learner could expect to hold their own copy of each prescribed textbook. Did it create a duty on the government to do everything possible to ensure that every learner had a textbook on time at the point when they start to study each year's curricula? In two judgments delivered in May and October 2012, Judge Kollapen answered both questions in the affirmative.[114]

The Kollapen judgments have gone down in the annals of jurisprudence on the right to basic education.[115] They are already studied across the world by education rights activists. But observers, particularly academics, often see only the type on a crisp page or computer screen. They seek mainly to decipher the judge's reasoning. What commentaries on public impact law do not see is the blood, sweat and tears that may go into winning a case. Through years of lawyering I have learnt that the process of public impact law requires a meticulous attention to detail. The judgment is just the visible tip of the iceberg. It talks about the law; in an orderly and logical fashion it distils the issues in dispute; it choreographs what was often chaos. But it is often an anaemic summary of the dilemmas that went into its gestation.

In commentaries on the Limpopo textbooks case you will not find any reference to intimidation. Yet in Karodia's 'wild west' we encountered a network of clumsy sycophants and spies. Teachers and principals at schools who provided SECTION27 with affidavits were visited by government officials and instructed or threatened not to give information to SECTION27.

The story of one fine public citizen, Mashangu Hlongwane, is a case in point.

Mr Hlongwane is the principal of Hanyani Thomo Secondary School in the village of Thomo in northern Limpopo. Thomo is a place of poverty and unemployment. It's a dry town, away from the main tarred road, subject to the scorching heat of summer suns and periodic storms that rage, howl and frequently take their anger out on school roofs.

Mr Hlongwane is the type of person who recognises mendacity and refuses to submit to mediocrity. His school has over 1 500 children, yet it was being starved of the resources it is entitled to by law. In his principal's office papers are piled high alongside tins of sardines for the school nutrition programmes, the carcass of a photocopier, trophies and the obligatory portraits of the Premier of the province. In his school, as many as 120 learners sit in some classes. Yet out of adversity he has moulded Hanyani Thomo into a school where the ethic of learning and teaching was more inspiring than the demotivating effect of dilapidated infrastructure. As a result his students achieved a 98 per cent pass rate in a school district where failure is generally the name of the game.

Mr Hlongwane was one of the small number of principals willing to speak to Nikki and Nthabi. He provided an affidavit about the shortages of textbooks at his school and how he tried to manage with these shortages. However, acting in the best interests of the children nearly cost him his job. Mr Hlongwane was singled out for special attention. He was phoned by a senior official in the department. His wife, also a school principal, was warned that she might lose her job. Initially Mr Hlongwane withstood the intimidation, quipping that after eighteen years as a principal he was beyond retirement age anyway.

In his first judgment Judge Kollapen had ordered that all textbooks be delivered by 15 June 2012. The Department of Basic Education failed to meet this deadline and after further delays we had no option but to go back to court. The department went on the offensive. The Minister of Basic Education's spokesperson, Panyaza Lesufi, told the media that the Limpopo textbooks litigation was being used by SECTION27 as a way to raise funds. They tried to suppress evidence of continuing textbook shortages. Schools that had formed part of our original application were visited by officials. Slowly the number of schools which had been applicants in the case dwindled, several claiming that they 'had never given SECTION27 a mandate to represent them'.

A few days before the second court hearing, Adila and I were attending the annual seminar of Students for Law and Social Justice (SLSJ) at Onrus, near Hermanus, a beautiful but brash tourist town that has been given layers of meaning and ambiguity in Zakes Mda's novel *The Whale Caller*. The seminar's aim is to inspire students by exposing them to practitioners of constitutional law, people like our good selves.

It was a Sunday morning. We were contentedly having breakfast en-joying the view of the sea when an anxious Nikki Stein broke the reverie. She told us that a new affidavit had just arrived from the Department of Basic Education. It sought to strike out Mr Hlongwane's allegations of textbook shortages, which they claimed he had retracted. This made it look as if SECTION27 had been lying to the court.

We faced a real difficulty. We could have asked the judge to refer the dispute to oral evidence. But this would have meant putting Mr Hlongwane in the witness box, cross-examining him and watching him perjure himself to protect his job. We did not want to do that. So, after careful consideration, we gave the department its way.

But that was not the end of it. When we arrived in court we found Mr Hlongwane seated with the government's legal team. He was nervous and fidgety, avoiding eye contact or conversation. During a break in the proceedings he told us that the day before he had been ordered to attend the hearing. His was a four-hour drive to Pretoria.[116]

Fortunately chicanery doesn't win out in every court. For a third time that year Kollapen once again ruled in favour of the rights of learners.

As the year progressed the combined effect of the litigation, the publicity and the demonstrations was to create a gathering wave that eventually washed away the government's wall of denialism about the extent of the textbook shortages. By the end of 2012 six million new books had been delivered to Limpopo, a presidential inquiry was established to look into the saga and make recommendations, and the Human Rights Commission undertook an investigation into the delivery of school textbooks nationally.

But commissions and inquiries do not a textbook spring make. SEC-TION27 therefore continued our monitoring.

In 2013 textbook delivery was much improved. But in 2014 Basic Edu-cation for All (BEFA), a Limpopo-wide organisation of teachers and par-ents that had been formed to monitor schools and educate people about their rights, began to report new shortages. The rigmarole of letters, accusations and denials repeated itself. In April that year, in the face of further howls about hidden agendas by the government, it became nec-essary to go back to court for a fourth time.

This time the lottery gave us a different type of judge. When Adila Hassim stood up in court to argue our case, Judge Neil Tuchten was im-patient and interruptive. One journalist, noticing this, described Judge

Tuchten as 'patronising', saying his attitude 'smack[ed] of sexism and patriarchy'. Quoting an exchange between Chris Erasmus, the department's Senior Counsel, and Tuchten, the journalist noted how Tuchten jokingly asked Erasmus whether he was 'addressing him as a judge.' But when he turned to Hassim he asked whether he was addressing her 'as a parent.' In the journalist's own words:

> Why don the 'judge hat' when addressing a male advocate but reach for the 'parental hat' when talking to a female advocate?[117]

Based on what we witnessed in court, Tuchten's understanding of the duties of government stipulated in section 29 of the Constitution seemed somewhat shallow. So we were taken by surprise when his order went further than Kollapen's. His judgment eulogised books in a way that would not be out of place in a Shakespearean soliloquy:

> Textbooks have been part of the stock in trade of the educator for centuries. There is something special about a book. It has a very long life, far longer than that of an individual reader. It is a low tech(nology) device. It is accessible to anyone who can read the language in which it has been written. During the hours of daylight it can be read (accessed) without any other supporting technology at all. It needs no maintenance except the occasional strip of adhesive tape. It can accommodate the reader's own thoughts in the form of jottings and emphases, it can accompany the reader wherever she goes, even to prison, to war and into exile. At night, it can be accessed with the help of the simplest technology, like a candle. What is written on one of its pages can readily be compared with what is on other pages by simply using bookmarks. It is always available, without mediation: a book in the hands of a reader cannot be censored or altered to distort what is written in it by anyone trying to exercise power over the reader. Books are the essential tools, even weapons, of free people. That is why tyrants throughout the ages have sought to restrict and even deny the access of their subjects to the written word and to burn and otherwise destroy the books of those whose cultures and ideas they seek to suppress.[118]

Then in his order he declared that the right to basic education includes the right of every learner at a public school 'to be provided with [every textbook prescribed for that learner's grade] before the teaching of the curriculum for which such textbook is prescribed is due to commence'.

With predictable stupidity the government decided to appeal this judgment and sent the matter up to the Supreme Court of Appeal. The core of their objection was that by requiring that every learner have their textbooks on time the judge had imposed an impossible standard of perfection upon them.

The impression we have gained is that government officials, ministers in particular, rarely read or seriously analyse the judgments made against them. They are quick to appeal even if the prospects of success are dim. This way court orders – and justice – are delayed. Rather than trying to understand the reasoning of the judiciary, an essential branch of government, they appear to treat as gospel the advice of their legal advisers. But this advice is not always disinterested. Senior counsel are entitled to charge their clients as much as R50 000 a day. This means the less ethical among them may develop a material interest in prolonging litigation. By dragging a case out for a few more months they are guaranteed to hit another jackpot in a fruit-machine filled with coins put there by the taxpayer.

This may not be fraud per se, but this common practice goes against the spirit of the Constitution and impedes access to justice. It is a practice frowned on by the Constitutional Court, which in 2012 stated that they can 'find no justification, in a country where disparities are gross and poverty is rife, to countenance appellate advocates charging hundreds of thousands of rands to argue an appeal'.[119]

This felt like one of those cases. The appeal had no merit. It was on a hiding to nothing.

In response to the appeal SECTION27 and BEFA mounted one of our most imaginative media mobilisations yet. Under the moniker #TextbooksMatter we organised marches in rural villages in Limpopo, held a public meeting in the iconic Morris Isaacson High School in Soweto and ran a unique social media campaign. In this campaign I was able to blend my love of literature with my love of activism. We persuaded a series of writers and respected public figures to record short spoken messages, which we broadcast on Facebook, on why textbooks matter and why access to reading is so important. Luminaries such as Njabulo Ndebele, renowned author of, among many books, *The Cry of Winnie Mandela*, and Mary Burton, former President of the Black Sash and former commissioner of the TRC, recorded poignant messages. This created a

A demonstration for
#TextbooksMatter,
led by school
students in Giyani
in Limpopo.

wide public awareness of the importance of the appeal and the issues
that were going to be at stake in the courtroom contest.

And so it came to pass that on 18 November 2015 members of BEFA,
TAC and SECTION27 could be found seated in the lovely old building of
the Supreme Court of Appeal (SCA) in Bloemfontein. The SCA was built
in the late 1920s for a very different purpose and type of law. Until the
Constitutional Court knocked it off its plinth in 1994, it was the highest
court in the land. For most of its life it was a court where mostly white
lawyers argued points of law before only white judges. But on this day
the visitors' gallery was packed with black people, members of BEFA
who had driven for ten hours from rural villages in Limpopo to attend
the hearing.

This time it was Erasmus SC who took all the hits. An angry and frustrated bench of five judges ripped into him. In my many years of watching court proceedings I have never seen such a savaging. The judges' questions showed they had carefully read the court papers. Their minds were clearly made up. It felt like poetic justice. Pay-back time for Adila Hassim.

Judgment came swiftly. Written by Judge Mohammed Navsa with the other four judges concurring, it continued the poetic tradition started by Tuchten. It was replete with assertions about 'the liberating power of books'. Its first line quoted Frederick Douglass, the great abolitionist who had himself escaped slavery in the United States: 'Once you learn to read, you will be forever free.' In South Africa's context, the judges said, 'It cannot be emphasised enough that basic education should be seen as a primary driver of transformation.'

The judges were brutal. Underlining the importance of literacy – the 'explosion of information . . . has rendered reading in the modern world all the more important' – they noted that the learners worst affected by textbook shortages were the rural poor, children who were 'overwhelmingly, if not exclusively, black learners'. With this in mind they declared '[w]e must guard against failing those who are most vulnerable', and concluded that 'those without textbooks are being unlawfully discriminated against', something that they found to be 'a violation of the learner's rights to a basic education, equality, dignity, the SASA and s. 195 of the Constitution'.[120]

That was the knock-out blow.

Zapiro's cartoon depicting the textbook scandal. (Zapiro)

At last wisdom prevailed. In early 2016 Angie Motshekga, the Minister of Basic Education, told a meeting of stakeholders:

> This judgement has far reaching consequences for the sector as a whole. It enjoins us to pull up our socks and get the basics right. We don't have a choice ... We have no choice but to comply. And in all honesty we should want to comply. We should be personally distressed that some of our children are not getting the education they deserve. In this regard, we should spare neither strength nor courage in ensuring that every child has an equal access to education and ... an equal chance to succeed.[121]

Suffer the children: death by toilet

SECTION27's first journey into the right to basic education was to insist that it included the right to textbooks. But on that journey what really shocked Nikki Stein and Nthabi Pooe was the state of the toilets they saw in the schools they visited. As they hunted for books they began a parallel process of inspecting each school's toilets, not something middle-class women would normally choose to do. Over several months they compiled a three-volume photo album of the pictures they took of school toilets, mostly filthy, broken, dangerous, brimming with shit, often riddled with maggots, their exteriors buzzing with flies, newspaper for toilet roll, some without doors, ventilation or running water to wash hands.

Greater indignity inflicted on young children is hard to imagine.

As I have already shown, travels in law and activism lead you down strange and unplanned paths. Polite society does not like to talk about this most basic of human functions, the great leveller of classes, the reductio ad absurdum of the human being. How humans shit and dispose of our waste is not a sexy subject for anybody. Even human rights advocacy steers away from it. But scratch and you will find that there are people who make this area of knowledge their business. I discovered that (as with everything else) there is a science to shitting and the disposal of human waste.

I had never thought of school toilets as having any relationship with education. I had never had to. I took toilets for granted throughout my life. The same mindset probably explains why they are one of the first amenities to suffer in the face of neoliberal budget trimming: 'kids go to school to learn, not to shit' is probably the thinking of those who have never wanted for a toilet. So, 21 years after freedom, 80 000 children in

Limpopo still went to schools without toilets. Perforce they relieved themselves in snake-ridden bushes.

Yet the vulnerability children feel when going to the toilet, the need to protect your privacy (partly because the stupid adult world has made such an issue of this most common of human necessities), is etched deeply into our psyche. It is 30 years since I left school but occasionally I still have bad dreams that bring back to life my neuroses about the toilets' lack of privacy, the saloon-style doors that were unable to properly insulate your sounds or smells from the child in the neighbouring stall. Toilets loom larger in a schoolchild's life than we allow: they are also good places for bullying, snogging, cigarette-smoking and even sex.

So how enduring is the trauma confronted by children who go to such schools in Limpopo (and elsewhere)? What memories or phobias do they carry with them into adult life? Because shitting is not a matter for polite conversation we don't even ask these questions. It would make an interesting topic for a radio talk-show.

SECTION27 staff kind of got used to these horror pictures. We joked darkly about how they entered our dreams. We started to prepare legal papers and to impress on the Department of Basic Education that litigation on textbooks would be followed by litigation on toilets if they did not demonstrate a will to address the problem. It seemed they heard us because Limpopo developed a plan to build and renovate school toilets which was presented to us by the Minister of Basic Education.

Yet our exposure to horror toilets in 2012 could not have prepared us for what we would soon become involved in.

A school is supposed to be a place of safety for children. Every day millions of parents release their children into the care of government and private schools believing it is just that. But for many poor children and their parents this is simply not true.

Monday, 20 January 2014. The first week of the new school year. A time of trepidation and excitement for parents and children across the country. On that day six-year old Michael Komape was starting his first week at Mahlodumela Lower Primary School in Chebeng Village, Limpopo. He was the third of the five children of James and Rosina. The few pictures of him show him as beaming and bright. His mum said he was a 'cute, smart boy' who was excited and in a jolly mood when he left for school.

During the mid-morning break Michael went to the toilets at the back of the school. At this point, the images that will come to your mind will divert. If you come from a background like mine the toilet you picture will be white, porcelain and flushed with drinkable water. If you are black and poor you will think of something more proximate to that I am about to describe.

The toilets at Mahlodumela Lower Primary were situated in three rectangular boxes made of corrugated iron. Once inside, the child faced another metal box, this one with a square hole cut into the middle. You either perched or sat above the hole and pissed or shat into the deep, dark pit that had been dug below.

This must have been what Michael attempted. Yet somehow the metal box on which he was squatting gave way. He tumbled into the foul liquids below. Some of Michael's little friends say they tried to tell the teacher that he had fallen into a toilet but were brushed away. After break class resumed without him, his empty seat not bothering the teacher.

It is hard to imagine the terror and pain felt by this young boy in the last minutes of his life: trapped in a dark hole, screaming, paddling desperately to extricate himself from quicksand-like shit.

Michael's absence was officially noticed by lunchtime. Then the school principal made a rigmarole of looking for him. His mother was phoned and asked if he was at home. He was not. His father was asked to come to the school urgently.

By the time James Komape arrived there was a gathering around the toilets. Michael's body had been found there still encased in shit. One hand poked out above the foul surface. A family friend, Charles Malebana, says he took a picture with his cell phone. But soon after he was confronted by the school principal and made to delete it.

Newspaper reports of Michael's death sparked a few days of outrage. Anger and disbelief were expressed by shocked callers to radio stations. Then the waters of acceptance rolled in. The storm in a toilet was stilled. Polite society got on with its business as if nothing had happened. There was no investigation by the police, no inquiry by the media, no sending of troops of journalists to Limpopo to investigate the deadly toilets of the province's schools. Little or no effort was made to reconstruct his brief life, to talk to his friends, or to reveal the grief of his family. Nothing was done to try to make the little boy a child again ... at least in our collective imagination.

At the end of January, Michael was buried. Shortly afterwards the guilty toilets were bulldozed and replaced by new toilets – demonstrating that sometimes the Department of Basic Education can respond with urgency to people's needs. School resumed.

According to our Constitution, we are all equal, we each have a right to life, to dignity, to equal protection and benefit of the law, which the state must respect, protect, promote and fulfil. All lives are equal. But, it seems, some lives are less equal than others.

But as with the media reports of textbook shortages that momentarily disturbed our urban complacency, Adila, who had also read the newspaper report, was restless and disturbed. Perhaps the fact that one of her own children was the same age as Michael made her feel a stronger and more purposeful empathy. She insisted that SECTION27's lawyers locate the family and offer them legal assistance. We did.[122]

There are millions of Michael Komapes among South Africa's poor and vulnerable, unemployed and marginalised. These are children whose parents – despite their love and best efforts – are unable to protect them from adversity. Each day they pack their children off to school, smartly uniformed. But once the children are out of their direct care they are unable to protect them from any threat the school may hold, be it death by toilet, rape, abuse by sexual predators in teacher's clothing or the dangers encountered getting to and from school.

In early March 2016, while I was writing this book, six-year-old Angel Sibanda drowned on her daily walk to her school in the 'informal settlement' of Diepsloot. It had rained heavily for several days and she was washed away by a flash flood as she tried to cross a stream. Her parents endured her absence fearfully. Two days later her little body was fished from the stream ten kilometres away.

Responsibility for Angel's tragedy lies in our inaction and neglect. Two years before her death some municipal official in Diepsloot took a decision to build two monumental footbridges over the main road that passes the settlement. The cost: R76 million. These footbridges lead to an empty field on the other side of the road. They have no purpose. Their only raison d'être must be that, faced with a pot of unspent money, somebody decided to award a tender for this unnecessary project to a friend. A far simpler and less costly bridge over the stream crossed by primary school children would have allowed Angel to become a girl, then a woman, maybe a mother, maybe a teacher, maybe a maybe.

The name 'Angel Sibanda' and that of the guilty official should adorn those white-elephant bridges.

Rarely is responsibility for these outrages tracked back to the highly intelligent and 'civilised' beings who work for the IMF or the World Bank or some accountancy consultancy with global tentacles; people who keep pads in cities like London or New York; people who insist on greater prudence in public spending as a condition for their investment or loans. The budget planner sitting at his oak-panelled desk demands fiscal prudence, cuts in 'non-essential' school infrastructure. In a fiscally constrained environment, out go school toilets or security fences. By the time the diktat gets down to the town planner it means not investing taxpayers' money to counter hazards along the route children take to school, an investment it is considered will serve no useful economic function.

This is how Charles Dickens expressed grief and anger about the death of Jo, the child street-sweeper, in *Bleak House:*

> Dead, your Majesty. Dead, my lords and gentlemen. Dead, Right Reverends and Wrong Reverends of every order. Dead, men and women, born with Heavenly compassion in your hearts. And dying thus around us every day.

The same anger belongs to Michael Komape, Thapelo Mlonyeni, Angel Sibanda and countless other children.

Bombs and birth

On 25 June 1997 our son Ciaran was born, carefully extracted by Caesarean section. Six years, three miscarriages and one never-say-never gynaecologist later he was followed by Aidan Nesta on 23 July 2003.

Both made a right meal of their births; Ciaran got yellow jaundice as his complication of choice, Aidan opted for feeding difficulties. However, by the time of their births Sharon and I were both wage-earners, able to purchase life-saving private neonatal care; without the clean hospitals, functioning respirators, on-call specialists there is a possibility that they too might have died. They would not have been alone. There is still a surprising amount of death attendant on birth. Reasonable estimates made by the Medical Research Council are that over 20 000 infants each year are either stillborn or die shortly after their attempted birth in a public hospital in South Africa. At the time when we lost our two children, one learned obstetrician tried to console us by telling us that 'two per cent' of births don't make it.

Cold comfort if you are part of the 2%.

But Ciaran and Aidan lived. From the get-go Ciaran was a child of our connections. Seen to birth by Paula McBride; named by Siobhan O'Hanlon, a colleague

Sharon, Aidan Nesta (named after the great Bob) and I, 2003.
Painful experiences of child loss taught us that birth really is miraculous.

of Sinn Fein leader Gerry Adams, a sparkling, laughing, serious young activist who died of cancer; fussed over in his early years by Zackie Achmat.

When Aidan's time came we were again stuck for a name. 'Aidan' was suggested by Jonathan Berger, the only instruction being that the name should have Irish roots. It means 'little fire'. Nesta, his middle name, was chosen by us. It ties him to the spirit of Robert Nesta Marley, keeping Bob forever present in our lives and hopefully his.

Both children unfolded the petals of their emerging characters to fill the empty spaces left by the would-be Joe and ne'er-to-be Caitlin.

During my years living on the bleak housing estates of Hackney I had sometimes wondered whether this dirty world was a place I wanted to burden my children with. Since those days I have witnessed living conditions that are far worse. Children have no choice. If you are born in Diepsloot, chances are you are born in shit. If you are born in Aleppo, chances are you are born into bombs.

But Ciaran and Aidan are children of fortune. From an early age, they were carried on paths into the Ukhahlamba Drakensberg mountains. After they learnt to tramp, we found a favourite haunt at a point where a stream runs down from Old Woman Grinding Corn, a mountain peak, slowly building a head of water that is then chiselled through ancient rocks at Marble Baths and becomes the source of the Injisuthi River. They have tasted the sea salts carried on the wind

that blows over the Wild Coast trails. *They travelled with us to the small moun-*
tain village of Nine Mile in Jamaica, the birthplace of Bob Marley.

Their lives are young and unmapped. They have quality education, choice and
opportunity.

I try gently to advise them. I try not to order or instruct. I learnt my lesson re-
belling against an intransigent father. I would hate to drive them away from a
belief in justice. There are many signposts in life. Parents are most important for
ethics. The best you can demonstrate to a child is love. I hope that they too will
understand that the greatest riches of life are not for sale, but are found in the
people, the places, the air, the water, the sea and the relics of our civilisation.[123]

The lonesome death of Dudley Lee

Textbooks and toilets were SECTION27's testing ground in education. The
first major test as to whether the ALP/TAC formula for public impact
litigation could be successfully applied to broader health issues came in
relation to tuberculosis.

TB is an ancient bacillus, estimated to have been with and in us for
over 70 000 years. Like human beings, its origins have been traced to
Africa. Over its long life it has felled many of us mortals and stilled the
great voices of a few immortals – John Keats, George Orwell and a whole
branch of Brontës. However, in the twentieth century medicine and better
sanitation have put it on the retreat. It used to kill indiscriminately. Now
it has sneaked away to dark corners of society where it continues its
rampage relatively undisturbed.

Prisons have always been breeding grounds for TB, whether they be in
America, Russia or South Africa. Wiser governments have recognised that
even if they don't care about the human rights of those in their prisons,
there is a public health benefit in preventing prisoners from contracting
or spreading TB. For example, in New York a programme of vigorous TB
screening and treatment in prisons in the mid-1990s caused a 66% drop
in active TB cases and was linked to a decline of TB incidence in the
general population.

I doubt that any prison is pleasant, but South Africa's prisons are bar-
baric. Approximately 160 000 people live in 240 prisons, 50 000 of them
awaiting trial. Many are held captive for months for lack of a paltry sum
set as bail. For many the penalty for petty economic crimes of poverty is
to be placed into a parallel dog-eat-dog world of gangsterism, rape and
infectious disease.

To have some sympathy with the plight of the prisoner you have to be or have been one. Thankfully I have been imprisoned only twice in my life. The first time is a matter of pride. In 1985 I spent six hours in an Oxford police station after being arrested at a student protest that aimed to prevent Margaret Thatcher from entering the gates of All Souls College to deliver a lecture. The second time is an experience I am coy about.

It requires a confession.

In early 2015 I was driving home from a relatively sedate dinner party at 10 pm on a Friday night. My route took me past Diepsloot, an informal settlement on the northern outskirts of Johannesburg. That evening the police had set up a roadblock on the edge of the township, anticipating a shoal of drunken drivers on a pay-day weekend. This was like placing a fishing net in the middle of a run of sardines. Fair enough. But rather than enforcing the law or protecting public safety, the primary objective of the roadblock seemed to be the illicit earnings that could be gathered through bribes.

I drove into the net. Then things happened so fast it could have been a hijacking. Like every other passing driver I was stopped and told to blow air into a yellow tube. Within seconds of doing so I was told that I was over the limit and pulled from the driver's seat – and suddenly I found myself the passenger of an unidentified policeman in my own car.

I was arrested and initially held at the nearby Diepsloot police station with about 30 other hapless fish. We each had our blood taken and were left in suspense as to what would happen next. I ended up lying behind the booking-in counter for the next three hours. Then at 2 am I was bundled into a police van and taken with six others to an unknown destination. Our police drivers were reckless and appeared drunk. Peering into the front cab, I could see the speedometer touch 140 km/hour. I gripped my seat fearfully as the police van ran a string of red lights. Then my cell phone battery ran out.

After half an hour we arrived at a bigger police station, Randburg, in Johannesburg. We were told that if there was no room in the cells there we would continue our journey to the notorious 'Sun City' prison. Thankfully there was room at the inn.

At Randburg police station we stood in an open courtyard for an hour. The sky began to grey with the dawn. Incoming detainees were humiliated and laughed at. Those who had enough money to hand – the asking price was R1 000 – paid bribes and slunk away into the night. I had never felt so powerless to circumstance. Policemen leered, bullied, ridiculed and threatened.

After our stint in the courtyard we were processed for a second time. Cell phones, belts and shoelaces were removed. Those of us without money for bribes found ourselves in an overcrowded cell. In its recesses was an open toilet. Shit was smeared over the walls. The obligatory filthy grey blanket was to hand.

I tried to sleep. But I wondered how it was that as an empowered human rights activist I felt so insecure and afraid. Then I realised a paradox: I was in the hands of the law but there was no rule of law protecting me.

Hours inched by. Brown bread and a beaker of tea were pushed through the bars in the early morning. As we waited, the shoal of now sober drivers began to establish a camaraderie. Only at 10 am that morning did the Diepsloot police arrive to do the paperwork that was a prerequisite for our release.

At last the cell doors were opened onto a courtyard. Thirty men and one woman formed a weary line, each waiting our turn with the arresting officer. Well into the computer age each statement with each person's details was filled in manually. Three times, in triplicate. To crown it all the policeman had the longest, slowest signature I have ever seen in my life. It must have had twenty loops, each one narrowing slightly to the final purposeful dot that marked the signature's end. Three times thirty.

I waited my turn anxiously: with the passing of the hours came the danger of another night back in the cell. It was slow torture. My time at the front of the line did eventually come. At around 5 pm the sluice gates were opened. Our exit felt triumphal.

The next day we had to appear in court. New-found friends refound each other, all the better for a shower and a sleep. This time the paradox was a different one. Each accused, most more vulnerable than me to the adverse consequences of a criminal record, was being asked by a crooked prosecutor to sign over their bail to him. In return he would see to the disappearance of their charge sheet. Of the 30 drivers I was the only one who turned down my get-out-of-jail-free card.

I make no excuses for myself. Drinking and driving is a criminal offence I won't repeat.

But allow me the purpose of this reflection.

I was caged in the cell itself only for eight hours. But in those hours I felt my nominal rights slipping off me. I had a glimpse of prison life that I would never want to repeat. I experienced how easy it is – without money and without concerned friends organising lawyers on the outside – to slip into the nether-world of the awaiting-trial prisoner. This was the world that the late Dudley Lee inhabited and that tens of thousands still inhabit.

The case SECTION27 got involved with concerned one such rather sad man called Dudley Lee.

For nearly five years, between 1999 and 2004, Lee was a prisoner in a prison called Pollsmoor, pressed up against the edge of the mountain near Muizenberg outside Cape Town. Pollsmoor was where Nelson Mandela had spent six years after leaving Robben Island. From the outside it could not be more beautiful, but its pretty surrounds and famous alumni hide another story. It is 300% overcrowded and run by gangs.

In April 2015 Pollsmoor was visited by Justice Edwin Cameron as part of the judicial prison-visiting programme. Cameron is not given to exaggeration but was moved to write in his report: 'The overcrowding is extreme. To know, statistically, that there is 300% overcrowding does not prepare the outsider for the practical reality. Again, with understatement, it can only be described as horrendous.' Words like degrading, hazardous, filthy, cramped spill off the pages of his report. According to him, 'the thickness of the air and lack of ventilation was palpable'.[124]

Many of South Africa's leaders have been prisoners, possibly more than any other government in the world. That may be why prisoners' rights are recognised and well protected in Section 35 of the Constitution. After all, ours was meant to be a humane society. But memories are short and there is little appetite and fewer resources to protect prisoners. Violent crime in South Africa is prevalent so there is little sympathy for those criminals who end up behind bars. We may have saved them from the death penalty but they are not protected from torture.

Small civil-society organisations like Lawyers for Human Rights and the Wits Justice Project do their best to expose the horrific conditions to which prisoners are subject. But for the most part, if you fall on that side of the law, well . . . forget it. You're on your own.

This was the space Dudley Lee inhabited.

I have a feeling Lee was born a victim. He struck me as one of those hapless people who are forever at sea in the world. Born to be buffeted. After four years he was acquitted on charges of fraud and set free. But while doing time for something he never did, he contracted TB.

Maybe he had one stroke of luck. One day, while waiting in the holding cells of the Cape Town Magistrates' Court, he bumped into a lawyer who referred him to another lawyer who later became his lawyer. His accidental encounter with one of the rare breed of public interest lawyers started a damages claim that focused on the failure of the Department of Correctional Services (DCS) to fulfil its constitutional duty to take proper steps to protect Dudley Lee from TB. The case ended nine years later in the Constitutional Court.

SECTION27 became aware of the Lee case somewhere between the judgment of the Cape High Court in February 2011, which Lee won, and the appeal in the SCA in March 2012, which he lost.

As I have told you, law can be a game of chance. Volumes of law reports, precedents, checks and balances are not failproof. It is not unknown for the subjective prejudices of a judge to overpower the written word, which, after all, is fairly defenceless and vulnerable to manipulation. Words have no armies with which to defend themselves from marauders. Ironically, words can't tell their own tales.

After they lost at the SCA, Lee's attorneys had decided to abandon the case. A phone call from SECTION27 attorney John Stephens persuaded them not to, and a discussion ensued on possible grounds for appeal to the Constitutional Court and the prospects of success. We had decided that if we could persuade Lee to appeal, we would be able to play one of our favourite strokes of law, the amicus curiae. We did.

Thus it was that on 28 August 2012 Adila Hassim, representing the TAC as amicus, stood robed before nine of the eleven judges of the Constitutional Court. Once more the Court was filled with activists. Adila's job was to advance a novel legal argument. She needed to convince the Court that the interests of justice (a prominent pillar of the Constitution) required an ancient common-law principle of damages to be reframed in order to provide relief to Dudley Lee and potentially many, many other prisoners. Although we could not say that *but for* Lee's being in prison he would not have contracted TB, the probability was that it was the prison authorities' failure to take precautions that had caused him harm. Get your head around that!

It was a complex legal argument on the complex subject of delict. Lovers of legal reasoning would relish it. The lives of hundreds of thousands of prisoners hung on the 'but for' test. To many observers it might have seemed removed and academic. But this did not make the case less important for each one of the 160 000 prisoners in our jails. Each prisoner stood to benefit from a clear ruling that the state has a duty to do its utmost within available resources to protect them from TB. Indeed, given the universal respect for South Africa's Constitutional Court, the case was important for prisoners worldwide – at least those in countries that claim respect for the rule of law.

With Adila Hassim outside the South Gauteng High Court during
the hearings of the claims by mineworkers for damages for TB and silicosis.

On 11 December 2012 the Court handed down judgment. Lee's long
journey through layers of law courts was vindicated. The Court expressed sympathy with him, noting how he had been to court on more
than 70 occasions 'stuffed into vans like sardines' and placed in 'jam-
packed' cells. The majority of judges found that he had been harmed
and that the harm could have been avoided if the prisons had done
more to prevent TB. In not-so-august language they agreed with the SCA
that 'Mr Lee has certainly had a hard time of it'. They declared that:

> The Supreme Court of Appeal acknowledged that an effective pro-
> gramme [of TB prevention] did not exist ... If the proper process had
> been followed, this would not have happened. In my view, it is legiti-
> mate to draw the inference that this is also probably how Mr Lee con-
> tracted the disease.[125]

The Constitutional Court ordered that the case be remitted back to the
Western Cape High Court to determine the quantum of monetary dam-

ages Lee should be awarded for his suffering. Eventually he received the rather paltry amount of R270 000. Lee's legal team were awarded costs of over R2 million. We do not know what defending the case cost the state, but an informed guess would be that an amount of over R5 million was probably spent – a fat sum that could have been used to purchase photosynthetic lights or put in place other measures that reduce TB in confined spaces.

I met Dudley Lee only once. In early 2013 SECTION27 organised a seminar with several partner organisations to discuss the implications of the judgment and determine how to monitor its implementation. We wanted to popularise the judgment and to start to build public awareness that might ensure that the state acted on the court's orders. In a brief conversation Lee showed me two of his state-issue identity documents. One was from before and one after his five-year incarceration. They could have been a TB-prevention advertisement: the pre-prison Lee was ordinary and anonymous, the post-prison Lee skeletal, emaciated and with drooping eyes.

Lee was free. But there was little left of his life and little to brag about. His health was shot. The man I talked to was evidently proud of having taken a stand. There is little record of Lee's life before he became a prisoner: a veritable Mr Nobody. But he has bequeathed his name for all time to a judgment of South Africa's Constitutional Court. I would imagine that at a point too late in life he discovered that there is a nobility in self-sacrifice and standing up for human rights. At least he had a taste of it. Most people don't.

Dudley Lee died on 21 May 2014 at the age of 68.

Law is forever restless. It is a murmuring sea of words and unrevealed meaning, never still, never closed. Law knits the fabric of our societies together, but it remains the sum of its threads. Each thread of law has a history and point of origin, sometimes dating back centuries. Many threads dangle, waiting for a chance moment to be picked up again and woven on into the future.

In 2015 the ghost of Dudley Lee would surely have smiled when his name cropped up once more in another courtroom. The case had nothing to do with him. It was a matter of seeking damages from 32 gold-mining companies for generations of mineworkers and their families who succumbed to silicosis and tuberculosis as a result of silica dust in the mines.

A group of about 60 miners had applied to the South Gauteng High Court in Johannesburg to try to certify as a class the hundreds of thousands of mineworkers, their names and whereabouts at that time unknown, who had suffered harm as a result of contracting TB or developing silicosis due to exposure to silica dust. The right to take action as a class is important for poor people. A class action recognises that, while systemic unlawfulness may inflict harm on thousands of people, poverty, inequality and ignorance often conspire to prevent them from taking legal action to protect their rights. Class actions allow a few people to come forward and argue that they represent a multitude of claimants.

Notwithstanding fierce opposition from some of the mining companies, a two-week preliminary hearing on whether TAC and Sonke Gender Justice would be admitted as amici was heard in October 2015 and resulted in their admission. Adila Hassim and Jonathan Berger, briefed by SECTION27, led by a silk, appeared as counsel for the amici. Nonetheless we were bit players in a battle of legal titans. One day, as lawyer jousted with lawyer, the ghost of Dudley Lee shimmered above the bank of advocates arguing the mineworkers' case. His name was referred to by one advocate because of the precedent 'the Lee case' had provided in relation to the legal test for causation of harm in delictual claims.

As I heard his name I felt his ephemeral presence and a shiver ran down my spine.

Judgment was handed down on 13 May 2016.[126] On that day the court ruled that 'Current and former underground mineworkers who have contracted silicosis, and the dependants of underground mineworkers who died of silicosis' constituted a class. This permitted tens of thousands of people to sue for damages. When the court came to the claim regarding miners with TB, it said that 'the courts [had] developed the law by finding that the "but for" test is not the only method of determining the issue of causation'. So the TB sufferers and their surviving dependants too could sue as a class. It was a profoundly important ruling. It may ultimately benefit millions. One day a Hollywood film may be made about this case.

If only Dudley Lee had known . . .

10

Seize power!
Endeavouring to build an independent and effective civil society

Wonder Woman: Man made a world where standing together is impossible.
Bruce Wayne: Man is still good. We break things, tear them down, but we can
rebuild. We can be better, we have to be . . .
Batman v Superman: Dawn of Justice, Warner Brothers, 2016

The fourteenth of November 2016: it was a typical spring evening on the Johannesburg Highveld. Great banks of clouds which had gathered during the day burst and sprinkled their loads over Johannesburg. Streaks of lightning cut horizontally across the sky, strobing silhouettes across the landscape.

That evening I sat at a large round table in a century-old house once owned by one of early Johannesburg's Randlords. Most of these grand mansions have been demolished and only a few remain. They sit on a ridge where they can watch over the city. From such a splendid vantage point I had a clear view of Johannesburg's urban forest, a suburban sprawl that spreads north all the way to the still-unspoiled rolling hills of the Cradle of Humankind.

As the sun sank the reds and browns of dusk mixed up with the purples rising from the blooms of the jacaranda forest. The clouds bled into the purple forest, now catching sparks of a departing sun. The dusk twinkled.

I was looking out. Anybody looking in would have noticed a dozen or so people gathered under a dim light around the table. They would have seen – but not heard – an earnest and intense conversation. Followers of South African politics might have recognised Sipho Pityana, Barbara Hogan, maybe me.

Had that picture been captured in a photograph and printed in a newspaper, purveyors of fake news might have misrepresented it as evidence of the involvement of 'white monopoly capital' in a 'conspiracy' aimed at 'regime change'. Intelligence agencies would have had a scoop. In Zimbabwe, Angola or Uganda, for example, such a meeting would be labelled treasonous – enough to land those at the table in prison.

But the truth is it was anything but treasonous. It was only a disparate group of concerned South Africans using their constitutional rights to freedom of expression and association to plan the next steps in a campaign to #SaveSouthAfrica from a rapacious and corrupt President. It was a week after #SaveSouthAfrica successfully held a People's Assembly Against State Capture to coincide with the concocted charges of fraud being brought against Finance Minister Pravin Gordhan. The discussion that night revolved around what should be done next to galvanise South Africans to grasp the power granted them by the Constitution to bring about the resignation of our President, Jacob Zuma.

On 31 March 2017, President Zuma sacked the Minister of Finance, his deputy and several other Ministers. In response, #SaveSouthAfrica immediately sought to build sufficient popular pressure to bring about Zuma's resignation. Whether this popular movement will succeed or not, time will tell – but the attainment of social justice in our country depends on restoring democracy, accountability and constitutionalism. If we cannot do this soon, the next few years will be dark and hard. It will be a second liberation struggle.

My present has caught up with my past. The #SaveSouthAfrica campaign raises old and new issues in our unfinished journey to freedom. This latest journey has grown out of our efforts to free South Africa from apartheid; out of years spent trying to use our newly-won political freedoms to realise the Constitution's promise of equality and dignity for all. It finds itself in the story of my and many others' attempts to broaden activism beyond single-issue campaigns, and instead to try to corral, cohere and converge individuals and organisations into a united front for social justice.

It is the story of trying to reconstitute civil society as a political power in South Africa.

Civil society . . . These two words roll so easily off so many lips. Across the world greater and greater store is being placed by civil society to right a myriad of wrongs. Yet the concept of civil society is ill-defined.

Let me tell you what it means to me. Civil society is the plural for thousands, possibly millions, of independent organisations across the world that work for human good on a thousand different issues, in hundreds of different ways. In my view and practice, civil society must always be independent of government or any other power. Yet it is intrinsically pro-government. This is because government is necessary – ever more so – to regulate people, to contain private powers, to assist people to live in harmony with each other and to achieve social justice.

It's only anti-government when that government is authoritarian, corrupt or murderous.

Civil society upholds a vision of equality. It will not be beholden to an ideology or party. Independence is power.

However, what many political observers, particularly organisations that provide funding to civil society, do not appreciate is that work to cohere civil society, to make its actions make sense, is arduous and difficult. We swim upstream. Capitalism makes a virtue of encouraging people to fend for themselves. This has made much of society of necessity selfish and uncivil.

Civil society emerges from within that uncivil society. The bricks that are needed to make society civil again are made of human flesh, blood and brains. The bricks are human beings with foibles, petty jealousies, their own needs, ambitions. From my experience in organisations such as TAC I can tell you that constructing a social movement is not an exercise in piling inanimate bricks upon one another and adding a thin layer of mortar.

In lighter moments I think of this process as something akin to the way in which Yul Brynner patiently assembled his team of gunfighters to defend a village of Mexican peasants from marauding bandits in *The Magnificent Seven* – but without Elmer Bernstein's uplifting musical accompaniment!

Getting civil society organisations to work together, in an environment that operates to keep them apart, is a stop-start process. Get on board. But be prepared for a long haul.

Demobilisation and doing away with civil society

In South Africa there has been a precedent for a united civil society. When it was launched in August 1983, the United Democratic Front (UDF) brought together over 400 organisations that were already fighting apartheid, including civics, faiths, notably the South African Council of Churches (SACC), trade unions and NGOs. In its seven-year life the UDF was able to do much more to galvanise the discontent with apartheid than the efforts of the ANC in exile did. The UDF made apartheid unworkable and then, counterintuitively, it disbanded in 1991 to clear the road for the unbanned ANC. In February 1991 an internal commission presented its leaders with two options: either 'disband and give their support and help to the ANC' or 'continue as a civil society organisation helping with reconstruction and development'.[127]

It disbanded and, after that, organised civil society took a back seat in politics. After the democratic victory in 1994 civil society was further marginalised. On the other side of 27 April 1994 a handful of NGOs, such as Lawyers for Human Rights, the Legal Resources Centre, the Black Sash and the Centre for Applied Legal Studies, continued to operate independently. But most of civil society – the UDF leadership in particular – allied itself formally with the ANC. Many individuals took up positions in the new government, some went into business. According to Kumi Naidoo (whom I will come to in a minute), NGO came to stand for 'Next Government Official'.[128]

One or two people stayed behind. The South African National NGO Coalition (SANGOCO) was established in 1997. It grew out of the National Literacy Coalition. In a very different context its coming together seems to have been driven by the same striving for an independent political voice for civil society as the process I am about to describe. In the late 1990s the offices of the AIDS Consortium were in the same building as SANGOCO, and some of its buzz rubbed off on us. Under the leadership of Kumi Naidoo, its first Director, and Jackie Boulle, its Deputy Director, SANGOCO seemed to offer some hope.

Naidoo came from the frontline of the anti-apartheid struggle, deeply involved in community structures, the UDF and the ANC. According to him there was an expectation that SANGOCO, and civil society generally, would subsume itself in delivering services and programmes in support of the new government's Reconstruction and Development Programme (RDP), an expectation he did not disagree with. However, a number of unexpected and bitter clashes with the new government over policy issues served as a rude awakening and led to SANGOCO developing a principle of 'critical solidarity' with the government. However, the ANC wanted the solidarity without the criticism, and the attack on civil society was launched by none other than Nelson Mandela himself at the ANC's 50th National Congress in Mafikeng in December 1997. Using language that is strangely familiar, Mandela told the delegates:

> Many of our non-governmental organisations are not in fact NGOs, both because they have no popular base and the actuality that they rely on the domestic and foreign governments, rather than the people, for their material sustenance.
>
> As we continue the struggle to ensure a people-driven process of social transformation, we will have to consider the reliability of such NGOs as a vehicle to achieve this objective.

> The success achieved by many CBOs [community-based organisa-
> tions] based on the contribution of 'sweat equity' by very poor commu-
> nities, points to the need for us seriously to consider the matter of the
> nature of the so-called organs of civil society.[129]

This massive pressure worked against the SANGOCO project. Consequently, by the end of the 1990s its light too had dimmed. After Boulle
and Naidoo left in 1998 it became the shadow of an idea whose time was
gone – or maybe still to come.

So, in many ways TAC represents the first attempt to rebuild a politically independent civil society movement. In its early years Zackie
Achmat and I spent many hours deliberately building bridges between
TAC, COSATU and church organisations. Time and time again we had to
reassure COSATU leaders such as Zwelinzima Vavi and Willie Madisha
that civil society independence and opposition to anti-poor policies were
not 'counter-revolutionary' or 'anti-ANC'.

With hindsight it is possible to see how TAC's 1999–2002 mobilisation
to demand a national programme to prevent mother-to-child HIV transmission and our ultimate victory in the Constitutional Court provided a
fillip to civil society as a whole. In its wake have come a number of potentially powerful new movements and networks. Nevertheless, the new crop
of organisations that emerged still worked in silos and were politically
cautious. Many tried to find a space outside politics to operate. When they
couldn't find it, they imagined it and then took comfort in a disorienting
and debilitating apolitical neutrality.

Get used to it, there's no such space, dear friends.

'Regime change': the 2010 labour-civil society conference

When Adila Hassim and I decided to form SECTION27 in 2010 one of our
aims was to try to do more to re-establish coherence between the different parts of civil society. We sought to build partnerships and networks
around actual campaigns. We were aided by the fact that at its 10th
National Congress in 2009 COSATU had resolved to convene a conference
of labour and civil society. We had invited Zwelinzima Vavi to be one of
the keynote speakers at the launch of SECTION27, an experience which
may have influenced his rush to organise a labour-civil society conference
later that year. Thus it came about that in late October 2010 COSATU,
SECTION27 and TAC co-hosted 58 NGOs, churches and trade unions gathered together to discuss undeniable evidence of deepening inequalities.

The question was whether it was possible to combine forces to do something about it.

The conference was, as far as I know, the first time since 1994 that independent progressive organisations met in the same room. Among the delegates there was a feeling of deep disappointment, even betrayal by the government. It was palpable. If you'd touched it your fingers would have been singed. Delegate after delegate told sad stories of a failure to provide decent healthcare services, quality basic education and effective, democratic local government.

That was also the first time I heard such dismay about flagrant corruption. Politicians who made few bones about their rise to riches became lightning rods for anger. One such was Sicelo Shiceka, then Minister of Co-operative Governance and Traditional Affairs. It was alleged that he had spent over R1 million on personal travel expenses. Shiceka was one of the first politicians to be investigated and have serious findings made against him by the new Public Protector, Thuli Madonsela.[130]

Reflecting this discontent, the Conference Declaration stated presciently that 'corruption goes to the heart of social justice ... we need a civil society anti-corruption mechanism [which] should be a civil society owned initiative'.[131] Two years later discussions that started at the conference brought about the formation of Corruption Watch by COSATU and SECTION27.

The conference was held at the Birchwood Hotel on Johannesburg's East Rand. The Birchwood is a soulless expanse of halls and meeting rooms, purpose-built to meet the growing market for conference facilities. Conference centres are a bit like shopping malls. They are places for rote performance of platitudes. From the outside they look as if they are built to deaden emotion and imagination, and once you're inside you're in a vacuum. Paradoxically, this almost always generates a sense of power and possibility. This was a case in point.

After two days several ambitious resolutions and a ten-point plan were agreed to. Yet, as also happens with many such conferences, most of these lofty ideas came to nothing. Hot air aside, the real significance of the event was that once more civil society and the trade unions had begun to talk to each other and explore alliances.

Things that previously could not be said openly about the ANC were starting to be said.

Holding a meeting of partners of the 'tripartite alliance' without the leaders of the ANC and SACP was straying into uncharted waters. Many ANC leaders, particularly those who lived in exile, were heavily influenced by Stalinism. They are deeply insecure. They had never tolerated criticism within their own ranks. Critics were expelled (like my friends from the MWT) and sometimes even murdered.

Consequently the conference unleashed a torrent of anger from a paranoid ANC. A couple of days later an ANC National Working Committee (NWC) statement warned that the conference 'might be interpreted as the first sign in a step to implement regime change in South Africa'.[132] Vavi and I were accused of secretly planning to start a new political party. Parallels were drawn with Zimbabwe's Movement for Democratic Change (MDC), which in 1999 was established by the Zimbabwe Congress of Trade Unions (ZCTU) to challenge Robert Mugabe's ZANU-PF. Ludicrous and laughable as all this may sound, it was dangerous. To be accused of planning regime change makes you a legitimate target for investigation and manipulation by intelligence services and other parts of the political netherworld.

Yet, if truth be told, the decision not to invite the ANC was not intended as a snub. We simply wanted to create a space for debate free from defensiveness and accusations. We wanted to break the mould where at meetings like these a holder of high political office is always invited to speak and the delegates then sing the praises of what they know are men (and women) of straw.

For me the most important achievement of this conference was that it kick-started a renewed effort to coalesce civil society around the pole of social justice. It set the scene for a new contest of ideas about how to achieve social justice. It was a kind of civil society speed-dating session. It laid the foundation for further experiments in how to build civil society coalitions. Two new coalitions, Corruption Watch and Local Government Action (LGA), were conceived as a result of this foreplay. And after the ANC/SACP-generated sound and fury had subsided, SECTION27 had become a household name.

Predictably, within months most of those who participated had fallen back into our silos. Activists returned to work in single-issue organisations fighting isolated campaigns on issues such as gender equality, housing and education that were pared back from their social context. Except these issues are anything but narrow. They demand to be politicised.

Amandla! Awethu! Marikana and its aftermath

On 17 August 1982 Ruth First was killed by a letter bomb. It had been sent by the notorious apartheid spy Craig Williamson. First was one of only a

handful of ANC leaders in exile who resisted Stalinist ideological pre-
scripts. She was ardent in her belief in socialism and respected the need
for organisational discipline in the ANC. But she also believed this should
not be in opposition to debate and dissent. Had Ruth First lived, it would
have been interesting to see what role she staked out for herself in the
post-apartheid period.

In 2008 the Wits University Journalism Department established an
annual fellowship to remember Ruth First. The Fellowship usually cul-
minates with a public lecture on the anniversary of her death. In 2012,
the 30th anniversary, she was remembered instead with a day-long seminar. When I was asked to speak on one of the panels I felt immensely
privileged.

However, little did anybody know that the day before would mark a
watershed in South African history. On the afternoon of 16 August 2012
as I was driving in Braamfontein, chilling recordings of gunfire began to
cut across the radio-waves. Reports told of the shooting down of a group
of striking mineworkers at the Lonmin Platinum mine in the hitherto
unheard-of town of Marikana in the North West province. By the time
the dead bodies were tallied 34 striking mineworkers had died of police
gunshot wounds.

That day South African politics changed irredeemably.

A cloud hung over the opening of the Ruth First seminar the next day.
There was shock and disbelief. Obviously most of the delegates were
activists from the liberation struggle. Several senior ANC leaders were
among them. Deputy Chief Justice Moseneke was there to give the keynote speech.

My speech came in the second session of the day. I started it by asking
whether the killings were 'a terrible tragic aberration or whether they
pointed to something deeper'.[133]

For my input I had chosen to reflect on the relevance of First's seminal study of the post-colonial African state, *The Barrel of a Gun*.[134] The
book's title seemed eerily appropriate. In it First explores coups d'état
that had taken place in West Africa, a political phenomenon involving
capture of the state by the military through the barrel of a gun. In her
study she points out how coups usually occurred after the liberation
movement had failed to transform society, succumbing instead to gross
self-enrichment and corruption. I knew about coups from my childhood
in West Africa. They were talked about in white expatriate communities
as a feature of post-colonial life, an occupational risk of working in Africa.

For example, in early 1966 my mother had to return to England to give birth to my sister, Mandy, after 'the coup of the five majors' in January that year. This was Nigeria's first coup after its 1960 independence and led to a period of instability and, before long, to the Biafran civil war.

The centrepiece of my argument that day was that the nature of and motives for the coup d'état have evolved: while what First called 'the iniquity of politicians' remains a cause of instability, the capture of a state no longer requires its seizure by the military or by any armed group of men. The state can be captured by stealth. You can have a coup without the old accoutrements of a coup! This, I tried to persuade the audience, had already happened in South Africa, starting with the 1999 Arms Deal, when elected politicians had sold themselves and their influence to members of a corrupt and mostly faceless shadow world.

I'm not sure if I persuaded anybody. And little did I realise that 'state capture' would become a central theme in our politics in the years ahead.

What I also did not appreciate that day was how deeply felt the aftershocks of the Marikana massacre would be, how they would rumble on through South African politics for many years to come, how they would impact negatively and positively on SECTION27's project of trying to cohere civil society.

The Marikana massacre shattered a consensus that ANC muscle had tried to impose on our country – one many ordinary people wanted to believe in. This was that the ANC *alone* was tasked with 'the historic mission' to transform South Africa. The bullets of Marikana ripped through an illusion that the ANC was intrinsically benign and benevolent. It suddenly looked as capable of butchery and betrayal as the liberation movements First had analysed in her book.

The bullets also freed many people from the chafing chains of party-political loyalty. The chilling footage of the massacre played over and over on TV screens helped to dispel the notion that all is well in the Rainbow Nation. Liberated from a myth, people felt that now they had good reason to speak truth to power.

Around this time SECTION27 was once again trying to help coalesce civil society. Consultations were held with grassroots organisations across a number of provinces. They wanted in. A number of activists who had played a part in civil society many years before and retired hurt put their hands back up. So it was that in November 2013 we tried to kick off a new movement, one which – after much agonising – we had decided to call Awethu! the People's Platform for Social Justice. Awethu! would prove to be still-born. Awethu! was an idea whose time had not come. It didn't cohere as easily as we imagined. Something was missing.

With hindsight I can see that the problem was that we did not appreciate how profoundly Marikana had reshaped the socio-political landscape in South Africa. In our imagination Awethu! was going to be an organisation that would join fragmented and sometimes discordant civil society voices, uniting them in a harmonious choir for social justice. In my mind it would rally more people to appreciate the transformative power of the Constitution.

But unfortunately Awethu! was born in the spray of several more significant baby showers. These unforeseen births delivered raucous children who would tear up the post-apartheid political landscape and – at that moment – make a new civil society initiative seem less necessary.

The first midwife was the activist and academic Dr Mamphela Ramphele. Her blood is liberation-struggle red. In February 2013 she declared the ANC 'irredeemably corrupted' and announced a new political 'platform' called Agang. Agang would spectacularly self-destruct hardly a year later, but in the early months of 2013 Ramphele's dissident voice was fresh and seemed to resonate deeply across the land.

Hot on her heels came Julius Malema, now the bastard scion of the ANC, Jacob Zuma's baby Frankenstein's monster. In July 2013 Malema officially launched the Economic Freedom Fighters (EFF) at a rally within sight of the koppies where the massacre had taken place at Marikana. Malema and the EFF promised 'economic freedom in our lifetime'. This too resonated.

Finally, in the embers of 2013, NUMSA, the metalworkers' union, passed a resolution at a special national congress to launch a United Front that would be made up of a coalition of trade unions, faiths and civil society organisations. Although I didn't admit it at the time, the UF seemed to make irrelevant the Awethu! objective of marshalling and emboldening civil society voices to demand social justice. NUMSA, a far more powerful force, stole most of Awethu!'s clothes.

In early 2017 we closed Awethu! down. It was an anaemic and stunted shadow of what we had hoped for. It had shrunk to be little more than another NGO. Unfortunately – for reasons I will go into at the end of this chapter – much the same fate has befallen the UF.

Building a united and effective civil society isn't easy.

Farewell, Madiba

Nelson Mandela had been with me on my journey from the earliest days of my political consciousness. One of my first poems was written after looking over to Robben Island from the top of Table Mountain – a 16-year-old white boy with privilege and no inkling of how much Mandela and all he stood for would become integral to my existence.

Mandela died on 5 December 2013. He had had 95 years. Despite enduring slings and arrows, outrageous misfortune, he had outlived most of his captors. After ten days of weeping, wailing, railing, reflection and then reorientation to a world without Mandela, what people call his 'mortal remains' were moved from Johannesburg to his ancestral home in Qunu in the Eastern Cape province of South Africa.

A ceremony to bid him farewell was held at the Waterkloof Air Force Base, on the outskirts of Pretoria. Like millions of others I sat rapt watching the service unfold on television. A rogues' gallery of South Africa's nouveau riche had tickets to sit alongside his real friends and comrades. But this could not denude the event of its pathos. The death hymns of the liberation struggle, 'Hamba kahle, um-khonto' ('Go well, soldier') and 'Senzenina' ('What have we done?'), rumbled and unravelled, filling the space of the hangar.

As the crow flies the air force base is a few Highveld hills away from my home. I watched Mandela's coffin as it was rolled out onto runway, lifted deli-cately into a plane. I watched the plane taxi and take off. I watched the cameras trailing it as it disappeared further and further away into a blue sky.

At the same moment that the plane disappeared from view a low humming, droning sound crept into earshot. I stepped away from the TV and saw Mandela's plane and its two escorts fly slowly above my home. I stood amidst the bird chatter and followed their flight onward into the distance. The three planes formed a triangle shape and drifted slowly out of sight. I stood until the black dots had faded into nothing.

That really felt like a goodbye.

I felt I knew this man better than my father. The closure was more complete.

Combating hate: xenophobia and its aftermath

On 15 March 2015 Goodwill Zwelithini, the Zulu king, told a meeting of his subjects in the rural town of Pongola that foreigners were to blame for much of the moral decay and crime they were experiencing in their communities. He exhorted his followers to 'fix what troubles us, take out lice, fleas and put everything in the sun for the heat to take out what's needed'.[135] Within hours a new wave of murderous xenophobia had broken out in several communities around Durban. Over the following weeks the attacks continued, mainly in the Durban area, but there were threats that, once again, the violence would spread across the country.

As I have explained, during the first outbreak of xenophobic violence in 2008, the civil society response in Gauteng (where it was at its most hateful and murderous) was inadequate. This (you may remember) had been a major cause of the tension between Zackie Achmat and myself. I think that somewhere deep down I wanted to make amends for my part in our omission. So, somewhat fortuitously, on 15 April 2015 I had a prearranged chat with Zwelinzima Vavi. We met on the edges of a conference on socialism being organised by NUMSA – once again at the Birchwood Hotel. Vavi was late, so I sat in on the conference for an hour. The speeches harked back to my days in the MWT. It was as if nothing in the world had changed. It felt, sadly, like a religious gathering of ageing proselytes.

Once Vavi arrived our talk quickly homed in on how to halt the xenophobia. He suggested that a mass demonstration would be a powerful way to show another face of South Africans, one that was welcoming and understanding of migrants. An hour later I got in my car, switched on my phone and set the plan in motion. I discovered civil society was better prepared to respond this time. The networks we had formed for Awethu! were dormant but they weren't dead; they made it far easier to contact people and float the idea of a mass march.

In the following days the SECTION27 offices became the hub of an ad hoc organising committee of activists from diverse backgrounds. Migrants from the African Diaspora Forum (ADF) and the Consortium for Refugees and Migrants in South Africa (CORMSA) played a leading role. Together we appealed to people to join the march in a language that was inclusive and energising. Together we advocated equal rights, respect for diversity, protection of Africa's common culture, solidarity and equality. Together, we encouraged people to invoke their own power, agency and solidarity.

We called out to people to reimagine the country we want to live in. And to demonstrate against the one we don't.

Sadly, as is so often the case, the stormtroopers of petty factional politics did what they could to block the march. Because of the involvement of Zwelinzima Vavi and NUMSA, the SACP, COSATU and parts of the ANC called on their members not to participate. They even planned rival marches! But these bodies have less hegemony than they imagine. Ordinary people will respond to politics when it's in their language. Our efforts were generating an excitement and belief in the march. You could feel it in the air.

At the last minute the Premier of Gauteng, David Makhura, contacted us to offer his full support. The night before the march a hasty meeting with the Premier and his staff took place. They promised to provide a stage, a sound system and hundreds of marshals from community policing forums.

On 23 April 2015 protesters began to gather at an inner-city park. I watched as they just kept coming. Then we spilled out of the park and onto the streets. This was the warm heart of South Africa. The marchers were an impromptu carnival of solidarity. Bands played, a real rainbow of peoples gathered under different flags, hand-made posters proclaimed people's deepest feelings. As we squeezed through Hillbrow the occupants of abandoned blocks of flats – many of them migrants – waved and clapped.

I felt hope, a glimmer of possibility, a joie de vivre in the discovery of others. So did many others.

The police estimated that 30 000 people marched. That night the international news networks, CNN, the BBC, the lot, fed it into homes all over Africa as well as to people in Asia and Europe. Images of hatred were displaced with images of community. Respected Cameroonian academic Achille Mbembe painted the picture for his followers on Facebook:

> ... children (and I mean children) carrying placards proclaiming our common belonging to a common humanity; school kids in their uniforms riffing on older, slower hymns with a faster, energetic and combative tempo; thousands of young people of all genders and sexual orientations bringing the street to life; anti-xenophobic chiefs wearing their best outfits; women of all ages, colours and professions; old veterans of earlier struggles beaming with joy and vigour, happy to be back in the arena and throwing their fists in the air.

As Mbembe said, 'It was as if South Africa at its best was back.'

The hastily convened People's Coalition Against Xenophobia (PCAX) had pulled off one of the biggest marches in the post-apartheid period. We had done so in eight days. In my view civil society once more demonstrated its potential power, this time its power to wash away artificial borders and hate. It revealed a possibility that is largely latent. It will come out of the bottle when summoned, but only if a language is used that sparks a sense of hope. Otherwise it sulks. I won't claim the march stopped the xenophobic attacks, but it did draw a very bright line between decent people and thugs.

After the march we had hoped that the PCAX would live on beyond its initial purpose. It didn't. Within a month people had demobilised, back to their pet struggles. But as with Awethu! the PCAX left the high-water mark of what can be achieved by civil society working together a little higher up the beach.

The next bona fide attempt at alliance-building could start from there . . .

Overcoming division: #UniteAgainstCorruption and state capture

As I've already mentioned, the COSATU/SECTION27/TAC conference in 2010 was the first time that I really noticed the depth of anger about corruption. At about the same time an investigative journalist, the late Mandy Rossouw, had uncovered and published the first evidence of massive state expenditure on the private homestead of President Zuma in the village of Nkandla in KwaZulu-Natal.

Over time 'Nkandla', as the scandal came to be known, grew to symbolise the corruption of the Jacob Zuma administration. Details emerged, drip by drip, of expenditure of over R250 million of public money. It was a slow-burn crisis. The media exposed it, the President laughed and made light of it in Parliament, the Public Protector investigated it. Then in March 2014 she issued her weighty report, *Secure in Comfort*.[136] At that point the executive and the ANC-controlled Parliament went into overdrive to cover up for Number 1.

In May 2015 – over a year later – Nathi Nhleko, the Minister of Police, told Parliament that a government investigation of the Public Protector's report had contradicted its most damning findings and found that allegedly nonsecurity-related improvements were in fact security-related. The 'investigation' decided that what she considered to be a swimming pool was in fact a 'fire pool', that the chicken run was a device to keep animals away from security systems and that the amphitheatre was an emergency assembly point.

#UniteAgainstCorruption was not born in the Birchwood Hotel. Instead it started in a bunker-like meeting room in the basement of the NUMSA offices in central Johannesburg, where various strands of civil society met to weave the narrative for a new campaign. Present were church leaders such as the Anglican Bishop of Pretoria, Jo Seoka (whom I had first encountered at Wilgespruit in 1983); dying-hard socialists from the MWT (now called the Democratic Socialist Movement) still trying to push their Marxist newspaper, now renamed *Izwi Labasebenzi*; and social justice activists from TAC and Equal Education, people (like me) who have unhitched the quest for social justice from ideologies and moored it instead to the Constitution and the human rights it promises.

At times it feels as if the suffering public have resigned themselves to political profligacy. But in response to Nhleko, the outrage barometer had rocketed to record levels. It seemed that not all the blue waters of the fire pool were enough to douse public anger. Temperatures rose, talk radio stations buzzed at white heat, anger became tangible. Nkandla seemed to be the bridge too far. On the back of this wave the #UAC (as it became known) decided to organise a mass protest march to the Union Buildings, the seat of the Presidency. We dreamed of 'a million' people marching. We compared the ANC's corruption denialism to AIDS denialism, warning that it carried a similar price tag.

Although the issue was simple enough, the campaign was not. Right from the beginning there was haggling over the contents of a 'Call to Action'. Social justice activists were looking for a language that could strike a chord with millions of angry people and excite them enough to join the planned marches. Marxist revolutionaries (their label, not mine) on the other hand felt the need to spice the 'Call' with references to Lenin and the treachery of neoliberalism.

But we were all prepared to try. So between June and October 2015 the SECTION27 boardroom once more became a hub for efforts to unite civil society.

Emissaries were sent out to woo the Christian churches. On the 30th anniversary of the Kairos Declaration, a letter was written asking them to witness in the present-day corruption the need for a second 'Kairos moment' – the first having occurred in 1985 when several Christian churches resolved that their theological teachings required that they take a public stand against apartheid.[137] In a simple twist of fate the letter was hand-delivered to Allan Boesak and Frank Chikane, two of the founders of the UDF, at the famous Regina Mundi Church in Soweto.

After a meeting I had with the playwright Mike van Graan at the Franschhoek Literary Festival, artists were rallied and rediscovered their political voice. Over 600 artists, including such legendary writers as Zakes

Mda and Njabulo Ndebele, endorsed the campaign, developing posters, poems, pamphlets and a short drama.

By such means civil society was discovering traditions last seen in the UDF. Student activists joined the daily meetings. Churches were back in the same pen as trade unions. NGOs were working alongside social movements of the poor. There was energy and intention. Something was happening . . .

There was much that was positive about the #UAC. It helped corruption to become a national talking point, debated on radio stations, dissected in the media. Civil society began to cajole business leaders (including Sipho Pityana) to take a stand on social issues. A request was submitted to Nedlac for a protected general strike.

But ultimately the campaign delivered less than we promised. The plan had always been that it should climax with mass marches, whose sheer numbers would announce the coming-out of a more united civil society. However, the marches were postponed several times, thus losing the momentum. On 30 September 5 000 people marched to the Union Buildings. In Cape Town about 7 000 marched to Parliament. On 14 October NUMSA and other unions led a workers' march through Johannesburg.

The marches were vibrant and energised. But there was no getting away from the fact that they were far smaller than we had hoped for.

There was a bright side. It was unprecedented to see so many civic leaders on a march that had been denounced by the ANC. We had set up a tent on the steps of the Union Buildings. In it you could see political-party leaders, including Julius Malema, Bantu Holomisa and Terror Lekota, trade union leaders from all three federations, and Christian, Jewish, Muslim, Hindu and many other brands of religious leader. Deride it as they would, the ANC could not ignore it, and the Minister in the Presidency, Jeff Radebe, came down to graciously accept the memo in the face of a rude and uncompromising roasting from Julius Malema who had stolen the stage moments before.

But a cold truth was that church leaders were present but not their flocks, trade union leaders but not their members. Only a small number of citizens joined spontaneously. Why?

For me, #UniteAgainstCorruption was a qualified success, a few more steps on the road to a more unified citizenry. Compared to Awethu! and PCAX the number of civil society organisations working with each other had increased. By October 2015 more people from more constituencies were haltingly defining their post-democracy vision, shaking off distrust and beginning to be a part of each other's struggles.

Our own worst enemies

Two questions keep me awake at night.

How can it be that when so many people know what's wrong with our country and the world – when there are so few people who defend the status quo – we continue to career down a path to destruction?

What holds us back from building organisations that will bring social justice and equality?

From experience I know that people's power is built on trust. It's built when people focus on winning a tangible good that will improve other people's quality of life. And your own.

Paralysis occurs when people try to jump the possible in order to reach the impossible, to use other people's desperation to try to win points in the game of politics. For such people politics is mostly a game of dethroning.

Distrust foments paralysis. It turns activists into naysayers and doubting Thomases. Paralysis takes hold when people allow differences that have been superimposed on the human being, such as our class or race or nationality, to blind us to what we have in common.

One of the greatest frustrations in my efforts to help build civil society has been the debilitating distrust between socialists and those who now invoke a more pragmatic, results-driven approach to social justice. This is derided as 'reformism'.[138] After the socialist wheat is sorted from the reformist chaff the amount of wheat that remains is minuscule. At times meetings of socialists resemble an aviary of peacocks, each one out to fluff its feathers and incanting Hail Marys to Karl Marx.

Such experiences have made me concerned about how ideology creates the fault lines that inhibit the convergence of people in a real united front for social justice.

I too am an anti-capitalist. But we socialists have failed. Let's admit it, for many years we lost our grip on reality. We saw nothing strange in our compulsive need to cull quotes from the twentieth-century Lenin to include in pamphlets about twenty-first-century corruption. Simple struggles for fundamental human rights like access to water, health or education – struggles that can be won – are rerouted into conflicts over complex concepts like the fight against neoliberalism and capitalism. We need workable alternatives. We need to be able to fire-up hope.

We often lose battles because of the way in which we talk to other people. Words are so important. Do the words we choose alienate or inspire? Do they dull or drive? Do we come across as irritating salespeople for a flaky ideology or catalysts for change?

In 1946 a world-weary George Orwell wrote an essay he titled 'Politics and the English Language'. Orwell lamented how '[o]rthodoxy, of whatever colour, seems to demand a lifeless, imitative style' and how 'political dialects to be found in pamphlets, leading articles, manifestos, White papers and the speeches of undersecretaries . . . are all alike in that one almost never finds in them a fresh, vivid, homemade turn of speech'.[139]

Let there be no doubt. Capitalism is a profoundly inefficient, immoral and dangerous economic system. Neoliberalism, through which we saw the almost complete unfettering of 'the markets' from restraint and regulation, was the logical progression of a world in which, in the early 1990s, capitalism appeared to have triumphed.

Make no mistake. Capitalism is an economic system that should have been controlled long ago.

That's not at issue. What is at issue is that so many worthy leftist initiatives are condemned to stillbirth by their leaders' desire to manipulate such campaigns to bolster alienating ideological claptrap, rather than to improve people's life on earth. The truth is the poor already have plenty of churches to choose from as they contemplate heaven. What they don't have is an organisation that has a realistic prospect of changing life on earth.

The Comrades Marathon between the cities of Durban and Pietermaritzburg has been run almost every year since 1921 and is one of the landmarks of South African society. I first ran it in 1996 and since then have run it another sixteen times. It has taught me that when you are on a long-distance race you measure success not just by when – or even whether – you cross the finish line. You attach equal weight to the arduous work that goes into the effort. There are moments of light and moments of darkness, moments when you enjoy human company and solidarity and moments when you are alone. You need emotional as well as physical fitness.

Our quest is also an ultramarathon. It started hundreds of years ago. Social justice will not be achieved in a year. Trying to put humanity back on a path to equality and dignity for all is an incremental process. Some of my friends called the anti-corruption marches a failure. I saw them as just one more mile on that journey.

Twenty-three years have elapsed since we won freedom. Today people whose dreams have been realised live side by side with others whose dreams are . . . dreams. A stark contrast exists between legal equality and lived inequality. The cheek-by-jowl lives of ultrarich and ultrapoor have created a society that is highly combustible. South Africa erupts like a rapid-fire volcano. At the moment most of its eruptions are spectacular, some beautiful. Some reveal the latent energy in our people, others our dormant creativity. Up to this point people have been demonstrating their desire for change by engaging in strikes, service-delivery protests and student rebellions. They challenge issues from racism to neocolonialism and fee increases. In contrast to greyer climes with greyer peoples, ours remains a mobilised, vibrant people. We are a country in flux, a country remaking its identity.

But the waiting time is almost up.

Saving South Africa

The latest chapter in our efforts to restore power to people began on 9 December 2015. It was a Wednesday. Weary South Africans were counting down the last few days to their annual summer holidays. Late that evening, President Zuma unexpectedly announced on television that he had 'removed' the respected Minister of Finance, Nhlanhla Nene, and replaced him with a largely unknown MP.[140] Shock, then anger followed. Senior ANC leaders claimed no knowledge of the decision. There had been a Cabinet meeting that day, but the matter was apparently not discussed there.

This was a putsch, a coup by any other name. Currency speculators pushed buttons. The rand did a nose-dive. Value evaporated.

What to do? The next day there were calls for mass protests. Despite year-end lethargy, a handful of UAC leaders pulled ourselves together again to announce and organise marches in Johannesburg and Cape Town on 16 December – the Day of Reconciliation. On 13 December public pressure forced Zuma into a humiliating reversal of his decision and the reappointment of former Finance Minister Pravin Gordhan. Despite this, such was the anger we decided to continue with the marches.

On 16 December what became known as the #ZumaMustFall movement flared brightly – but controversially. In Johannesburg the march across Nelson Mandela Bridge attracted thousands of people. The march was racially diverse, the mood defiant. Among those who were there a sense of rising civic power pervaded. In Cape Town a similar march drew predominantly white people onto the streets. The day after, almost every newspaper in the country featured the marches.

Surprisingly, though, the marches also caused divisions within civil society. Some of civil society's most important allies, NUMSA in particular, didn't participate, arguing that it didn't matter who was the Minister of Finance – 'the real enemy was capitalism and neoliberalism'. Then, as if to confirm a self-fulfilling prophecy, the marches were portrayed as predominantly an uprising of moneyed people (black and white), people primarily concerned with their bank balances in the face of a falling rand.

These criticisms were inaccurate and unfair, but they stuck – for a while. I penned an angry article to try to set the record straight.[141] It elicited a volley of vituperation, much of it focused on my race. I chose not to read the attacks. Thus ended 2015, with me feeling somewhat demoralised and deflated.

Civil society down, apparently divided. But not out.

Is activism futile?

Sometimes as I sit through my umpteenth meeting of TAC or SECTION27, more recently of #SaveSouthAfrica, I can't help wondering whether we are making any progress, or whether activism is ultimately futile. I hear the same old themes recur again and again. Old voices and new voices struggle with old issues of inequality and injustice. I witness organisations divided around personalities. I have become an expert observer of the best and worst behaviour of activists.

In 2016, for example, SECTION27 made its best efforts to prevent over 2 000 long-term psychiatric patients being moved from Life Esidimeni, a health facility where they received appropriate care and were stable. We failed. Government wouldn't listen. They saw us as the enemy. They lied in court. As a result more than 100 patients died horrible deaths at the unregistered NGOs they were moved to.

As a result of painful experiences like these, from time to time I wonder whether it's worth it. My conscience asks whether there's something I'm not seeing. Is it possible to rally humanity to stand up for human rights or are we wired to be selfish? In which case . . . but perish the thought.

For hundreds of years, day after day, individuals like me have done everything we can to advance people's rights. We notch up victories here and there, we better and save many lives. But it doesn't feel like the world is getting better. The data show it's getting worse.

All our efforts couldn't prevent the age of inequality.

At the end of his history of those who resisted World War I, Adam Hochschild conjures up an imaginary cemetery 'not of those who were confident they would win their struggle, but of those who often knew in advance that they were going to lose yet felt the fight was worth it anyway, because of the example it set for those who might someday win.'[142] He quotes Bertrand Russell as saying, 'I knew it was my business to protest, however futile protest might be.'

Their example remains important.

We live once again in a dangerous world; an un-brave new world; a planet of the powerful; we are prostrate before cruel bombasts shorn of empathy.

But blaming this world on the powerful is not good enough. It has arrived on our doorstep because millions and millions of good people, people who have some power, surrendered that power. It is time to reclaim that power.

When we surrendered that power we let go of our and others' destinies. We let the waves of politics carry us hither and thither – forgetting our imagination and empathy, powers of thought that make us different from sheep and other animals. Rather than capturing the world and forcing it onto a more humane course, we were captured.

The struggle for social justice can be enormously uplifting. But I admit it can also be exhausting and draining.

Often I feel very alone, very vulnerable. In recent years I returned to writing to try and change the world. People like my articles, some say I am a wordsmith. But I feel very uncertain about the words I send out into the world – including these.

After many years as an activist I am still frustrated and angry. 'What's wrong with you?' I want to scream at each leader who chooses to focus on our small differences rather than our large swathes of agreement.

Why can't people work together? I ask myself.

I hate the pettiness, the divisiveness, the selfishness that I must often witness.

I admit, there are days when I want to give up, succumb to a spreading sense of exhaustion, deep-dumbing depression. For many years whisky offered the fastest way to close down each day. I became a functional alcoholic. I gave up alcohol in 2016, to better manage the moments of despair.

As I get older the temptation to cut and run gets greater. My time on earth is diminishing. I am tempted to just enjoy life. I face no barrier of class or race or education. I have no dread disease or disability. I could choose to be another person, immerse myself in literature or theatre, trawling through our civilisations, laughing and loving.

I won't.

I won't because I've had the privilege of glimpsing the beautiful minds of our activists and writers, people who celebrate value and beauty – but who don't want to own it just for themselves. People who will risk murder or years of torture in prison cells to ensure that what they have seen and understood of the beauty of life is equally available to others.

The struggle for social justice may be long and arduous, but ultimately it is a struggle that will set you free.

I won't give up while I can run on mountain paths or read poetry, while I can still feel uplifted by Bob Marley's 'Redemption Song' or smile at the wry anger John Lennon expresses in 'Working Class Hero'.

I won't give up because my being human is dependent on my marriage to a *long line of writers, singers, composers, thinkers, and murdered and imprisoned activists.*

After all these years I still believe that humans are civilised and I still believe in the possibility of human civilisation. Surrendering that belief is not an option.

During the first few months of 2016 the political embers burned low until they were suddenly blown back into flame when, on 30 March 2016, the Constitutional Court handed down a unanimous judgment to settle the dispute between President Zuma and the Public Protector over whether her remedial powers were binding.[143] That day I was due to give a graduation address to Humanities students at the University of the Witwatersrand. On the spur of the moment I decided that a ringside seat in the Constitutional Court would be a fitting place to seek a bit of inspiration.

So there I was witness to one more moment in history. At 10 am all eleven robed judges filed in. Their faces were fixed in give-nothing-away expressions. They took their seats and Chief Justice Mogoeng Mogoeng began reading their judgment. Half an hour was all it took to divert the course of politics. A unanimous Court declared that the Public Protector is '. . . one of the most invaluable constitutional gifts to our nation in the fight against corruption, unlawful enrichment, prejudice and impropriety in State affairs and for the betterment of good governance'. It was an office to 'give even to the poor and marginalised a voice, and teeth that would bite corruption and abuse excruciatingly'.

The Court found President Zuma had 'failed to uphold, defend and respect the Constitution as the supreme law of the land' and had shown

2016:
Upholding the
Constitution in the
struggle to save
South Africa.

'substantial disregard for the remedial action taken against him by the Public Protector in terms of her constitutional powers'.

He had also failed to fulfil his shared obligations under section 181(3) of the Constitution because: 'He was duty-bound to, but did not, assist and protect the Public Protector so as to ensure her independence, impartiality, dignity and effectiveness by complying with her remedial action.'

Zuma was ordered to pay back (some of) the money.

This was history. A few hours later I tried to draw a link between what I had heard in the court with what I called the 'first green shoots of a new rebellion by students, one that has put a primacy on education and meaningful far-reaching non-racialism'. I affirmed the importance for all of society of tertiary education, particularly in the Humanities, and quoted one of my favourite writers, J M Coetzee, on how 'indispensable to a democratic society – indeed, to a vigorous national economy – is a critically literate citizenry competent to explore and interrogate the assumptions behind the paradigms of national and economic life reigning at any given moment'.[144]

But somehow my speech missed the mark. I didn't feel I connected with the students or their parents. Perhaps that's the nature of keynote speeches at graduations. Everyone's mind is elsewhere. Mine was too. I was already planning a meeting that evening of the hastily reconvened #UniteAgainstCorruption coalition.

A day later I was back at the Constitutional Court, this time for a press conference that we had called on its steps. Present were trade-union, church and civil society leaders. They were joined by several well-respected heroes of yesteryear, including Cheryl Carolus, one of the founders and first General Secretary of the UDF, Mavuso Msimang, once a member of the High Command of Umkhonto we Sizwe, and 'red' Ronnie Kasrils, one of the last of a generation of heroic activists, who embodies the values of the ANC's underground struggle against apartheid.[145] The Court's judgment had emboldened these stalwarts to declare 'SeKwanele' (enough is enough) and call on President Zuma to resign.[146] At their feet was a scrum of national and international media.

I wasn't a speaker. I was still smarting from the 'white agenda' accusations. I didn't want my presence to become another titbit for social media trolls. As I stood in the shadows I felt a little teary and overwhelmed, perhaps because it was a blustery day with sprinkles of rain. But it was more likely that the moment felt like initiation day for the

Constitution: recognition of the pre-eminence of the Constitution was something we had struggled to have popularly accepted since the earliest TAC campaigns. Now, as a result of the Nkandla judgment, that little booklet had been brought out of the wilderness and onto the streets. Talk of its power was on a million lips. Very few people questioned its authority or power. Not even the President.

I slept better that night.

President Jacob Zuma is not a democrat. He is a hybrid of chief, spy and strongman. Knowing this makes it naïve to imagine he will be responsive to democratic norms. He has used his power to enrich his family and his faction. He must therefore protect himself (and the extensive clique that has captured parts of the state during his Presidency) from possible prosecution. He will pay lip service to the Constitution, but he defiles its spirit.

The call on Zuma to resign thus fell on deaf ears. Instead Zuma offered a half-hearted apology admitting only that 'the matter has caused a lot of frustration and confusion for which I apologise on my behalf and on behalf of government'.[147] The same day the ANC 'welcomed and appreciated' his apology, deciding that there was 'no intention on the part of the President and ANC Members of Parliament to deliberately act inconsistently with the Constitution'.[148] It promised to consult its members on whether or not to accept this apology. Only one province, Gauteng, was principled enough to recommend that the President stand down.

Stalemate.[149] In the months ahead, civil society once again floundered. Once again we found ourselves too weak and too fragmented to make good our demand. Another bout of inertia settled in. NGOs went back to what they know best: providing relief to the victims of a failing state.

Then an unanticipated voice broke the silence. It came from Sipho Pityana. Pityana is a former ANC and government leader of enormous pedigree. He had started his political life as a student activist and comrade of Steve Biko. Since the early 2000s Pityana has been in business and now chairs AngloGold Ashanti. On 23 August, out of the blue (or so it seemed), he used his address at the funeral of another ANC leader, the Rev. Makhenkesi Stofile, to speak with an unusual directness and passion about why Jacob Zuma was unfit to be President.[150] The speech struck with the power of a thunderbolt. In my view it marks the beginning of the #SaveSouthAfrica campaign, although nobody – Pityana included –

knew that. At the time many people commented on it as a watershed, although what was on the other side of the watershed was unclear. When I saw a YouTube recording of Pityana's speech, I posted it on Facebook, asking:

> Is this the beginning of a serious fight-back against corrupt ANC leaders from within? Rubicon I. Recommend you watch every minute. Ironically, it reclaims the tradition of the political funeral, except this time the regime that is being harshly and justifiably criticised is ours. Yes ours. Every rights bearer must take some responsibility for it.

A few weeks later I received an invitation signed by Pityana to attend a consultative meeting of civil society organisations. The meeting was to discuss 'the crisis point in our nation' and 'urgent action that is required to change the socio-political and economic trajectory'. I needed no persuading. I had a feeling of portent.

I was a few minutes late and when I walked into the boardroom of the Nelson Mandela Foundation I could see from those already seated that this might be the start of something. There were only 25 people, but I'd first read about many of them as a young virgin activist over 30 years before.

Since that meeting events have moved fast. First came the announcement in October 2016 that Finance Minister Pravin Gordhan and two former senior officials of the South African Revenue Service, Ivan Pillay and Johann van Loggerenberg, were being charged with fraud. In response, civil society mobilised. #SaveSouthAfrica was barely a month old but we pulled out the stops. On 2 November we organised a dignified, politically resonant 'People's Assembly Against State Capture' at St Alban's Cathedral in Pretoria. It was attended by a thousand people and watched live on TV by over a million.

Just two days before the Assembly, the charges against Gordhan were dropped – mainly as a result of the litigation instituted by the NGOs Freedom Under Law and the Helen Suzman Foundation, and the outrage expressed by the public. But it was only a stay of execution.

The axe eventually fell for the Minister just after midnight on 31 March 2017 when a 'cabinet reshuffle' was announced. Actually, it was an old-fashioned coup. The Zuma gang would not be stopped in their haste to rob the Treasury.

Within a day, #SaveSouthAfrica had a tent up in Pretoria's Church Square and an activist occupation started. More meetings, more mobilisation. More talking, persuasion, cajoling, introspection … Then on 7 April, 30 000 people marched to the Union Buildings to demand that Zuma resign – the biggest, most non-racial march since the days of marching against apartheid.

Those were tough days. There were moments when I loved people and moments I hated people. I saw the generosity of the human spirit. I saw its dark corners when a group of thugs from the ANC Youth League threatened us and claimed that I was party to the overthrow of Gaddafi of Libya.

But you have to push on. People do have power when they organise together!

#SaveSouthAfrica was the reason I was in a Randlord mansion looking out over a stormy Johannesburg on 14 November 2016. #SaveSouthAfrica is how I ended up typing these last few words in our tent on Church Square.

The #SaveSouthAfrica movement is a work in progress.[151] To my regret several campaign leaders described in this chapter have retracted support, largely because of ideology and flimsy political purism. My friend Zwelinzima Vavi, for example, talked about 'his nervousness about the class orientation of this campaign'. Others worried about an imaginary influence from 'big business', or complained about the prominence of individuals such as Pityana, ignoring the years he gave to the struggle, not getting to grips with his real character.[152] As we teetered on the edge of the cliff of state capture, NUMSA declared that it 'was not part of any of the political parties and organisations that are calling for mass protests against Zuma or for Pravin'. Their General Secretary Irvin Jim reasserted his ideological purity on behalf of the 'industrial proletariat' and promised instead 'the mother of all strikes over the government's decision to shut down 5 Eskom power plants'. His statement 'on the crisis facing the country', available at the NUMSA website, is a masterpiece of ideological fog worthy of a dissertation of critique on why some socialists will remain irrelevant to the real struggles of the 21st century. These 'radicals' are wrong. Their actions make them conservative. I call this scabbing.

Of course, only time and hard work will tell if this initiative will contribute to restoring accountable, honest government to South Africa, and to building an effective civil society. Success is not guaranteed. But it never is. However, sitting on the fence makes you dizzy. I know where I will always be . . .

11

Journeying the present – beliefs lost, values gained

Life runs into literature. Literature drips into life. 'Truth and illusion, George, you can't tell the difference,' screamed Martha – nine words I still remember from reading *Who's Afraid of Virginia Woolf* at school.[153] Words, sentences or songs often surface unbidden from some deep recess in my soul, putting their hands up like keen-to-please kids in a classroom. 'Miss, miss, miss, miss. Use me. Look at me.' Literature is a tonic for life.

Talking of the wonderful Virginia Woolf . . . trying to make sense out of my life's journeys made me remember Orlando, the man/woman whom Virginia Woolf created as the literary persona for *her* journey of fantasy and imagination between the sixteenth and early twentieth centuries. The androgynous Orlando consorts with kings, queens and authors. She visits Constantinople and plods the streets of London. Orlando's journey is a metaphor for Virginia's self-realisation, inventing locations and scenes in which she can reflect on and parody her own life's epiphanies in love, gender, politics, literature, class, women and sex.

In the years since her suicide in 1941 we have all become time-travellers. But, unlike Orlando's, the journey I have tried to describe in this book is not a voyage of the imagination.

I was always a punk but never a head-banger. For those of us who persist with our journeys along well-worn if outmoded paths that, we hope, will lead to social justice, now is a time to take stock.

I set off on my life's journey during the dying days of the post-World War II economic boom. I was travelling in England during the 'winter of discontent'; as a young boy I saw Thatcher survive the Brighton bomb, then later witnessed 'Thatcherism' morph into 'neoliberalism'. At the age of 23 I saw the self-immolation of socialism, the fall of the Berlin Wall and the start of the transmogrification of the USSR into a tawdry capitalism. I was around when Freddy Mercury died of AIDS in 1991. The year before I had heard the radio crackle out the news of the death of

Bob Marley. I lived before cell phones and after; before the World Wide Web, the internet and email. And I lived after.

As a child I accompanied my parents on their journeys through Africa. I was still a child when I fell in love with the people and places of the former colonies and decided to make them my home. I wasn't meant to do that. My love set me on a new path. In time it took me to a ringside seat at the fall of apartheid, then the realisation of the dream of freedom for people who had been colonised and oppressed on the basis of race for over 300 years.

I have travelled through wars. I huddled in a shack with Lennox, Dan, Philemon and others – members of an SDU who nursed Russian-made automatic weapons to protect citizens from terror in the heart of the Dark City. I helped to found a movement of people who have journeyed together through the deathly heart of the AIDS epidemic. I stood at gravesides singing the laments of loss for people who never had a chance to become:
Senzenina?

By the time I was old enough to decide where I was going, I thought I was on a journey towards a distant light of freedom, a Golden Fleece. Many of the sirens and harpies I encountered were slain. Stalinism, apartheid, the so-called Cold War . . . all have evaporated. They are caged now in literature, books of history or the imagination of artists. But their overthrow has not brought about the freedoms we thought it would.

By the time freedom arrived in South Africa, I had become an adult. I was still an adult when I saw freedom depart again.

2017 is a good time to cash up on 30 years of time-travel. What sense does one make of these journeys?

Is there any sense to be made at all?

During my lifetime one of the great journeys undertaken by science has been to build on the knowledge of the gene by sequencing the human genome.[154] Humans now understand the scientific base for heredity, what we inherit from our parents. But the deeper digging into the genome is also revealing our individual predisposition to illnesses through the identification of 'corruptible genes'. It is thought by some that DNA may even have memory, particularly of trauma.

However, knowledge of what it is that shapes our mind and consciousness still eludes us. As far as we know, the shape of our soul is not inherited. Nor are the beliefs that form within it. At birth our minds are a tabula rasa. The beliefs and values that our minds acquire are things we test, refine, adopt, reject, affirm.

When I set off on my journey it was with the deceptively simple belief that all people should be equal. Racism was wrong. Class inequality took a little longer to get to grips with. The discovery that not everybody thought equality and non-racism should be the natural order of things, indeed that there was resistance to this notion, hardened my own beliefs. The resistance required understanding and helped turn me towards an ideology: in my case the theories of Marxism. For ten years I employed Marxism, a very, very broad genre of political thought, as a driving manual. Marxism is both enormously helpful and enormously wanting. Karl Marx was a giant of philosophy and economics but, it is important to remember, there are many giants in the land of human thought.

I have been fortunate to encounter some of them, both in books and on the streets. The men and women we meet should cause us to constantly check our beliefs along the road. When beliefs get too rigid, when they start to shut out other emotions, they make us stop learning. Shining individuals like Nelson Mandela and Chris Hani revealed for me the power of literature as an animating force. Because literature is harder to encounter without access to education, they brought me back to the centrality of the right of access to quality education.

In 2016, during the #FeesMustFall protests, I sat one evening in late October in a mass meeting of students and civil society leaders in Solomon Mahlangu House at Wits University. I was in awe of the power of the words used by some student leaders. I witnessed the effect their words had on the raw emotions of the students. But I was troubled by the way words were used to steer away from the possibility of compromise and towards defeat and possible disaster for many of the young lives.

A day later, an understanding came to me that is not new, even to me, but that suddenly I felt I could articulate and that made deep, deep sense. It was 5 am. I was driving to the start of a trail running-race in the Free State. The last of the night hung in the air. It was light but not yet dawn. The great sandstone walls of the Maluti mountains were being lit, one by one, valley by valley, by an exploring sun. By pure coincidence I was listening to a Beatles song called 'The Word' from *Rubber Soul*.

> In the beginning I misunderstood
> But now I've got it, the word is good
> Spread the word and you'll be free
> Spread the word and be like me
> Spread the word I'm thinking of
> Have you heard the word is love?

At that moment I realised how essential it is that progressive politics be driven by love, the two must be inextricably intertwined if the people who arise as leaders of other people are to be trusted. This sounds corny. But it isn't. If the wellspring of a person's politics is their love of humanity, and of people, not ideology or anger, then they can be trusted to do the right thing in the heat of battle.

If not, beware.

Beware, because we are living in a time of rupture.

Times of rupture are times of foolishness, war, revolution or disintegration. We have miseducated ourselves into thinking that rupture always brings progress. Our belief that progress must inhere within human society is just that. A belief. Call it the teleology of getting out of the woods.

Increasingly I feel that we have arrived at a time when we have got to redesign everything, to question assumptions about our being that may have sufficed for hundreds of years. Angry students refuse to play by the rules, not because they are anarchists but because they dispute the legitimacy of the rules.

Could it be that since the advent of public education in the nineteenth century the powerful parts of the world have miseducated ourselves concerning 'beliefs' as fundamental as those we hold about gender, race, sex and sexuality, morals – and, as importantly, the rules and regulations we build around these beliefs?

What if History has taught us to look for the wrong things? Public education has taught two centuries of children that History is largely about remembering the names of the Big People, the dates of periods of rupture, the points when Father Time would no longer be constrained by contemporary laws of doing and regulating – even if those ways had sufficed for decades or centuries. We do not teach ourselves to identify and examine the currents that flow under the Big Names and Big Dates.

The Big People assert that the last 30 years have been a time of advance. On the contrary. We are journeying deeper and deeper into the time of disintegration.

When I left my cocoon in St Peter's School in 1982 it was at the end of a relatively long period in human society during which there had been a temporary flicker of hope. Then Conservative Party leader Margaret Thatcher was elected as the British Prime Minister in 1979. She wasted little time before garrotting hope. For 30 years laws and ways of living had entrenched a belief that class inequality should be ameliorated by ensuring quality basic services for all, including health, education and social security. Equality was considered an order we should all aspire to, providing some succour to the poor and working class not only in Britain but globally. But the notion of equality was considered by Thatcher and her Band of Merry Robbers to be a straitjacket on the rich, a system that constrained the further development of capitalist economies.

The little market was chomping at the bit. Chomp. Chomp. Chomp. It wanted to grow up and be the (big) Market.

I was there as Margaret Thatcher violently ushered in a cold post-Cold War-neoliberal-anti-equality world and changed the rules of the game. She removed those simple certainties that the poor of developed countries had been promised by the 'welfare state'. If the working class of the developed world had no such entitlement, then the logic that one day the poor of the South could also expect First World living conditions became ludicrous.

Thatcher and Ronald Reagan were luddites. Thatcher's depiction by the anarchist group Class War was closer to home than I imagined at the time.

Thatcher and Reagan may both be six feet under, but society is now paying the price for their extremism. We journey now through the era of man-eat-man and the devil take the hindmost. We are living in a time of inequality, economic instability, desperation, new forms of war. That's the name of our 21st century game.

The triumph of the Market necessitated the destruction of notions of solidarity and empathy, ethics that underpinned socialism. The so-called unipolar world, centred on the victor of the 'Cold War' and its economic

Margaret Thatcher on a
Class War poster form the UK.

system, temporarily destroyed the idea that there are alternative systems by which human beings can live.

For millions of people this destroyed hope.

My father was a banker all his working life. Even over domestic matters he had a puritan attitude to money. He didn't give it out easily. You had to earn it. But he died very disappointed in the Bank. Something had happened to money and banking that he didn't understand. The Bank's money put me through private school. Through the Bank I accessed a quality education and came to know of people like Chaucer who had lived centuries before me.

Geoffrey Chaucer's *The Canterbury Tales* is a ribald collection of stories written in the fourteenth century. They are told by a diverse group of mostly men journeying towards Canterbury on a pilgrimage. Like so much of literature, we were made to read the *Tales* at school long before we could appreciate their import. One evening the Pardoner, a man who by his own admission makes his money by exploiting religion for self-enrichment, tells his tale. His story is about Death and how three ebullient young men end up killing each other as they plot for sole ownership of the eight bushels of gold they had found under a tree. Centuries of English pupils have been asked to discuss the same question arising from this tale: 'Is the love of money the root of all evil?'

Five centuries later, in an era when almost everything has been monetised, this is an appropriate question with which to commence a planetary introspection. People like my father would say it's a non-question. Money just is, they will say.

But my journey for social justice has taken me to many places where money just isn't. The prospect of ever having any money has been withdrawn from hundreds of millions of people. While I was a student at Oxford one of the few gigs I ever attended was to listen to Billy Bragg, a troubadour of the resistance to Thatcherism, a made-in-England slimline equivalent of Bob Dylan. One of the songs Bragg sung that night was titled 'To Have and to Have Not'. The song laments the changing nature of capitalism and the dashing of youthful dreams, noting how 'At sixteen you were top of the class' but 'At twenty-one you're on top of the scrapheap', and concluding how . . .

I've come to see in the land of the free
There's only a future for the chosen few[155]

I had no idea that this was a lyric of prescience.

As a result of these changes, as I think my father understood, the old story about money just doesn't hold water any more. Being jobless means not having any money. Not having those little bits of paper cripples a person and his or her family.

In bygone days children of the developed world were brought up with the expectation that at the end of their education they would get a job, even if it was a low-paid one. That way they would earn Money. Full employment was the norm, not an anachronism. Now full unemployment is the norm. The last time I looked, in 2013 202 million people were unemployed across the world: 74.5 million of them were young people.[156]

But it gets worse. Of those who do work nearly a billion people (839 million to be precise) earn less than two dollars per day. They constitute 26.7 per cent of all those employed. Forty-eight per cent of them are in what is called 'vulnerable employment' with limited or no access to social security or a secure income.

The very idea of a 'welfare state' has crumbled. Everything has been monetised. So not having money means a return to King Lear's lament about those who live with 'houseless heads and unfed sides, looped and windowed raggedness'.

For many, not having money means not having a home or food. Endemic and ongoing hunger is normal. In 2014 12 per cent of the world's population – that is, 842 million people – were experiencing hunger 'in its most extreme form', according to the UN Special Rapporteur on the Right to Food. A hundred and sixty-five million children were 'so malnourished that they do not reach their full physical and cognitive potential; 2 billion people globally lack vitamins and minerals essential for good health'.[157] Never mind the foodstuffs needed by the soul. Hunger robs a person of autonomy. In the words of Tsitsi, the lead character in *Sweet Medicine*, a novel by Panashe Chigumadzi, young people's dreams of 'self-actualisation have morphed into stomach actualisation'.[158] Hunger is so 'normal' we've stopped seeing it. Yet there's no absolute shortage of food in the world. Yet.

That's a lot of misery and a lot of pain inflicted on a lot of people.

All because they don't have money.

The journeys that can't be told

There's one character I have left out of this journey. She is a continuous presence but one whose story can't be told. She is the love two people can find for each other and how this love lights up life's journey. Love is lit. It is sad that I can't unfold this story. Many other storytellers face the same dilemma. It's more than an absence. It's a calculated omission. As a result of this lacuna, this ellipsis, the love stories of public figures often end up being told by prurient others, denuded of their sensitivity, tied to pejorative and judgmental words like 'infidelity', 'affair', 'unfaithful'. Love leaves a hole in many autobiographies, an empty attic where biographers exercise their imagination to become fictionalists. Love is easier described in poetry, where it can be clothed in its essential ambiguity. Readers of poetry feel more refined. They don't need love to be given a name to appreciate it. But anyway, love defies categorisation. It is everything and its opposite. It's our most universal feeling.

The person whose love most transcends and infuses this journey is Sharon Ekambaram. During our many years together we built a home, built young people, built campaigns, drank from mountain streams, crossed river estuaries, felt horror and loss.

At the outset of our relationship, when we were first deeply in love, I told Sharon that I/we should never attach the word 'forever' to the words 'I love you'. I so desperately wanted to use them, so desperately believed in them. But I said we must avoid them. I refused to say them and by so doing said them. Our love has survived. But it is not the same love.

Love may be permanent or transient, a thing of years or a thing of forever. It may be entirely given over to and sated in one person, or it may bumble along trying to find and rediscover itself through experience of several people. It may be in hiding. The feeling of love will almost always arise innocently but the practice of love will sometimes be made to feel guilty. It may put you in the path of betrayal, or that is the word you yourself may reach for when a person you love leaves you before your love has expired. Love is our deepest and most consistent emotion, we can't 'teach' it, predict it or prepare for it. But we could do far more to understand it. Back in 1980 one of the first poems I wrote was to a girl called Sally Shuttleworth (I can name her without risk of embarrassment

```
IF I SAID I LOVE YOU .

IF I SAID I LOVE YOU
WOULD I LOSE YOU
WOULD YOU DRIFT FROM ME
LIKE A BIRD ON THE WIND
WOULD YOU TALK BEHIND MY BACK
CALLING ME NUTS
WOULD THE FRIENDSHIP THAT BOUND
    US
            SNAP ?

I'VE TOLD YOU I LOVE YOU
IN MY DREAMS AND MY PRAYERS
BUT REALITY REMAINS
A MOUNTAIN UNCLIMBED
TO FACE YOU WITH A STATEMENT
SO NATURAL AND PLAIN
COULD ENSUE, DENIAL, LOST FRIENSHIP
            INSULTS,
                        AND PAIN.

SO THAT STATEMENT REMAINS BURIED
IN THE FOLDS OF MY MIND
TO BE DUG UP IN FANTASY
AND A DREAM WORLD OF MINE
THAT GAP REMAINS UNBRIDGED
THAT MOUNTAIN UNCLIMBED
THAT QUESTION STILL BURIED
OUR FRIENSHIP
            STILL
                    FINE.
```

My first love poem.

now!). Girls joined our all-boys school only in the sixth form. Sally, who was one year above me, became a close friend. In my poem I tried to give expression to love's double edge. Thirty-five years later I still think I chanced upon some truth in that poem.

The 21st century is not yet eighteen. Many young people have lost hope. Older people have shed long-held beliefs. But all still strive for something profoundly different from their lot. No one can articulate it yet, or make it into an –ism. Yet by their actions they have shown that people are revolted and revolting. The new normal is abnormal.

Between 2006 and 2010 the number of protests in China doubled, rising to 180 000 reported 'mass incidents' in 2010. This trend has continued. Protests and strikes take place in different times and towns, against official corruption, land grabs, low wages, for Tibetan autonomy and against environmental degradation.

Even in the most oppressive theocracies people have attempted to dislodge the elites. The 'Green Revolution' in Iran in 2009–10 saw sustained – but ultimately unsuccessful – protests by millions of people against the rigging of presidential elections.

In December 2010 26-year-old Tunisian Mohamed Bouazizi set himself alight in an act of desperation and anguish. Bouazizi was not a leader or an adherent of any –ism. He was a street-trader. Yet millions of people identified with his anguish. They knew why he had killed himself, because there must have been times when they had thought of killing themselves. Their anger rippled, gathering momentum as it rolled across artificial borders. It was the beginning of the Arab Spring.

By December 2013, corrupt elites had been prised from power in Tunisia, twice in Egypt, Libya, and Yemen. Civil uprisings had erupted in Bahrain and Syria. Major protests had broken out in Algeria, Iraq, Jordan, Kuwait, Morocco, Sudan, Mauritania, Oman, Saudi Arabia, Djibouti, Western Sahara and the Palestinian territories.

Revolts have also spread within newly established and sometimes ancient democracies. In the last few years there have been mass demonstrations and uprisings in Brazil, Great Britain, France, Turkey, the United States, Spain, Greece, Portugal, Ukraine and Romania.

In South Africa 'service delivery' uprisings now occur at a rate of 50 a day, many of them involving violence by protesters and police. They have been aptly described as 'the smoke that calls'[159] – a way people are trying to draw political attention to the horrendous conditions in which they are forced to live. South Africa's uprisings are but a microcosm of the global striving for freedom.

All over the world people are flexing their muscles. The sans-culottes are bypassing the old forms of politics. People recognise that political institutions that worked in the past have been hijacked. Democracy and many democratic institutions are manipulated for self-interest by the people we now call the '1%', the ultracapitalists. A coup has taken place in many of the nations on Planet Earth. This coup did not need a military conspiracy, it has not required the physical seizure of power. Elite rule is the endgame of neoliberal economics, the logical outcome of Thatcherism.

While writing this book I journeyed into the writings of other contemporary writers. Looking for clues. One day I came across Carne Ross. Until 2004 Ross was an Establishment boy through and through. He is a thoroughbred of the British elite, a loyal servant and diplomat of the British Queen and Country. At the turn of the century he represented the British government on the UN Security Council. Around this time Tony Blair, the Prime Minister, had decided to go to war against Iraq. Blair was meant to be a Labour Party leader, a party that had traditionally opposed war. But Blair was using the Weapons of Mass Destruction alleged to be controlled by Saddam Hussein (so-called WMDs) as a pretext to launch a war. Through his work Ross realised that the WMDs didn't exist. He tried to stop the war with truth-telling but his leaders weren't interested. So he resigned from the Queen's service. In his words, 'I couldn't sit with the Prime Minister or Foreign Minister and do what I used to do for them.'[160]

Ross says it was then that he recognised how

> incredible and seismic changes of the late 20th and early 21st century
> have forced dramatic and sometimes revolutionary changes in almost
> every realm of human activity – finance, technology, culture – save
> one, politics . . .

Yet, he fretted:

In this most crucial forum, the institutions and habits acquired in ear-lier and different times have endured, even when their effectiveness is less and less evident. On the contrary, the evidence is accumulating that these inherited bodies and rules are less and less able to compre-hend and arbitrate the forces swirling around us.[161]

These words struck me with the force of bullets. Greased lightning. Yes. Shapes of economy, science, technology and communication have under-gone a revolution. But the political forms of a bygone age have remained the same.

In the late twentieth century political forms and institutions ossified, yet the twenty-first-century game of politics goes on as if nothing has changed. We persist in trying to make forms of social and political or-ganisation that we have inherited from the nineteenth and twentieth century work, even though they clearly don't. And they won't. They have become impotent or incompetent. The people who occupy high govern-mental office don't seem to care because they are conflicted. They are elected by the people but they must serve the Market. No bones about it.

The structures of the old politics are our parliaments and councils. Above them the IMF and World Bank, our United Nations. These are tan-gibles. The structures of the new politics are more opaque and amor-phous. They are found in the emerging elites of China, India and Russia. Above them are the ratings agencies and the Market.

The new elite seeks to perpetuate the dysfunctional institutions of gov-ernment primarily for self-interest. Let the people eat nostalgia. Political parties, elected governments and most parts of the vast bureaucracy of the United Nations have been captured, to use a word that has become common currency in South Africa. These spaces offer comfortable careers and opportunities for people who often start out as do-gooders but then become detached from the people they claim to do good for. Instead they zoom around the world notching up carbon emissions.

Crushed underneath all this are the ordinary citizens of the earth who now live in a world of hybrids and paradox. Trade unions are progressive and regressive; workers' parties are sometimes more conservative than their business counterparts; civil society can be both a catalyst for and a brake on change. There is a maelstrom of agendas, hidden and real; sus-picions, justifiable or not; internal and external conflicts; lazy old ideologies that have morphed into quasi-religions and attach themselves to progressive movements like dog shit. We live in an Idiot Wind where, in the words of Bob Dylan, 'What's good is bad what's bad is good / you'll find out when you reach the top / You're on the bottom.'[162]

Yes, ours is a time of rupture. So-called movements of people to the right are evidence of this. The narrow majority that voted for Britain to exit the European Union; the 61 million people who voted for the racist Donald Trump in the American presidential election; the support given by some ordinary people to Islamic State. Each in their different way evidences the alienation of millions of people from the institutions and elites of government.

Whether it be from the left or the right (popular terms that seem less and less distinct from each other), underlying each revolt is the desire for freedom and democracy and a revulsion for the various cliques that have usurped power on the basis of their ethnicity, class, caste or control of armed forces. Each uprising is fuelled by anger at austerity, declining living standards, perpetual youth unemployment, unaccountable government, unbridled corruption, profiteering and inequality. Some are rebellions of despair and desperation, others are against the loss of hope. They are modern slave uprisings against various forms of state, structural or private violence, against the '1%' who have usurped power across the planet.

The protests reflect the decay of democracy.

Yet so far, not one of these bursts of energy and discontent has succeeded in establishing a state based on dignity, human rights and equality. People have shown the power to take power, but they have also revealed our inability to reorganise economic and political power so that it benefits everybody, and in particular the poor.

The 21st century cries out for new shapes and methods of organisation. The institutional forms we have inherited, whether they be trade unions, political parties or NGOs, have failed to change the modern world. Some of them are a danger to it. Where there could and should be a new political and economic imagination about alternative ways of organising human society, there is a Hawkingesque black hole that threatens to gobble us all up.

What do we need to do to bring about lasting change?

In twentieth-century democracies the contest over ideas and ideals took place between classes and was waged primarily through political parties. Political parties were said to be either left-wing or right-wing, just as workers were said to be blue-collar or white-collar. For people like me left was good, right was bad. No more. Today political parties are left and right within the same shell. Right and left. Today, the primary contest takes place between different interests *within* political parties. Before and after they are elected as governments, the opaque but powerful forces I have mentioned are already seeking to control them.

So is joining a political party still what activists should do? In my early strivings for justice I was encouraged to believe a political party was what you joined to advance social justice. I spent my Oxford years as a Labour Party Young Socialist. For almost ten years I was a member of the MWT of the ANC. But evidence overwhelmingly suggests that to believe that political parties can advance social justice just doesn't hold water any more.

The decline and degeneration of the ANC from the highs and hopes I described in the early part of this book to disappointment, denialism and capture is a tragic example of this. To this I have been a witness.

It was the murder of Steve Biko in 1977 that woke me up to injustice. The account of his life and death written by Donald Woods launched me on my journey. It made me look deeper into injustice. I came to romanticise the ANC. I idealised and envied the heroism of its leaders. I wrote poems about Saul Mkhize, Solomon Mahlangu and Nelson Mandela.

During the South African youth uprisings of the 1980s, support for the ANC grew rapidly. Vast hopes were pinned on it by South Africa's black poor, especially young people. The sacrifices made by many ANC leaders seemed proof of their intention to transform our society for the better.

The election of 1994 was a catharsis for the soul. But such, such was the joy that we forgot how steeply the odds were stacked against the new South Africans. The world economy was labouring into a transition in which the structure of industrial economies was evolving. Economies that for a century had made profits through the exploitation of human beings and given them a wage in return were being replaced by knowledge and finance economies, more and more dependent on capital investment and new technology.

The world the freedom movements inherited after the 1970s was an unstable and rapidly changing one. The newly independent states of Africa, Asia and Latin America had no colonies to milk and provide a comfortable cushion to partly quench the expectations of their peoples. Neither did they have industry. The possibility of their economies following a 'normal' process of development had been profoundly distorted by years in which agricultural and industrial production had been tuned to the needs of other peoples. Their weakness made them little more than pawns in the Cold War between the great powers.

Racists imply or state outright that there exists an African predisposition to corruption: hence our many state failures. Their claptrap overlooks the objective economic factors that condemned independent states to failure. Countries with colonial names were born with cerebral palsy as a result of being asphyxiated during birth.

South Africa lives in the vortex of these new realities. In 1994 our streets were bedecked with the ANC's election billboards promising 'Jobs, Land, Peace'. But the economy that this promise depended on was 'modernising' away from its traditional base of migrant slave labour, primarily in gold mining.

An internal discussion document that I helped write for the MWT soon after the 1994 election warned: 'As far as the bosses are concerned it is necessary to transform the economy from one based on cheap black labour to one that is more capital intensive. This means holding down wages, and replacing human labour with machines. Put simply it means further retrenchments in major industries such as motor, clothing and textile. But how does this square with the need to create jobs, and extend the buying power of the black population (to boost the local market)?'[163]

As predicted, for a decade South Africa experienced 'jobless growth'. When the growth stopped after the 2008 financial crisis we just got joblessness.

The problem was that the economy was not open to truth or reconciliation. Indeed, it was not even asked to play the game. So, while the owners of property and capital lauded the 'rainbow nation' they declined to meaningfully share their economic power or any of their 300-year pickings.

Looking back it seems inexplicable that the first real economic policy of our democratic state, the misnamed Growth, Employment and Redistribution (GEAR) policy introduced in 1998, would start to cut back on public spending at the very moment when a legally binding constitutional obligation to improve access to healthcare services and provide quality education came into being.

This Constitution made social justice one of its cornerstones.

While world leaders saluted our far-sighted and transformative Constitution, they allowed traps to be set, baits to be placed, leaders to be caught or compromised. The notorious Arms Deal, struck in 1999 with arms manufacturers located in the great democracies of Europe, was the start of the rot of corruption.

Twenty years later we are seeing the price that was to be paid for the failure to advance social justice. The weak and insecure economic position of our government left it unable to finance quality education and health services, as well as other crucial public services needed for development and transformation. Poor-quality public education left the economy uncompetitive and the offices of the government staffed by people without requisite skills.

Ultimately, sad as this may sound, where a real economy is suffocated, for many the road to riches lies through petty or grand theft. An understaffed, under-trained public service leaves the state's coffers unguarded. And thus dawned South Africa's age of corruption.

For a time the country was blighted by hundreds of what we called 'cash-in-transit' robberies, a modern form of highway robbery. It was suspected that behind the desperate young men hired to risk their lives to take out well-armed cash convoys were networks of more sophisticated criminals. In recent years cash-in-transit robberies have dropped off. Corruption wears a white collar. Corruption has become a refined form of bank robbery mainly practised by the elites. Each year billions of rands are siphoned from the public purse. Billions more are prevented from ever being put in the purse by tax evasion and illicit capital transfer to developed countries and off-shore bank accounts.

In 2011, as this problem became more apparent, SECTION27 undertook to conceptualise and then establish Corruption Watch, an NGO dedicated to combating corruption. As part of this process we commissioned research to try to establish the scale and shape of corruption in the health sector. We were shocked to find that up to ten per cent of all funding for health was being stolen, approximately R20 billion a year. That's as much money as funds the annual ARV programme, which keeps 3.5 million people alive.[164]

South Africans have been free for 23 years. So far our democratic government has failed to deliver black people from poverty and inequality.

We have entrenched 'democratic values' without social justice, recognition of 'fundamental human rights' without budgets for their fulfilment.

My journeys towards social justice have led me to believe that a political party has become a necessary evil. Parties will not die away, nor should they. But they are no longer a potent instrument for advancing equality and social justice.

The alternative is organised, active citizenry, the forming of diverse organisations that work for a common good, and for these organisations to shape themselves into a force that has the power to bend politics and economics to the will of the people and the interests of the planet.

In *Blessed Unrest: How the Largest Movement in the World Came into Being and Why No One Saw It Coming*, Paul Hawken claims: 'All social justice organisations can trace their origins back some 220 years ago, when three-fourths of the world was enslaved in one form or another.' He traces the start of the human quest for social justice to a day in 1787 when 'a dozen people began meeting in a small print shop in London to abolish the lucrative slave trade'.[165] Thereafter he documents the slow rise of non-governmental movements, their coagulation into what we now call civil society and their growing influence on governments.

Hawken argues that the joining together of the environmental and social justice movements would create a new force in world politics. The road to social justice now lies through mobilising people to be political, not mobilising people into political parties where they surrender autonomy to their leaders. What is needed are diverse organisations of informed and competent people who will hold *any* government and *every* level of government, as well as vast and powerful multinational private companies, firmly to account according to a set of global norms based on human rights and environmental sustainability.

In South Africa the Constitution gives us the power to do just this.[166] In the world the Universal Declaration of Human Rights is the foundation for a global framework of law based on human rights.

We need to act and we need to act soon. A black hole is forming. It threatens to suck in our civilisation. Theories and analyses about our planetary crisis are a dime a dozen. There is a stellar blizzard of words. Philosophers of the right and left, with names like Fukuyama, Žižek and

Piketty, come and go. Superficial critiques about our world line up on bookshelves side by side with others containing deep wisdom. How do we sift the wheat from the chaff? In this vacuous mishmash people and powers that are destructive of people and our planet continue to run riot.

Yet in the winter of despair for billions of people there is a spring of hope. I do not exaggerate about the despair. We talk about a coming catastrophe but for many hundreds of millions it's already here. Can you, dear privileged reader, imagine what it must be like to be living in a nightmare that doesn't have a happy ending, or that you go to sleep to get away from? Think about it. You will find it on a street corner near you.

What's most frustrating is that this need not be.

Among us, the privileged, more and more people sense that something is profoundly wrong. From different locations and experiences more and more people are groping towards alternative ways of living, thinking and organising.

The biggest problem is *within us*: it is what we tolerate, what we consider 'normal' or unalterable. Or perhaps it is that we no longer ask ourselves what the meaning of life should be. For me, a world in which your purpose is just to make money is a mucky one. But it helps explain the lack of imagination needed to fire the engines, the lack of a catalytic idea or pole of attraction where previously there was the ideology of socialism.

As a result the prevailing ideology of the middle classes could be described as 'leave-us-alone-ism': rid us of some taxes, privatise education and parts of the health system, limit crime and let us get on with it.

This will not do. Together with the marginalised and excluded, the middle classes suddenly have an important role to play. We need to work to construct an alternative, but what is it?

We will not find it in an ideology. We are looking in the wrong place if we expect to find it in a single organisation. We will not find inspiration in old forms of politics but in literature, music, each other, innovation, love. For those of us with privilege the hope that others may have what we have seen for ourselves should make us activists and advocates of social justice.

It is not my place or ability to prescribe – in fact prescriptions are what we don't need any more. But I finish with some suggestions as to how we may remake our country and world:

- We can't get away from money but, to go back to the Pardoner, it's the love of money that is the problem. For a long time I have tried to find ways to reconcile my beliefs with the Big C, 'Capitalism', but it's not possible. Capitalism is not a conspiracy of elites. It's a way of doing. Inequality is built into its DNA. But the notion that we can overthrow it is redundant. We can't rid ourselves of the marketplace or the fact that there must be a medium of exchange. But we can change the rules and we have the power in law to do so.

- The question our greatest thinkers should be applying their minds to is how we may continue economic development through meeting human needs in a way that protects and strengthens the environment. This needs different business models and ethics.
- Finally, we should seek to restore the Universal Declaration of Human Rights to the position of a global constitution.

Let me part from you with hope. In all my travels I have met many, many more good people than bad. I have spent a bit of time with some of the people who inhabit the top 1 per cent and many more people in the bottom 20 per cent. I have never lost the belief that there are more good people than bad people.

Early in the morning of the last day that I worked on this book, 28 March 2017, news came in of the death of 'Uncle Kathy', Ahmed Kathrada. On the one hand I felt bereft. On the other hand I felt uplifted and inspired. This gentle and kind soul had lived his 87 years without blemish. His whole life, including 25 years in prison, had been given to the service of others and to making a reality of the dream of social justice. He had lived a rich and fulfilling life – while shunning material riches.

There are beacons for us to follow in this dark night. I work every day with people who are inhabited by the same spirit as Ahmed Kathrada. Most are unknown. Many are just beginning their journeys. I think their numbers are growing. They help me to believe that we have the power to set ourselves free.

Epilogue –
the journey we must take together

Then they'll raise their hands
Sayin' we'll meet all your demands
But we'll shout from the bow your days are numbered
And like Pharaoh's tribe
They'll be drownded in the tide
And like Goliath, they'll be conquered.
Bob Dylan, 'When the Ship Comes In'[167]

February 2005 was a hot summer in Cape Town. For the third year in a row TAC had organised a march to coincide with the opening of Parliament and the annual State of the Nation address by President Mbeki. We had made a great breakthrough in 2003 when a national ARV treatment plan had been published, but implementation of the plan was being frustrated by the Minister of Health, who was supported by AIDS denialists and probably the President himself. The deadly delay was keeping medicines from people whose lives depended on them. To try to speed things up TAC had launched a new campaign demanding '200 000 people on ARV treatment by 2006'. Once again the march ended at the gates of Parliament. But this year we had set up 400 white plastic chairs on the square outside the National Assembly, so that MPs could come out to hear our demands.

Only one MP, ANC stalwart Ben Turok, took a seat.[168] We were undeterred. The TAC speakers directed their words to the ghosts in the empty chairs. When my turn came I told the empty chairs that although the prescription of ARVs at state hospitals had commenced, it was happening too slowly. People were still dying. I warned:

> TAC's journey has not ended just because a policy is now in place. TAC will continue to protest for as long as one person is being denied treatment. 'Each life counts equally.' That's what our Constitution says. Every human body feels pain and fear and indignity. Everyone mean *every* one.

That was twelve years ago. As we said, TAC's struggle goes on, for *every-one*. I remain part of it. So too does the centuries-old struggle for social justice continue. The denial of socio-economic rights – of housing, education, clean water, sufficient food – to *anyone* on our earth is an injustice. The denial of the opportunity for decent employment in a country that is awash with the need to employ people as teachers or nurses or civil servants is a travesty. Let's be clear, social justice is affordable. We have ample resources. It is outrageous that in our world a small minority of people command and own unimaginable wealth and use it to usurp the fruits of our shared civilisation. Meanwhile for several billion people the prospect that they will ever experience dignity and a meaningful life is receding. For as long as these unnecessary and unacceptable injustices endure, it will be incumbent on good people, like you and me, to take a stand and challenge them.

My journey towards social justice will end only when there is social justice for all – that is, when there is substantive equality between peoples. That day is a long way away, unlikely in my lifetime. But as you can see, it's been an interesting road. I hope you are ready to join us.

As we approach the end of this book, permit me to make some suggestions that may help you on your own journey:

What is it that divides us?

I am a person of the white race, middle class, privileged with a high-quality education. I am a man. To people who are oppressed each part of my character carries some culpability. I have tried to grapple with this culpability.

At the age of thirteen I commenced my one-boy rebellion against racism. Since then I have taken a stand against the privileged among my race, the white people of this century and the last.

But looking back I understand that apartheid is more than a political construct dreamt up by Hendrik Verwoerd and the National Party in South Africa. It is a global phenomenon. We have allowed separateness to be constructed within us, or at least we the middle classes, we the privileged, we the whites. Apartheid is not a part of the poor, because poverty forces people upon and against each other.

Once upon a time and not so long ago, separation was possible. But in today's world separateness is as unsustainable as apartheid. People are connected to each other whether they like it or not. You and I are connected.

While it is true that it was the rise of capitalism that created and then exploited racial inequality, the fact is that my race, people who are white, have surfed atop the great waves of capitalism, colonialism and neocolonialism. We have almost always stayed on the crest of the wave, glorying in the sun, the sky and the sea, as millions of others have been drowned beneath it.

So we must understand that race does matter. In late September 2016 I spent an afternoon with some of my family beside a swimming pool at a sports club in Tuxedo Park, a forested suburb of New York state. Young white children frolicked in a swimming pool, carried squash racquets, called up food and drink from the bar, took kayaks onto a glassy lake that mirrored the mountains around it. These children were oblivious of the larger world they live in. These children are insulees.

In that very same hour across the Atlantic Ocean on the edge of Fortress Europe, a place that can be reached in a second by email, children of this same world lived through horror and fear as they were swept along in a refugee flood into a hostile and often racist Europe. They sought to escape bombs, beheadings and constant insecurity.

In those same moments the body of Alan Kurdi, a little boy of three, was being fished off a beach in Turkey, as if he were a beached seal. Images flashed at the speed of light to every corner of the world. Evoking howls of anger from some, compounding inertia in others. I doubt that even one of the children beside the swimming pool noticed or cared.

Unless children of privilege can learn to see themselves as common citizens of a common world, not part of an elite, they will be the problem when they grow up. The actions or inactions of their parents, and their parents before them, have contributed to the civilisational crisis we now face. Their job is to help to undo it.

But how?

It is important to call out white people's complicity and complacency. In the free South Africa inequality has become more stark and more visible than it was under apartheid, when it was tucked away in homelands and townships. Poverty leers into car windows at every road intersection, seeking a few cents or rands. Poverty holds pathetic handwritten placards. Yet most white people still seem oblivious of the silent roar of suffering inside the human beings around them. Most white people remain mentally shackled in their own privilege.

My journey took me through apartheid, then through AIDS denialism. Three and a half million people have died of AIDS in South Africa this century. But most people carry on as if this holocaust had never happened.

The lack of response to the pain caused by inequality is another form of denialism. Feeling denialism. Affinity denialism. Pain denialism.

Empathy denialism. Solidarity denialism. Inequality denialism. Human-ity denialism.

Call it what you will. It's the name of the game in our brave new century.

Denialism is deadly.

Denialism may cost us our planet.

When I started my journey I chose to get involved in 'the struggle'. You do not have as much choice as I did. Taking a stand is now a matter of survival.

In the past, people of privilege could live out their lives largely un-touched by others' pain and suffering, by social dislocations, even by wars. This has changed. The world has grown much smaller. Poverty and peo-ple have exploded to such an extent that they are pressing in more and more – even on those who consider themselves secure. The levels of in-equality, the environmental crisis and climate change constitute a civili-sational emergency that will be very hard for anyone to keep at bay, even if a wall's built. If people do not act together we will not be able to avoid wars over water or food or new shapes of 'terrorism' from people whose alienation or hatred is so complete that it has freed them from what were once considered the rules of civilised behaviour, even in war.

You have a self-interest in joining forces with the poor to advance equality and human dignity.

We must make social justice the heart of our quest and defend gains made in the centuries-long struggle to have it accepted that all human beings have equal human rights.

During the twentieth century many social justice activists made ideo-logy the centre of struggle. We fought for –isms. We can no longer afford to be chained to big ideas that do not take all of society forward. We should act with a clearer articulation of the type of society we want.

Those of us who live in South Africa are well placed to do this. The Preamble to our Constitution enjoins us to bring into being 'a society based on democratic values, social justice and fundamental human rights'. These three pillars differentiate South Africa from many other rights-based constitutions, which may protect democracy and human rights, but make no reference to social justice.

Lawyers and constitution-writers are fastidious about words. So the words 'social justice' must be there for a reason. They are. They tilt our country towards what earlier generations once considered should be the fruits of socialism – human equality and dignity. But they do so without binding the state to any ideology. Who can disagree with the idea that we should actively pursue substantive equality between peoples to try to ensure *each* person's fundamental rights, housing, health, water, food, basic education?

We all often feel powerless but we must recognise that this is only a feeling: In fact we have a great deal of power.

In this book I have described several successful campaigns for social justice. There are many more. I have shown how TAC linked up with activists all over the world and bettered millions of lives. These campaigns have unleashed the power of ordinary people and have usually depended on two things: the existence of legally binding frameworks which, on paper, protect and advance human rights, and the presence of organisations and individuals who wanted to put them into practice.

Do not forget, the South African Constitution is our *supreme* law. It sets clear parameters for both government and corporate power. It inclines society towards social justice. It is an antidote to neoliberalism because it mandates that South Africa should have a strong government that places each individual's well-being at the centre of all law, politics and – vitally – economics. Our Constitution is one part of a framework of laws based on human rights that exists internationally.

The logic of neoliberalism led to many evil things but it has not yet dismantled this legal framework. It acted outside them, outside the law. It has been aided in doing so by us, because with its bright light dazzling us and with the confusion of ideologies fogging our minds we did not take advantage of instruments to advance social justice that lie at our feet.

Let me put my cards on the table: human society is too vast and complex and contradictory to escape regulation and restraint. Law is the best means for doing this. There are many forms, areas and divisions of law, but our supreme laws should be human rights laws.

But law is not self-enacting. It needs people to wield it.

In some ways each of the movements for social justice that I have described in this book has been an experiment to test the power that organised people can really exert, including through the law.

When it comes to the rights to ARV treatment for AIDS and to basic education, single organisations have proved sufficient to win tangible victories such as access to a class of life-saving medicines or a clearly defined right to have textbooks. But sustaining and extending these achievements requires something much larger. It requires that people start to gnaw at the roots of power. It requires that people start to redis-cover a common vision of an alternative society. In South Africa it re-quires that we join the dots, connecting ourselves to the millions of people elsewhere in the world who are already trying to do this.

Can civil society globalise its force and become a political power that cuts across all the artificial distinctions that have been imposed upon and accepted by us – nationality, ethnicity, gender, race, ability, even age? Can civil society emerge with power strong enough to corral and direct corporate and governmental powers? Can civil society on its mil-lion different frontlines launch an offensive on every localised expression of injustice and cruelty? Can the good people of the world, you and me, raise our hands and create a planetary wave that demands that the Uni-versal Declaration of Human Rights be the foundation of a truly global compact and constitution? Can we make social justice the lodestar that will help revive our humanity?

That's the question you have to answer.

About the author

MARK HEYWOOD has been the Executive Director of the public interest law centre SECTION27 since 2010. Before that, he headed the AIDS Law Project (ALP) for 13 years. Heywood also serves on the executive of the Treatment Action Campaign (TAC), an organisation he co-founded in 1999.

Among several other organisations he helped create, the #SaveSouth-Africa campaign, started in 2016, #UniteAgainstCorruption, started in 2015, and Corruption Watch (2012) are among the most prominent.

Heywood chaired the UNAIDS Global Reference Group on HIV and Human Rights from 2006 to 2012, and served as deputy chair of the South African National AIDS Council from 2007 to 2012.

He has been involved extensively in successful human rights litigation, including:

- South Africa's first Constitutional Court judgment dealing with HIV (*Hoffman v SAA*, where the ALP was amicus curiae);
- *Pharmaceutical Manufacturers' Association v SA Government*, where he co-ordinated TAC's legal team, and assisted with drafting the TAC's affidavits (TAC was admitted as amicus curiae);
- The case brought by the TAC against the South African government on mother-to-child HIV transmission, which also led to a ground-breaking judgment in South Africa's Constitutional Court (*TAC v Minister of Health and Others*, 2002).
- *NM and Others v Smith and Others*, where the Constitutional Court ruled in favour of the right to privacy.
- Cases on the rights of learners to basic education, particularly the duty of the government to provide each learner with textbooks in each prescribed subject, in 2012, 2014 and 2015.

Author of more than 300 op-eds, essays, peer-reviewed articles and book chapters on legal, ethical and rights questions linked to HIV/AIDS, health, politics, law and literature, Heywood has also published a volume of poetry, *I Write What I Fight* (Echo Press, 2016).

Heywood holds a BA (Hons) from Oxford University, and his proposal for turning his Masters into a PhD in African Literature was accepted by the University of the Witwatersrand.

He is a member of the editorial board of the *Journal of Human Rights Practice* (Oxford University Press), and co-editor of the National Strategic Plan Review, *HIV/AIDS and the Law: A Resource Manual*. His other publications include, as co-editor (with Adila Hassim and Jonathan Berger) *Health and Democracy, A Guide to Health, Law and Policy in Post-Apartheid South Africa* (Siber Ink, Cape Town, 2007), and (with Jonathan Berger, Adila Hassim, Brian Honermann and Umunyana Rugege) *The National Health Act – A Guide* (Siber Ink, Cape Town, 2008 and 2013).

Heywood has undertaken consultancy work for UNAIDS, the UNDP, the ILO, the Southern African Network of AIDS Service Organisations, the World Bank, and the International HIV/AIDS Alliance. He was a Distinguished Visitor at the O'Neill Institute for National and Global Health Law at the Georgetown University Law Centre, and the Phyllis W Beck visiting Professor of Law at Temple University, Philadelphia, both in the United States.

A veteran of more than 150 marathons, he has run over 30 ultra-marathons and completed the iconic Comrades Marathon 17 times. He lives in Johannesburg.

Acknowledgements

Many of my friends and comrades encouraged the writing of this book and their enthusiasm and encouragement helped nurse it to life. I shared drafts with different people at different stages. Leisl Algeo, Edwin Cameron, Brian Currin, Robin Gorna, Paula McBride, Ralph Mathekga, Hugh McLean, Rob Petersen, Faranaaz Veriava, Tish White and Irma Wilson gave me helpful suggestions or prodded my memory.

Anso Thom looked after this project (and me) from the beginning. Sisonke Msimang helped me unravel a few things in myself that even I didn't know about. Adila Hassim made me confront some questions the text was trying to avoid. Sharon Ekambaram read it twice, despite mixed feelings caused by the pain and loss it evoked, and corrected my memory in a number of places. Kate Paterson helped me edit it at a time when it was making me weary and provided ideas and encouragement over the last mile.

After I made a false start, Tony Morphet gave me the clue about how to write this book. A big thank you to Erika Oosthuysen who persuaded me to put it back on the road after a chance meeting at the 2015 edition of the Daily Maverick's Gathering. She encouraged me throughout. Mark Gevisser made me admit the problems in the penultimate draft that I had been trying to ignore. His advice confirmed this hint to a writer: when you get down to editing, be willing to sacrifice your favourite sentences, paragraphs and even chapters first. His advice was enormously helpful. Betty Welz did a masterful job editing and fact-checking. Only she is fully aware of the prevalence of my bad habit of malapropism.

Thank you to Michele Pickover, Zofia Sulej and Gabi Mohale, the staff in the Historical Papers section of the William Cullen Library at the University of the Witwatersrand. Archivists of the highest calibre.

Thanks to Google. For the writer and researcher, Google has become an externalised part of the brain, capable of providing almost instant gratification and making you look far more erudite than you really are.

Thank you to the Rockefeller Foundation Bellagio Center for awarding me a month's pure peace as a resident of the Villa Serbelloni. In those 28 days I went running or cycling every day, visited churches, climbed mountains. As a result, in March–April 2014 I was able to make a start to the book and, as importantly, to meet inspiring writers such as Anne Nelson who made me question what I was really trying to write.

One disclaimer: This book is a subjective recollection of my friends, my passions and the campaigns I have participated in. In places it may be incomplete and even slightly faulty. I have done my best to reconcile memory and fact. Nonetheless it reflects my state of mind at the time I wrote it. What bobs on the surface of the narrative reflects the undercurrents of my mind and memory, feelings that even I probably don't fully understand.

Finally, and most importantly of all, I want to thank comrades and friends, alive and dead, especially from the Treatment Action Campaign (TAC) and SECTION27. You are too many to list and I am sure my narrative omits important names in relation to some of our campaigns. But it is your lives, efforts and commitment that are the stuff of this book.

Endnotes

Opening remarks

1   T S Eliot, 'Portrait of a Lady' (from *Prufrock and Other Observations*, 1917) in *Collected Poems 1909–1962*, Faber and Faber.

Chapter 1

2   Susan Williams, *Colour Bar: The Triumph of Seretse Khama and His Nation*, Allen Lane, 2006.

3   P Larkin, *Collected Poems*, Faber and Faber, 1988, p. 180.

4   Jimmy is the lead character in *Quadrophenia*, a 1979 film version of The Who's album of the same name. Floyd 'Pink' Pinkerton is the lead character in Pink Floyd's 1982 film version of their album, *The Wall*. These two films about alienation and anger within an unfriendly world hit my teenage self at more or less the same time, adding ingredients to the eclectic mix that was shaping my character.

5   J D Salinger, *The Catcher in the Rye*, Penguin Books, 1958, p. 181.

6   Sex Pistols, 'Bodies' on *Never Mind the Bollocks, Here's the Sex Pistols*, 1977.

7   J Dury (ed.), *'Hallo Sausages': The Lyrics of Ian Dury*, Bloomsbury, p. 109.

8   The Stranglers, *Rattus Norvegicus*, 1977. This album is still essential listening.

9   Andrew Motion, *The Pleasure Steamers*, Carcanet, 1978.

10   W Shakespeare, 'King Lear', Act III, Scene iv, lines 28–33.

11   Donald Woods, *Biko*, Penguin edition.

12   Hugh Masekela, 'Stimela (Coal Train)', *I Am Not Afraid*, Blue Thumb Chisa, 1974.

13   Joseph Lelyveld, 'South African Flees His Trial For Treason', special to the *New York Times*, 19 April 1983. http://www.nytimes.com/1983/04/19/world/south-african-flees-his-trial-for-treason.html. The ways in which the law, even under apartheid, could be used to advance justice became a theme of my later life. Again, it's about connections. Little did this young white boy know then that later life would introduce him to the greatest practitioners of anti-apartheid law, notably Arthur Chaskalson and George Bizos.

Chapter 2

14   John Lydon, *Anger Is an Energy: My Life Uncensored*, Dey Street Books, 2015. This quote is from chapter 4, 'Into the Inferno'.

15   *Never Mind the Bollocks, Here's the Sex Pistols*, 1977. Lyrics quoted from http://www.sexpistolsofficial.com/nmtb-lyrics/.

16   Samuel Beckett, *Collected Shorter Plays*, Faber and Faber, 1984.

17   Jean-Paul Sartre, *Iron in the Soul*, Penguin Books, 1950.

18   The Stranglers, 'No More Heroes' on *The Stranglers*, 1977.

19   Jon Savage, *England's Dreaming*, Faber and Faber, 1991.

20   Linton Kwesi Johnson, *Selected Poems*, Penguin, 2006.

21   Leon Trotsky, *Problems of Everyday Life*, Pathfinder Press.

22   'Lincoln Steffens', Wikipedia, https://en.wikipedia.org/wiki/Lincoln_Steffens.

23   The Iconic Orgreave Photograph, http://news.bbc.co.uk/local/sheffield/hi/people_and_places/history/newsid_8217000/8217946.stm.

24   Florence Reece, 'Which Side Are You On?' Adapted and sung by Billy Bragg, 1984.

25   K Luckhardt and B Wall, *Organize . . . or Starve! The History of the South African Congress of Trade Unions*, Lawrence and Wishart, 1980. Nimrod Sejake is another person whose life story needs to be told. He returned to South Africa after years in exile and died on 27 May 2004, still an ardent and unapologetic socialist. The *Irish Times* carried a fitting obituary of him: http://www.irishtimes.com/news/tireless-activist-who-spent-30-years-in-exile-1.1145648.

26   Billy Keniston, *Choosing to Be Free: The Life Story of Rick Turner*, Jacana, 2013. This book is an essential introduction to Rick Turner and his time. See also, https://www.dailymaverick.co.za/opinionista/2014-08-04-is-the-continuation-of-the-present-a-possible-future-in-honour-of-richard-turner-1941-1978/#.WNScGGXBaSM.

27   John Cooper Clarke, *Ten Years in an Open Necked Shirt*, Vintage, 2012.

28   A Wainwright, *A Coast to Coast Walk*, Westmorland Gazette, undated (c1972).

29   Karl Marx, *Capital*, Volume 1, 'Preface to the French Edition', Penguin Books, 1976.

30   A Wainwright, *Memoirs of a Fellwanderer*.

31   Martin Legassick, *Towards Socialist Democracy*, University of KwaZulu-Natal Press, 2007.

32   *Inqaba ya Basebenzi*, issue 13, March–May, 1984. Available in Mark Heywood Papers, 1981–2012, A2562 (box A1.2), Historical Papers Research Archive, Wits University.

33   'Inkatha – This Spear of Counter-Revolution Must Be Broken', by Peter Davies and Daniel Lakay, *Inqaba ya Basebenzi*, February 1986.

34   'The Freedom Charter – Is It a Worker's Programme?', by Sean Kelly, *Inqaba ya Basebenzi*, April 1988.

Chapter 3

35   Linton Kwesi Johnson, 'Mi Revalueshanary Fren', *Selected Poems*, Penguin, 2006.

36   Rob Petersen recalled in an email of 10 September 2016: 'James Motlatsi fleetingly agreed to join the Tendency after brief discussions in London. Weizmann and I thereafter travelled to Stockholm and had a brief discussion with Ramaphosa when he and Motlatsi were visiting there, urging him to take the NUM into COSATU when it was formed, and arguing that the ANC would become the movement of the great majority. Later, when he had made his career in the ANC, Ramaphosa would say that we had "nothing to do with the ANC".'

37   A C Jordan, *Ingqumbo Yeminyanya*, Lovedale Press, 1940.

38   M Heywood, *Lovedale at War: William Govan versus James Stewart – Conflict and Continuity, 1860–1890*, unpublished MA thesis, 1996.

39   Colin Bundy, *Govan Mbeki: A Jacana Pocket Biography*: Jacana, 2012.

40   When Jordan published the novel in English 40 years later, he left out the quote from Shakespeare. That too tells us something.

41   M Heywood, MA dissertation, pp. 82–83, 1994.

42   M Heywood, *A Colony for a Stage: Shakespeare, the English and the African Writer*, unpublished, 1996.

43   *The American Night: The Writings of Jim Morrison*, volume II, Vintage Books, 1991, p. 61.

44   I left Violet, Thembeka, Stella Chepape, Germinah Dunn, Nana, Sara and other brave women activists behind when my Alex journey ended in 1994. I have since heard that Thembeka died. She was a bright, articulate and out-raged young woman who worked in a lighting factory on Louis Botha Avenue. I wish I had known more of her life than the moments we spent together.

45   *Philemon Dipulelo Mauku vs The State*, Case N SH 555/91, Southern Transvaal Regional Court (held in Brakpan), transcript of the trial, p. 8 (evidence of Sgt Cornelius Van Den Berg). Translated as: 'I asked the accused for an expla-nation. He reported to me that he was on his way to Alexandra township in Johannesburg. He said that he was going to use the weapons to establish a "defence unit".'

46   Philemon Mauku, 'Report on His Involvement in the Struggle and How It Start-ed in Alexandra', 25/10/92. Smuggled from prison. Mark Heywood papers.

47   Oliver Schmitz, *Philemon Mauku on Trial for Self Defence* (video), in Mark Hey-wood Papers, box A4.1.4, Wits Historical Papers.

48   Letter from 'Andrew' to Philemon Mauku, 6 April 1992. I am grateful to Robert Petersen for providing me with an electronic copy of the trial transcript and other documents. These are now stored as part of the Mark Heywood col-lection at Wits Historical Papers.

49   Magistrate P J Fourie, Reasons for Decision and Sentence, 18 May 1992.

50   Legal papers were prepared to appeal against the judgment and sentence. After the first advocate we appointed as Philemon's counsel produced an affidavit that made an unprincipled concession, he was fired. The great Arthur Chaskalson was then approached to act as his counsel but declined. Eventually we abandoned the appeal.

51   'Paula Leyden', Walker, http://www.walker.co.uk/contributors/Paula-Leyden-9126.aspx.

52   Bryan Rostron, *Till Babylon Falls*, Coronet Books, 1991.

53   John Carlin, 'ANC 'terrorist' released: Pretoria is freeing one of its most hated political prisoners', *Independent UK*, http://www.independent.co.uk/news/world/anc-terrorist-released-pretoria-is-freeing-one-of-its-most-hated-political-prisoners-john-carlin-1553995.html.

54   'TRC Final Report: Volume 2, Chapter 4, Subsection 5', http://sabctrc.saha.org.za/reports/volume2/chapter4/subsection5.htm.

55   Mark Heywood Papers, box A4.3.

56   Mark Heywood Papers, box A4.4

57   David Beresford, *Ten Men Dead: The Story of the 1981 Irish Hunger Strike*, Atlantic Monthly Press, 1997.

58 W Wordsworth, 'The French Revolution as It Appeared to Enthusiasts at Its Commencement', *Poetical Works*, Oxford University Press.

59 Steve Jolly, *Eyewitness in China*, Congress Militant publication (no date).

60 Subsequent to the split the remaining members of the MWT took the organisation through various permutations. Today it is known as the Workers and Socialist Party (WASP), an independent party. WASP stood in the 2014 general election and got 0.05% of the votes. It did not present candidates in the 2016 local government elections. Its newspaper is now called *Izwi Labasebenzi*. Further information is available at: http://workerssocialistparty.co.za.

Chapter 4

61 Counting AIDS deaths has been notoriously difficult owing to poor reporting on causes of death. This figure is considered the most accurate estimate, calculated from the most advanced actuarial model. Information about the model is available at: http://www.thembisa.org/about#.

62 William Shakespeare, *The Merchant of Venice*, Act III, Scene ii.

63 The deaths of Joe and Caitlin made me understand the pain being suffered by parents whose children were infected with HIV. But for the most part I have kept this pain private. I have only written about it in one other place. On 17 August 2000 I penned an article for the *Sowetan*, advocating for a PMTCT programme. I wrote: 'I have lost two children, more importantly, my wife has. I have watched two pregnancies take place over nine months. I have seen the bond that grows between a mother-to-be and her unborn child. I have felt the bond that develops as a father.

'Late in pregnancy, this bond becomes physical. For the father it is expressed in the little kicks and movements that dent the mother's stomach. For a mother the kicks are an expression of the imminence of life – a life that she has created and nurtured.

'I have also learnt the meaning of loss. Two of my children died shortly before or after birth. So I can remember their faces. I also know the look of a mother when she is told that her child is dead – the harrowing cry of "give me back my baby, it's not true" as it echoes through a maternity ward that is suddenly emptied of life and promise.

'And years of pain that follow it.'

64 R Jennings, 'Your Victory is Our Victory', A versus SAA, October 2000, ALP Papers; see chapter 3, 'The Applicants Who Grounded SAA' in Didi Moyle, *Speaking Truth to Power: The Story of the AIDS Law Project*, Fanele, 2015, pp. 60–82.

65 *Hoffmann v South African Airways* (CCT17/00) [2000] ZACC 17; 2001 (1) SA 1; 2000 (11) BCLR 1235; [2000] 12 BLLR 1365 (CC) (28 September 2000).

Chapter 5

66 E Cameron, *Witness to AIDS*, Tafelberg, 2005.

67 'Andrew Natsios', Wikipedia, https://en.wikipedia.org/wiki/Andrew_Natsios.

68 Advances in medical science on how to utilise ARVs to prevent a pregnant woman with HIV from infecting her child during or shortly after birth accelerated in the late 1990s. The research focused on finding drug regimens that could be implemented in developing countries where weak health systems and affordability are issues. The first breakthrough came when it was found

that one drug, AZT, used only in the last trimester of pregnancy and for a short time after birth, had a dramatic effect in reducing infant infections. However, using AZT was expensive and its use fiercely opposed by the South African government under the influence of Thabo Mbeki. By the early 2000s, an even simpler regimen, using the drug Nevirapine required only one pill to be taken after onset of the mother's labour and a single dose to be given to the new born child after birth. After TAC's victory in the Constitutional Court it was this regimen that was introduced by the South African government. As a result of the roll-out of this programme, today the rate of mother-to-child HIV transmission is under 2 per cent.

69 L Kramer, *Reports from the Holocaust: The Makings of an AIDS Activist*, St Martin's Press, 1989.

70 M Heywood, 'Debunking "Conglomo-talk": A case study of the amicus curiae as an instrument for advocacy, investigation and mobilisation', *Law, Democracy & Development* 5: 2001(2), Butterworths.

71 G Oppenheimer & R Bayer (eds), *Shattered Dreams? An Oral History of the South African AIDS Epidemic*, Oxford University Press, 2007; Thys von Mollendorff, *Dare to Care*, Reach Publishers, 2003.

72 Joe Slovo, *The Unfinished Autobiography*, Ravan Press, 1995.

73 Charles Dickens, *A Tale of Two Cities*, Collins Classics, 2012.

74 Affidavit of Sarah Hlalele, *TAC v Minister of Health*.

75 Albie Sachs, *The Strange Alchemy of Life and Law*, Oxford University Press, 2009, p. 184.

Chapter 6

76 Mike Cherry, 'The President's Panel' (pp. 16–36), in *The Virus, Vitamins and Vegetables: The South African HIV/AIDS Mystery*, edited by Kerry Cullinan and Anso Thom, Jacana, 2009.

77 M Mbeki, letter to Professor Michael Cherry, 19 January 2000. Mike Cherry has kindly provided me with a copy of the letter together with its annexures.

78 The tragedy of AIDS denialism in South Africa has been extensively documented and discussed. See in particular N Geffen, *Debunking Delusions: The Inside Story of the Treatment Action Campaign*, Jacana Media, 2010; N Nattrass, *Mortal Combat: AIDS Denialism and the Struggle for Antiretrovirals in South Africa*, 2007. What is still missing is an explanation or more importantly an apology from the protagonist himself, Thabo Mbeki. In *The Things That Could Not Be Said: From A(IDS) to Z(imbabwe)*, Picador Africa, 2013, Frank Chikane, the Director General in the Mbeki Presidency, makes a rather pathetic effort to explain and justify Mbeki's position, which he describes as 'this matter', 'unfortunate' or 'Mbeki's HIV and AIDS story'. By doing so, though, he makes matters worse for Mbeki. For example, he contradicts Mbeki's repeated games of work play, claiming that he never said HIV does not cause AIDS, by asserting that '(at least up to 2000) Mbeki still believed there was a virus called HIV, which was related to AIDS . . .' (p. 276). He also admits that 'because of unresolved ethical questions' research into Virodene was 'forced . . . to go semi-underground' (p. 273). It seems Mbeki will never apologise. In early 2016 – after a decade of silence – he re-entered the fray with two further insensible 'letters' on AIDS. These letters re-opened old wounds by

revealing a man who clung religiously to arguments regardless of the weight of scientific evidence against the view he propagates through them. T Mbeki, 2016, Letters on AIDS: http://cdn.bdlive.co.za/images/pdf/MbekiLetter.pdf; http://www.timeslive.co.za/ilive/2016/03/14/FULL-LETTER-Mbekis-observation-on-HIV-deaths. Interestingly, when I attempted to access them from the Thabo Mbeki Foundation website on 19 August 2016 the letters on AIDS appear to have been taken down. Also significant is ANC Treasurer-General Zweli Mkhize's response to Mbeki's letter: http://www.timeslive.co.za/sundaytimes/opinion/2016/05/08/Dear-Mbeki-now-is-the-time-to-apologise-for-Aids-denialism.

79 Dira Singwe, *Talking Back* interview: Nono Simelela, 2013, available at: https://www.youtube.com/watch?v=JDLm-HhMaV8.

80 A Brink, *Debating AZT, Mbeki and the AIDS Drug Controversy*, Open Books, 2000.

81 Address by President Thabo Mbeki at the Inaugural ZK Matthews Memorial Lecture, www.nelsonmandela.org/omalley/index.php/site/q/03lv03445/04lv04206/05lv04302/06lv04303/07lv04304.htm.

82 Nawaal Deane, 'The Madness of Queen Manto', *Mail & Guardian*, 11–16 April 2003.

83 Jack Lewis (Director) *Taking HAART*, produced by Community Media Trust, 2011. Available at https://www.youtube.com/watch?v=eGwvv0z7--Y.

84 An obituary by Mongadi Mafata in the *Sowetan* quoted Edward Mabunda's last message in full: 'People must support TAC because the government has been dragging its feet for four years. TAC is negotiating with the government to implement a national treatment plan. So now I think it is high time TAC started a civil disobedience campaign to show the Government that 600 people a day are dying of HIV/AIDS. We want ordinary people in South Africa to have these anti-retrovirals. So I am urging the people all over the world to support TAC to show solidarity with South Africa – we are dying. As a person living with HIV/AIDS I am very fortunate to be a member of TAC. What about the person who comes off the streets, who knows nothing about the treatment? So please – the world must support us, the world must be with us. I want to salute all the comrades who went on this civil disobedience and I want to pledge to give them my . . . I wanted to be part of it. Unfortunately I am sick and TAC is doing everything for me. Please, I beg you . . .'

85 Len Kumalo, for *The Sowetan*.

86 Private email from Sharon Ekambaram, 2 October 2016.

87 P Chigwedere et al, 'Estimating the Lost Benefits of Antiretroviral Drug Use in South Africa', *Journal of Acquired Immune Deficiency Syndrome*, 49(4), 1 Dec 2008, pp. 410–415.

88 S Friedman and S Mottiar, *A Moral to the Tale: The Treatment Action Campaign and the Politics of HIV/AIDS*, Centre for Policy Studies, University of KwaZulu-Natal, 2004. Available at: https://www.escr-net.org/sites/default/files/Friedman_Mottier_-_A_Moral_to_the_Tale.pdf.

89 Oppenheimer and Bayer, p. 200.

90 Obituary: Winstone Mwenda Zulu, *The Lancet*, Vol. 378, 12 November 2011.

91 M Heywood, *I Write What I Fight*, Echo Press, 2016.

92 Remarks by Stephen Lewis, http://www.terry.ubc.ca/2006/09/08/remarks-by-stephen-lewis-un-special-envoy-for-hivaids-in-africa-to-the-closing-session-of-the-xvi-international-aids-conference-toronto-canada/.

93 Paul Hawken, *Blessed Unrest: How the Largest Social Movement in History Is Restoring Grace, Justice and Beauty to the World*, Penguin, 2007.

94 Arundhati Roy, *Capitalism: A Ghost Story*, Haymarket Books, 2014.

95 Sex Pistols Winterland concert; Phil Strongman, *Pretty Vacant: A History of Punk*, Orion Books, 2007; J Savage, *England's Dreaming: Sex Pistols and Punk Rock*, Faber and Faber, 1991.

Chapter 7

96 Peter Piot, *No Time to Lose: A Life in Pursuit of Deadly Viruses*, W W Norton & Company, 2012.

97 The Ebola response in 2015 has now been roundly criticised by public health experts. It was confirmation (if confirmation is needed) of how global public health priorities are determined more by Western fear than good public health sense. See: 'Will Ebola Change the Game? Ten Essential Reforms before the Next Pandemic. Report of the Harvard-LSHTM Independent Panel on the Global Response to Ebola', *The Lancet*, November 2015.

98 David France (director), *How to Survive a Plague*, 2012.

99 The Chinese Human Rights Defenders website: https://www.nchrd.org.

100 Transcript of interview with Li Dan, by Jehangir S Pocha, http://archive.boston.com/news/world/asia/articles/2006/03/28/transcript_of_interview_with_li_dan/?page=2.

101 Shen Tingting, email correspondence with the author, 29 February 2016.

102 Attacks on human rights activists in China are continuous. The detention of artist Ai Weiwei in 2011 was a high-profile example. Usually the people who disappear are unknown and unlamented. Most governments, including ours, turn a blind eye for opportunistic economic reasons.

103 Email from Tian Xi with the author, 17 May 2013.

104 M Heywood, 'The Critical Importance of Engagement with Civil Society in National Responses to HIV', address to the Inaugural Meeting of the China Red Ribbon Beijing Forum, 5 July 2010.

105 L O Gostin, *Global Health Law*, Harvard University Press, 2014.

106 M Heywood, 'The Unravelling of the Human Rights Response to AIDS', *AIDS Today*, 2014. https://www.aidsalliance.org/assets/000/001/014/ESSAY1_Mark-Heywood_original.pdf?1412944701

107 These figures are sourced from the South African National AIDS Council, 'National Strategic Plan on HIV, TB and STIs 2012–2016'.

Chapter 8

108 John Lennon, *Double Fantasy*, 1980. This was John Lennon's last album, released several months before his murder on 8 December 1980.

109 B Beresford, *The Price of Life – Hazel Tau and Others vs GlaxoSmithKline and Boehringer Ingelheim: A Report on the Excessive Pricing Complaint to South Africa's Competition Commission*, AIDS Law Project and TAC publication, 2003.

110 The full tale is told by Didi Moyle in a chapter of her book, *Speaking Truth to Power*.

111 M Heywood, 'Victims of Success?', *The Star*, 11 March 2009.

112 S Peberdy and M Jara, 'Taking Control: Civil Society Responses to the Violence of May 2008', unpublished paper, 2010.

113 Christa Kuljian, *Sanctuary: How an Inner-City Church Spilled onto a Sidewalk*, Jacana, 2013.

Chapter 9

114 *SECTION27 & Others v Minister of Basic Education and Another*, 3[2012] 3 All SA 579 (GNP); 2013 (2) BCLR 237 (GNP).

115 F Veriava, 'The Limpopo Textbook Litigation: A Case Study into the Possibili-ties of a Transformative Constitutionalism', *South African Journal on Human Rights* Vol. 32(2), 2016, pp. 321–343; also, *The Limpopo Textbooks Crisis: A Study in Rights-Based Advocacy, the Raising of Rights Consciousness and Governance*, SECTION27, 2013.

116 In the end Mr Hlongwane had the last laugh. In July 2016, after not hearing from him for over a year, Nikki Stein received a message from him on WhatsApp. It read: 'Hi Nikkie! It is Hanyani Thomo High School principal. Thank you very much your organization turned our school into a former model C school. Physical structures of high quality were built as a way of silencing us. Good luck in all your endeavours!!'

117 'In this case, the judge is guilty', *City Press*, 21 April 2014. Available at: http://www.news24.com/archives/city-press/in-this-case-the-judge-is-guilty-20150429.

118 *Basic Education for All and Others v Minister of Basic Education and Others* (23949/14) [2014] ZAGPPHC 251; 2014 (4) SA 274 (GP); [2014] 3 All SA 56 (GP); 2014 (9) BCLR 1039 (GP) (5 May 2014).

119 *Camps Bay Ratepayers' and Residents' Association and Another v Harrison and Another*, CCT 76/12 [2012], ZACC 17.

120 *Minister of Basic Education v Basic Education for All* (20793/2014) [2015] ZASCA 198; [2016] 1 All SA 369 (SCA); 2016 (4) SA 63 (SCA) (2 December 2015) availa-ble at: http://www.saflii.org/za/cases/ZASCA/2015/198.html.

121 Keynote Address by the Minister of Basic Education, Mrs Angie Motshekga, MP, at the Basic Education Sector Lekgotla, 20 January 2016. Available at: http://www.education.gov.za/Newsroom/Speeches/tabid/950/ctl/Details/mid/3816/ItemID/3887/Default.aspx.

122 In 2017 an unprecedented trial seeking constitutional damages on behalf of the family of Michael Komape will take place in the Limpopo High Court. SECTION27 is acting as the Komape family's attorneys.

123 Sometimes the right words just find you. My most successful effort to find words to give my children and yours on advice on how to live their lives is found in a 'letter' I wrote in January 2015 published in the *Daily Maverick*: http://www.dailymaverick.co.za/opinionista/2015-01-05-living-in-the-21st-century-a-letter-to-my-children-and-yours/.

124 Constitutional Court report: Pollsmoor Correctional Centre – Remand Centre and Women's Centre, July/August 2015. Available at: http://www.constitu-tionalcourt.org.za/site/PrisonVisits/Cameron/Pollsmoor-Prison-Report-23-April-2015-Justice-Edwin-Cameron-FINAL-for-web.pdf.

125 *Lee v Minister of Correctional Services* (CCT 20/12) [2012] ZACC 30; 2013 (2) BCLR 129 (CC); 2013 (2) SA 144 (CC); 2013 (1) SACR 213 (CC) (11 December 2012). Available at: http://www.saflii.org/cgi-bin/disp.pl?file=za/cases/ZACC/2012/30.html&query=Dudley%20Lee.

126 *Nkala and Others v Harmony Gold Mining Company Limited and Others* (48226/12,
     31324/12, 31326/12, 31327/12, 48226/12, 08108/13) [2016] ZAGPJHC 97; [2016]
     3 All SA 233 (GJ); 2016 (7) BCLR 881 (GJ) (13 May 2016) Available at: http://
     www.saflii.org/cgi-bin/disp.pl?file=za/cases/ZAGPJHC/2016/97.html&query=-
     Silicosis%20judgment.

Chapter 10

127 South African History Online, 'United Democratic Front (UDF)', http://www.
     sahistory.org.za/organisations/united-democratic-front-udf.
128 Kumi Naidoo, interview, 11 January 2016.
129 South African History Online, 'Report by the President of the ANC, Nelson
     Mandela to the 50th National Conference of the African National Congress
     Mafikeng, 16 December 1997', http://www.sahistory.org.za/archive/report-
     president-anc-nelson-mandela-50th-national-conference-african-national-
     congress-mafik.
130 Public Protector of South Africa, 'In the Extreme: Report No 11 of 2011/12
     of the Public Protector on an Investigation into Allegations of a Breach of
     the Executive Ethics Code by the Minister of Cooperative Governance and
     Traditional Affairs, Mr Sicelo Shiceka, MP', http://www.pprotect.org/library/
     investigation_report/Shiceka%20Report-%20Final%20version%207-signed.pdf.
131 Treatment Action Campaign, 'Declaration of the Civil Society Conference
     held on 27-28 October 2010, Boksburg', http://www.tac.org.za/community/
     node/2959.
132 Politicsweb, 'ANC statement reminiscent of Mbeki-era paranoia – TAC/SEC-
     TION27', http://www.politicsweb.co.za/documents/anc-statement-reminis-
     cent-of-mbekiera-paranoia--ta; Sapa on Polity.org.za, 'ANC urges leaders to
     take legal action', http://www.polity.org.za/print-version/anc-urges-leaders-
     to-take-legal-action-2010-11-04; Stephen Grootes, 'Analysis: Will the dark
     recesses of the ANC ever learn?' on *Daily Maverick*, https://www.dailymaverick.
     co.za/article/2010-11-04-analysis-will-the-dark-recesses-of-the-anc-ever-
     learn/.
133 Mark Heywood, Ruth First Symposium Lecture, 17 August 2012: 'South Africa's
     Undeclared and Unnoticed Coup d'etat – How to restore democracy and
     people's power?', http://www.journalism.co.za/wp-content/uploads/RFMark-
     Heywood.pdf. An edited version of this speech was published in the *Mail &
     Guardian:* 'Coup by the connected and corrupt', 31 August 2012, http://mg.
     co.za/article/2012-08-31-00-coup-by-the-connected-and-corrupt.
134 Ruth First, *The Barrel of a Gun: Political Power in Africa and the Coup d'Etat*, Penguin
     African Library, 1970.
135 The report is available at: http://www.adf.org.za/documents/PRELIMINARY_
     REPORT_ADF_AND_30_OTHERS_VS_KING_ZWELITHI.pdf.
136 Available at: http://www.gov.za/sites/www.gov.za/files/Public%20Protector's
     %20Report%20on%20Nkandla_a.pdf
137 Kairos Southern Africa, 'The South Africa Kairos Document 1985', https://
     kairossouthernafrica.wordpress.com/2011/05/08/the-south-africa-kairos-
     document-1985/.
138 Polemics and political sparring are a tool of trade of the left. But they are

mostly about self-aggrandisement. A brief written contretemps between me and a former comrade, Norma Craven, is an example. I stopped it almost as soon as it started: Mark Heywood, 'Op-Ed: Twenty First Century Struggles for Social Justice', https://www.dailymaverick.co.za/article/2015-11-09-op-ed-twenty-first-century-struggles-for-social-justice/ and Norma Craven, '"What has social democracy ever done for us"? (With apologies to Monty Python)', https://www.dailymaverick.co.za/opinionista/2015-11-18-what-has-social-democracy-ever-done-for-us-with-apologies-to-monty-python/#.WHD0OmXBbos.

139   George Orwell, 'Politics and the English Language', available online at: http://www.orwell.ru/library/essays/politics/english/e_polit/.

140   ENCA, 'WATCH: President Zuma removes Nene as finance minister', https://www.enca.com/south-africa/president-zuma-removes-nene-finance-minister.

141   Mark Heywood, 'The small story of a small but significant march', https://www.dailymaverick.co.za/opinionista/2015-12-19-the-small-story-of-a-small-but-significant-march/#.WG0VBGXBbos; Irvin Jim, 'A small and insignificant march – a false step for the working class!', https://www.dailymaverick.co.za/opinionista/2015-12-22-a-small-and-insignificant-march-a-false-step-for-the-working-class/#.WG0UgmXBbos.

142   Adam Hochschild, *To End All Wars: A Story of Loyalty and Rebellion, 1914–1918*, Mariner Books, 2012, p. 376.

143   *Economic Freedom Fighters v Speaker of the National Assembly and Others; Democratic Alliance v Speaker of the National Assembly and Others* (CCT 143/15; CCT 171/15) [2016] ZACC 11; 2016 (5) BCLR 618 (CC); 2016 (3) SA 580 (CC) (31 March 2016). Available at: http://www.saflii.org/za/cases/ZACC/2016/11.html.

144   J M Coetzee, 'Universities Head for Extinction', *Mail & Guardian*, http://mg.co.za/article/2013-11-01-universities-head-for-extinction.

145   African News Agency, 'ANC veterans tell President Zuma to step down', *Mail & Guardian*, http://mg.co.za/article/2016-04-06-anc-veterans-tell-president-zuma-to-step-down.

146   http://www.news24.com/SouthAfrica/News/the-chorus-calling-for-zuma-to-resign-is-growing-20160409.

147   News24 (ed. Michelle Solomon), 'Zuma apologises to the nation for Nkandla', *Mail & Guardian*, http://mg.co.za/article/2016-04-01-zuma-on-nkandla-i-apologise0.

148   Statement of the African National Congress following meeting of the National Officials held on the 1st April 2016, http://www.anc.org.za/content/statement-african-national-congress-following-meeting-national-officials-held-1st-april-2016.

149   In my view one of the most balanced and well-thought-out critiques of the stalemate in the power-play between Zuma and his opponents is Ralph Mathekga's *When Zuma Goes*, Tafelberg, 2016.

150   A video of Sipho Pityana's speech is available here: https://www.youtube.com/watch?v=gWA1R986iOc.

151   More information about #SaveSouthAfrica and its campaigns can be located at www.savesouthafrica.org. Get involved!

152   M Heywood, 'Of Trust and High Horses', *Daily Maverick*, https://www.dailymaverick.co.za/opinionista/2016-11-03-of-trust-and-high-horses.

Chapter 11

153   E Albee, *Who's Afraid of Virginia Woolf?*, 1962.

154   S Mukherjee, *The Gene: An Intimate History*, Simon and Schuster, 2016.

155   Billy Bragg, 'To Have and to Have Not', *Life's a Riot with Spy vs Spy*, 1983.

156   International Labour Organisation (ILO), 'Global Employment Trends 2014: The Risk of a Jobless Recovery', available at: http://www.ilo.org/global/research/global-reports/global-employment-trends/2014/WCMS_233953/lang--en/index.htm.

157   UN Special Rapporteur on the Right to Food, Final Report: 'The Transformative Potential of the Right to Food', 2014.

158   Panashe Chigumadzi, *Sweet Medicine*, Blackbird Books, 2016.

159   K von Holdt et al., *The Smoke That Calls: Insurgent Citizenship, Collective Violence and the Struggle for a Place in the New South Africa*, Centre for the Study of Violence and Reconciliation | Society, Work and Development Institute, 2011. Available at: http://www.csvr.org.za/docs/thesmokethatcalls.pdf.

160   Carne Ross, 'An Independent Diplomat', TED Talk. Available at: https://www.ted.com/talks/carne_ross_an_independent_diplomat#t-18088.

161   Carne Ross, *The Leaderless Revolution: How Ordinary People Will Take Power and Change Politics in the 21st Century*, Simon and Schuster, 2012.

162   Bob Dylan, 'Idiot Wind', *Blood on the Tracks*, 1975.

163   'Analysis of the Elections, and Perspectives for the Post-election Period', Draft for NC members, 23 May 1994. From the Mark Heywood papers.

164   In 2013 I met the Minister of Health at his request. He asked me to come alone for a private tête-à-tête. Before being made Minister of Health he had been MEC for Basic Education in the province of Limpopo. He was proud of the work he had done to try to improve the quality of education. But, he told me, President Jacob Zuma's reward for then ANC Youth League President Julius Malema's support for his campaign to become President of the ANC in 2007 was to effectively hand over Limpopo to him and his supporters. Once they were in power Malema and friends reorganised tender systems in the education and other departments to make it easier to direct benefits to their allies.

165   This story of the campaign against the slave trade is essential reading for any activist. It is best told in Adam Hochschild's *Bury the Chains*.

166   Mark Heywood, 'Seize Power! The Role of the Constitution in Unifying Social Justice Struggles in South Africa', in *Capitalism's Crises*, ed. V Satgar, Wits University Press, 2015.

Epilogue

167   *Bob Dylan: Lyrics 1962–1985*, Jonathan Cape, 1987, p. 100. I confess that this is the only book I have ever stolen from a friend or, rather, wilfully forgotten to return. Apologies to Hugh McLean and his brother Glen.

168   Ben Turok is a role model for a life lived with complete integrity. B Turok, *With My Head above the Parapet: An Insider Account of the ANC in Power*, Jacana, 2014.

Index